FarmVille®

FOR

DUMMIES®

FarmVille®

FOR
DUMMIES®

by Angela Morales and Kyle Orland

WILEY

Wiley Publishing, Inc.

FarmVille® For Dummies®

Published by
Wiley Publishing, Inc.
111 River Street
Hoboken, NJ 07030-5774

www.wiley.com

For general information on our other products and services, please contact our Customer Care Department within the U.S. at 877-762-2974, outside the U.S. at 317-572-3993, or fax 317-572-4002.

For technical support, please visit www.wiley.com/techsupport.

Wiley also publishes its books in a variety of electronic formats. Some content that appears in print may not be available in electronic books.

Library of Congress Control Number is available from the Publisher upon request.

ISBN: 978-1-118-01696-1

Manufactured in the United States of America

10 9 8 7 6 5 4 3 2 1

WILEY

About the Authors

Angela Morales: Angela Morales, also known as "FarmGoddess" by FarmVille Freaks, is the founder, active contributor, and editor of `FarmVilleFreak.com`, one of the largest and longest running FarmVille fan sites. `FarmVilleFreak.com`, a blog-styled Web site, is updated daily and is dedicated entirely to FarmVille and FarmVille-related news.

Angela started playing FarmVille almost at its inception, in the summer of 2009. Soon after, she launched her site in September 2009 to fill the void of reliable FarmVille resources on the Internet. Since then she has helped keep a large community of farming enthusiasts informed with the latest FarmVille updates, changes, guides, upcoming items, news, and fan art.

Due to the success of the site and its reputation as a trusted source for FarmVille coverage, she is considered one of the foremost experts in all things FarmVille. Her FarmVille articles have been published in *The New York Times*, MSNBC, CNet, AOL's Games.com, and Inside Social Gaming and she has been cited as an expert by CBS Evening News with Katie Couric, Stevie "KillCreek" Case, Gamers Advocating Fiscal Responsibility, and several independent documentaries.

Kyle Orland: Kyle has been playing video games since he was seven and writing about them in one form or another since he started fan site Super Mario Bros. HQ (`www.smbhq.com`) at the tender age of 14.

From that humble beginning, Kyle has gone on to somehow make a full-time freelance career out of game-related writing, with work appearing in *Electronic Gaming Monthly*, *Paste Magazine*, National Public Radio's NPR.org, *The L.A. Times*, Gamespot, The Escapist, Joystiq, and many other outlets. He currently contributes regularly as a news writer for developer-focused game site `Gamasutra.com`, and has been quoted as a video game expert by *The New York Times*, *The Washington Post*, G4TV, and TheStreet.com, among other outlets.

This is Kyle's second *For Dummies* book, after 2008's *Wii For Dummies*. He also co-wrote and published *The Videogame Style Guide and Reference Manual* with coauthors David Thomas and Scott Steinberg in 2007. His favorite game of all time is Super Mario 64.

Dedication

For Sebastian — you will never know how much of a beautiful distraction you were, but you have changed my world forever . . . you are my world.

Mikey, my best friend, my husband, the love of my life — without you I am lost, with you I am free. Since 09.07.01 "we loved with a love that was more than love." I'm hoping we continue to conquer more fields of mushrooms in the rain, even when we're ninety.

Thank you to my family: my pumpkin Mary, Jason, and especially my parents for always supporting me and believing in me even when I didn't. Mom, you are my inspiration. Daddy, you are my strength.

To all the FarmVille Freaks — your love and support continues to overwhelm me. A special thanks to my favorite FarmVille Freaks: Amy "CabbagePatchKid" Costa for keeping me sane; Mike "Guru" Birch for cracking the whip; Dave_NC for your amazing talent; Kayyy my little mod queen; DarkFarmer, the most knowledgeable FarmVille player, Csh01, Link, Eva, and last but not least Dr. Green Thumb; without you this book would not be possible. — *Angela S. Morales*

To my wife, Michelle, one of the strongest women I've ever met.

To my family and friends, old and new, present and far away.

Finally, to everyone who was incredulous that an entire book about FarmVille could exist. The proof is in your hands, doubters! — *Kyle Orland*

Author's Acknowledgments

Thanks to my wife Michelle for tolerating all the late nights I spent chained to my desk meeting deadlines, and also for taking the wheel on drives across the state so that I could write even more. Thanks to A. Mike for helping set up my sweet dual-monitor desktop setup that made editing text and playing the game at the same time quite easy.

Thanks to Libe Goad, who gave me a shot at AOL's Games.com — The Blog and got me into this whole social gaming thing in the first place. Thanks to Susan Christophersen, Amy Fandrei, and all the other people at Wiley Publishing who saw our prose through to polished completion.

Thanks to Zynga for making a product that gets millions more people to realize that video games aren't just for teenage boys and social recluses. Thanks to Google for making the Chrome browser, which I used for all the Web-related things in this book and was quite pleased with. Thanks to 9gag.com for providing welcome distraction when I felt I just couldn't write another word about the Farmers Market.

Finally, thanks to the thousands of Internet commenters who wrote some variation of "I can't believe this book actually exists" or *"FarmVille For Dummies* . . . isn't that redundant?" I will think of you fondly on the way to the bank. —*Kyle Orland*

Publisher's Acknowledgments

We're proud of this book; please send us your comments at http://dummies.custhelp.com.
For other comments, please contact our Customer Care Department within the U.S. at 877-762-2974,
outside the U.S. at 317-572-3993, or fax 317-572-4002.

Some of the people who helped bring this book to market include the following:

Acquisitions and Editorial

Project Editor and Copy Editor:
Susan Christophersen

Acquisitions Editor: Amy Fandrei

Technical Editor: Michelle Oxman

Editorial Manager: Jodi Jensen

Editorial Assistant: Amanda Graham

Sr. Editorial Assistant: Cherie Case

Cartoons: Rich Tennant
(www.the5thwave.com)

Composition Services

Project Coordinator: Patrick Redmond

Layout and Graphics: Samantha K. Cherolis,
Timothy C. Detrick, Joyce Haughey

Proofreaders: ConText Editorial Services, Inc.,
John Greenough

Indexer: Sharon Shock

Publishing and Editorial for Technology Dummies

Richard Swadley, Vice President and Executive Group Publisher

Andy Cummings, Vice President and Publisher

Mary Bednarek, Executive Acquisitions Director

Mary C. Corder, Editorial Director

Publishing for Consumer Dummies

Diane Graves Steele, Vice President and Publisher

Composition Services

Debbie Stailey, Director of Composition Services

Contents at a Glance

Introduction 1

Part I: Basic Farming 5
Chapter 1: Welcome to FarmVille 7
Chapter 2: Getting Set Up to Play 15
Chapter 3: Getting Around in FarmVille and Starting Your Farm 29
Chapter 4: Won't You Be My Neighbor? 53

Part II: Seeking Your FarmVille Fortune 73
Chapter 5: For the Love of Virtual Money 75
Chapter 6: Agricultural Economics 101: Mastering the FarmVille Market . 93
Chapter 7: The Farmers Market 113

Part III: Expanding Your Reach 133
Chapter 8: Reaching New FarmVille Levels 135
Chapter 9: Adding Storage Facilities and Animal Shelters 153
Chapter 10: Looking for Special Items and Events 171

Part IV: Embracing FarmVille Fame and Community ... 179
Chapter 11: Earning Achievements 181
Chapter 12: Let's Cooperate: Co-op Farming 201

Part V: Staying Safe and Up-to-Date on FarmVille 211
Chapter 13: Staying Secure and Finding Support 213
Chapter 14: Technical Matters: Troubleshooting and Game Enhancements . 223

Part VI: The Part of Tens 233
Chapter 15: Ten Farming Personalities 235
Chapter 16: The Ten Most Wanted FarmVille Items 241
Chapter 17: Ten Go-to Crops 249

Index 255

Table of Contents

Introduction *1*

About This Book 1
Foolish Assumptions 1
How This Book Is Organized 2
  Part I: Basic Farming 2
  Part II: Seeking Your FarmVille Fortune 2
  Part III: Expanding Your Reach 2
  Part IV: Embracing FarmVille Fame and Community 3
  Part V: Staying Safe and Up-to-Date on FarmVille 3
  Part VI: The Part of Tens 3
Conventions Used in This Book 3
Icons Used in This Book 3
Where to Go from Here 4

Part 1: Basic Farming *5*

Chapter 1: Welcome to FarmVille 7

Why Millions Play FarmVille (and You Should, Too!) 8
  Ease of play 8
  The challenge of self-improvement and competition 9
  Creativity 10
  Entertainment and escape 11
Understanding the Key Concepts of FarmVille 11
  You get your own farm 11
  You grow crops, plant trees, and tend animals 11
  You decorate your farm 12
  You help your neighbors (and they help you) 12
  You upgrade your farm (and yourself) 12

Chapter 2: Getting Set Up to Play 15

Getting Your Computer's Ducks in a Row 16
  Getting on the Internet 16
  Choosing a compatible Web browser 16
  Getting the Adobe Flash Player 17
  Enabling JavaScript
  Optimizing your performance
Creating a Facebook Account So That You Can Play the Game ....

Installing the FarmVille App 22
 Bookmarking FarmVille on your Facebook account 24
 Playing directly from FarmVille.com 24
 Playing FarmVille from your mobile iDevice 26
 Turning Facebook friends into FarmVille neighbors 27

Chapter 3: Getting Around in FarmVille and Starting Your Farm 29

Using the Top Menu to Navigate FarmVille 29
 The Free Gifts tab: Sending gifts to your neighbors 30
 The Play tab: Heading down to the farm 32
 The My Neighbors tab: Keeping in touch with
  your FarmVille neighbors 32
 The Invite Friends tab: Recruiting more neighbors 33
 The Add Farm Coins & Cash tab: Increasing your farm's assets 34
 The Game Card tab: Redeeming your FarmVille Game Cards 34
 The FarmVille Requests tab: Taking care of
  actions awaiting your attention 34
Setting Graphics and Sound Preferences through the Options Menu 35
Keeping Track of your Farming Stats 36
 Viewing your farm close up or from afar 38
Getting to Know the Tools Menu 39
Starting Your Farm: Level 1 42
 Customizing your farmer 42
 Plowing, seeding, and harvesting 44
Diversifying Your Farm 45
 Farm animals 45
 Pets 46
 Trees 48
 Decorations 49
Tips for New Farmers 50
 Block your farmer 50
 Wait to decorate 50
 Add neighbors 51
 Watch your Facebook news feed 51
 Maximize your crop space 52
 Plant fast-growing crops 52

Chapter 4: Won't You Be My Neighbor? 53

Finding and Adding Neighbors 53
 Sending neighbor requests to Facebook friends 54
 Finding more neighbors 57
 Removing neighbors 60
Helping Your Neighbors 61
 Reaping what you sow by visiting your neighbors' farms 61
 Providing more neighborly assistance 64

Giving and Receiving Gifts 65
    Giving gifts 65
    Accepting and using gifts 66
Other Ways to Be a Good Neighbor: Farming Etiquette...................69
Posting Items and Bonuses to a Facebook News Feed 70

Part II: Seeking Your FarmVille Fortune 73

Chapter 5: For the Love of Virtual Money................................75
Acquiring Farm Coins for Essentials 76
    Earning Farm Coins...76
    Earning Farm Coins quickly 77
Acquiring Farm Cash for Premium Items 78
    Earning Farm Cash..78
    Knowing when to use Farm Cash...79
Spending Real Money on Virtual Goods 80
    Buying Farm Coins and Cash through FarmVille...........................81
    Using a nontraditional payment provider 82
    An alternative to paying online: FarmVille Game Cards 83
    Sending Zynga Game Cards as online gifts 85
    Earning "free" Farm Cash through offers and promotions............87

**Chapter 6: Agricultural Economics 101: Mastering
the FarmVille Market...93**
Browsing the FarmVille Market 93
    Seeds...96
    Trees..96
    Animals..97
    Buildings 98
    Decorations 99
    Farm Aides 99
    Vehicles...102
    Clothing...102
    Limited-edition items 102
Obtaining and Using Vehicles and Tools to Speed Up Your Harvest ...104
    Vehicles...104
    Getting fuel to run your vehicles 109
    Arborists and Farmhands 110
Maximizing Your Profit 111
    Farming on your schedule: Time is virtual money 111
    Expand on demand 112
    Frugal farming 112

Chapter 7: The Farmers Market **113**

Collecting, Sharing, and Using Bushels 113
    Setting up market stalls 114
    Collecting bushels 114
    Sharing bushels 118
    Using bushels 120
Crafting Goods to Increase Profits 122
    Setting up a crafting building 122
    Making a crafted good 123
    Leveling up and mastering crafted goods 126
    Buying crafted goods from neighbors 128
    Trading crafted goods for fuel 129
    Selling crafted goods 130
    Upgrading your crafting building 131

Part III: Expanding Your Reach *133*

Chapter 8: Reaching New FarmVille Levels **135**

Understanding Levels 135
    What are experience points (XP)? 136
    How to Earn XP 136
    What are levels? 138
    Unlocking new items and features by leveling up 139
Leveling Up Quickly 145
    The hay bale method 145
    The soybean method 147
    The news feed method 149
    The big-spender method 150

Chapter 9: Adding Storage Facilities and Animal Shelters **153**

Understanding Storage and Retrieval of Items and Animals 154
    Building storage facilities from frames 154
    A good ol' fashioned barn raising: Expanding storage facilities . . 155
    Storing items and sheltering animals 157
    Retrieving items from storage 157
    Removing animals from storage 158
Choosing the Right Kind of Storage Facilities 159
    Storage Cellar 159
    Barns and Tool Sheds 161
    Garage 162
    Garden Shed 162

Sheltering Your Animals 164
    Chicken Coop 164
    Dairy Farm 166
    Horse Stable... 166
    Nursery Barn 167
    Beehive... 168
    Pigpen 169

Chapter 10: Looking for Special Items and Events 171

Catching Limited-Edition Items and Events 171
    Discovering the benefits of limited-edition items........................ 172
    Checking in for limited-edition events 173
Solving the Mystery of Mystery Items 174
    Mystery Boxes and Games... 175
    Mystery Gifts 176
    Mystery Eggs 176
Giving Back: FarmVille Philanthropy in the Real World.......................... 178

Part IV: Embracing FarmVille Fame and Community........ 179

Chapter 11: Earning Achievements 181

Earning Ribbons.. 181
    Collecting ribbon bonuses 183
    Earning the next ribbon 184
Collecting Collectibles into Collections..................................... 187
    Differentiating between permanent and limited-time collections.....188
    Acquiring collectibles.. 189
    Storing completed collections 192
Mastering Crops 193
    Earning mastery points 193
    Earning mastery bonuses 199

Chapter 12: Let's Cooperate: Co-op Farming .201

How Do Co-op Jobs Work? 201
Starting or Joining a Co-op Job 202
Recruiting Friends to Help 206
Working on a Co-op Job 207
    Quitting a co-op job 207
Completing a Co-op Job 208
Rewards You Earn from Co-Op Farming....................................... 210

Part V: Staying Safe and Up-to-Date on FarmVille 211

Chapter 13: Staying Secure and Finding Support. 213
Avoiding FarmVille Scams 213
"Free" Farm Cash offers 214
FarmVille guides...214
Fake FarmVille Facebook groups 215
Fake news feed links 215
Protecting Yourself on Facebook 216
Contacting Zynga 217
General user support...217
Replacing lost items 218
Web Resources 220
The Official FarmVille Forum...220
The Official FarmVille Podcast 221
FarmVille Freak 222

Chapter 14: Technical Matters: Troubleshooting and
Game Enhancements 223
Taking a Picture of Your Farm 223
Getting ready to take a screenshot.................................224
Taking a screenshot on a Windows PC 224
Taking a screenshot on a Mac...225
Troubleshooting Common Bugs and Glitches 225
Out of sync...225
Facebook news feed posting 226
Performance 226
Loading..227
Gifts..227
Requests...227
Saving 228
Neighbors' profile pictures...228
Strangely clad neighbors 229
Full Screen mode not working...229
Avatar not displaying...229
Missing items on farm 229
Random text in pop-up messages....................................230
Handling the "FarmVille Has Been Enhanced" Notification 230

Part VI: The Part of Tens 233

Chapter 15: Ten Farming Personalities .... .235

The Functional Farmer.. 235
The Exterior Decorator.. 236
The Leveler... 236
The Happy Hoarder.. 236
The Breeder... 237
The Farm Master... 237
The Artist.. 237
The Collector... 238
The Zoologist.. 238
The Overachiever... 239

Chapter 16: The Ten Most Wanted FarmVille Items............ .241

Unwither Ring 241
Lawn Jockey 242
White Stallion 243
Black Stallion 244
Villa... 244
Platinum Gnome 245
Farmhands and Arborists... 246
Lake Nessy.. 246
Farm Expansion 247
Unlimited Storage 247

Chapter 17: Ten Go-to Crops... .249

Peas 250
Raspberries 250
Asparagus 250
Black Berries 251
Pumpkin 251
Onion... 252
Rice 252
Tomatoes 252
Grapes 253
Sunflowers 253

Index 255

Introduction

*I*f you're already on Facebook, you've probably received dozens of invitations to play FarmVille from some of the game's more than 50 million active players, complete with cryptic messages about sharing carrots; adopting lost, lonely animals; and hatching golden Mystery Eggs. Even if you aren't on Facebook, chances are you've heard about the game that's been making international headlines as the most popular Facebook application created to date. Or maybe you have absolutely no idea what FarmVille is and picked up this book by accident, perhaps thinking it was about hobby farming. If that's the case, you want *Hobby Farming For Dummies,* by Theresa A Husarik (Wiley), instead. But you might want to stick around and try FarmVille anyway, because it's a blast.

About This Book

FarmVille is a strictly virtual farm, and this book tells you everything you need to know about living the life of a virtual farmer, starting with an introduction to what FarmVille is all about.

The wonderful world of FarmVille is an agricultural bliss of perfect weather and animals that never die. Get ready to slap on some overalls, sharpen your pitchfork, and saddle up for your journey into virtual farming — all from the comfort of your climate-controlled home.

Okay, you don't really need overalls or a pitchfork. Your most useful tool for your farming adventure is actually your computer's mouse, but a comfy chair and this book won't hurt, either.

If you're new to FarmVille, you can use this book to find out how to get your farm up and running — and get playing. If you already play FarmVille, this book provides tips and tricks for fine-tuning your current farming skills and maximizing both your profit and enjoyment as you play the game. Either way, we hope you'll have some fun along the way as we provide you with everything you need to know to develop your alternative life as an Internet farmer.

Foolish Assumptions

You do not need to be a computer nerd or a skilled gamer to use this book, but we do assume that you have a computer and an Internet connection, and that you know your way around a Web browser enough to download some simple software applications. We also assume that you're willing to get a Facebook account if you don't have one already, because you can't play FarmVille without one.

Otherwise, you don't need to know much else; in this book, we tell you everything you need to know to play the game. You can get caught up in the technical aspects of gaming if that's your thing — but if it's not, that's fine, too: FarmVille is meant to be an enjoyable experience that anyone can master!

Sometimes, the best way to learn is by doing, and FarmVille is no different. Don't be afraid to try things out and click around your farm to see what different things do. Remember, you have this nifty guide as a resource to help you cross any technology gap you may be facing and overcome any fear of the unknown that virtual agricultural entails.

How This Book Is Organized

This book is designed so that you can read it from cover to cover or use it as a reference for specific situations as they arise. We've organized the material into the following six parts, described next.

Part 1: Basic Farming

This first part introduces you to FarmVille, including what the game is, how it fits into the social gaming genre, and why so many people play it. You find out how to set up both a Facebook account and a FarmVille account. You also find out how to navigate through the basic FarmVille menus and start to set up your first farm. Finally in this part you can gain an understanding of why having neighbors is so important to your farming endeavors.

Part 11: Seeking Your FarmVille Fortune

Part II is all about the virtual money. We introduce you the various virtual currencies used in FarmVille and tell you how to earn more of them. This part is also where you see how to spend your money (both virtual and real, if you so choose) in the FarmVille Market and the Farmers Market, and how to be a success at your chosen in-game crafting profession.

Part 111: Expanding Your Reach

In this part, we explain the levels of FarmVille and ways that you can "level up" as you play. We also tell you about storage facilities, animal housing, and some of the more mysterious aspects about FarmVille, including how to obtain limited-edition items.

Part IV: Embracing FarmVille Fame and Community

Part IV describes the achievements you can earn in FarmVille. You find out how to earn all the rewards of blue-ribbon farming by arriving at specific achievements, obtaining collections of items, gaining crop masteries, and successfully completing co-op farming endeavors.

Part V: Staying Safe and Up-to-Date on FarmVille

The Internet can be a scary thing for many people, but don't worry — we've got you covered. In this part we discuss some ways that you can play FarmVille more safely and make yourself a more informed user. You also find out how to contact Zynga, the game's developer, and make use of Web resources to help you get your farming fix.

Part VI: The Part of Tens

What would a *Dummies* book be without the Part of Tens part? In this part, you find out about ten different types of FarmVille players, the ten most-wanted items, and the ten go-to crops that you can always rely on.

Conventions Used in This Book

In this book we use numbered steps, bulleted lists, and graphics for your reference. Sidebars contain information that's not strictly necessary but may help you understand a topic a little better.

Web addresses appear in a special monotype font that looks like this: www.dummies.com. Also, when we provide a series of menu commands to follow, we present those commands in this format: Start➪Programs➪Accessories. This means to click Start, followed by Programs, followed by Accessories.

Icons Used in This Book

We use various icons in the margins to draw your attention to specific information, as follows:

This icon calls points to a tip or trick that you can use to enhance your gameplay.

This icon emphasizes points that can make you a better farmer.

If you see this icon, please read it! Warnings can prevent you from making a big mistake that could be hazardous to your farm (or computer).

This icon, which appears rarely in our book, is the geeky stuff that you can safely skip but may find interesting.

Where to Go from Here

If you have specific questions or comments about this book, or maybe a lingering question that we didn't address, you can contact Angela at farmgoddess@farmvillefreak.com or Kyle at kyle.orland@gmail.com

Thank you for buying our book, and we sincerely hope that it is helpful to you as a FarmVille player.

Note: All the information in this book was accurate to the best of our knowledge at the time of writing: October to November 2010. FarmVille is in a constant state of change. There are sure to be many changes and new content introduced to FarmVille in the future that will obviously not be addressed by this book. (We know a lot about FarmVille, but we're not psychic, after all.)

For the most part, what we have written about the fundamentals of farming should not change significantly and will remain useful for you as a reader well into the future. Specific information contained in tables and regarding Market prices and bonuses is more likely to change after the book goes to press. New in-game functions and items are sure to appear that don't exist yet, but then again, that's what future editions are for!

Part I
Basic Farming

The 5th Wave   By Rich Tennant

"Jim and I do a lot of business together on Facebook. By the way, Jim, did you get the sales spreadsheet and the bushel of soybeans I sent you in FarmVille?"

1 n this part, we tell you about the basic
concepts involved in playing FarmVille.
You find out how to create a Facebook
account (necessary for playing the game)
and install the FarmVille app. We familiarize
you with your game's menu controls and
take you through the process of starting
your first farm. Finally, we discuss the
importance of neighbors in FarmVille and
give you some tips on where to find more
neighbors.

facebook

1

Welcome to FarmVille

In This Chapter

▶ Understanding the key concepts of playing FarmVille

▶ Understanding why people play FarmVille

▶ Watching out for FarmVille addiction!

*F*armVille is a Web-based farming simulation game produced by a gaming company called Zynga. In contrast to many computer games that you have to buy on a disc, anyone with an Internet connection and a Facebook account can load FarmVille in his or her Web browser and play for free in an instant. The ease of access is one of the reasons FarmVille has become so popular.

The basic concept of FarmVille is relatively simple. You manage your virtual farm by planting, growing, and harvesting virtual crops; tending livestock and trees; constructing buildings such as barns and chicken coops; and buying and selling goods made on the farm. By completing these tasks, you earn coins that you can spend to expand and upgrade your farm. You also gain experience points, which go toward earning new levels, new items, and new gameplay opportunities on your farm. Through weeks and months of dedicated farming, you can build your initial small, empty farm into a massive, thriving mega-farm bustling with life.

Whereas most games cease to exist when you turn them off, crops and other items on your FarmVille farm continue growing and ripening in real time, even when you're not actively playing. Fully grown crops can wither on the vine if they're not harvested promptly, meaning that you may have to plan your daily schedule around your FarmVille play time to some extent. This time-sensitive gameplay can be a little annoying, but the game doesn't require a heavy time investment — just a half hour to an hour each day is enough to keep up with most basic farming tasks. Of course, you can play much more than that — the sheer time-sucking amount of stuff to do and collect on your farm helps make FarmVille one of the most addictive games out there (as more than 50 million users, as of this writing, can attest).

This chapter tells you what FarmVille is and the basics of playing the game. It also provides some tips to help you avoid getting too engrossed in the magical world of digital crops. Welcome to green pastures and the simple life — all controlled with the click of your mouse.

Why Millions Play FarmVille (and You Should, Too!)

Surely there has to be some common factor that makes FarmVille appealing to so many millions. Maybe deep down inside, we all want to be farmers. Perhaps we're intrigued by farming's Zen-like simplicity. Or could it be some innate desire to own land and return to days of simple, natural living?

Whatever the case, FarmVille is attracting people from all walks of life. The virtual farmers of FarmVille represent a broad range of backgrounds and professions. Business professionals, stay-at-home moms, doctors, the unemployed, stockbrokers, technology gurus, college students, and retirees are living second lives as diligent Internet farmers. Even if you don't play, chances are good that you know somebody who enjoys virtual farming.

Ease of play

Satisfying gameplay sessions in FarmVille can last as little as a few minutes, and real-world interruptions won't ruin your progress, because the game saves your progress constantly. What's more, playing FarmVille doesn't require your full attention. You can easily play the game while multitasking on a conference call, watching a mindless TV show, or waiting for dinner to cook.

With a laptop or mobile device, FarmVille can even help fill those wasted wait times that can seem to fill up a day. Whether it's a lull in your work schedule, an otherwise boring airport layover, a long delay in a doctor's waiting room, or a ride on the subway, you can make it more tolerable by cashing in on coins from the day's harvest.

Aside from the occasional withered crop, FarmVille has few of the frustrating setbacks that can sour the experience of traditional games, such as impassably tough challenges, frustratingly obtuse puzzles, or "game over" screens.

Additionally, in contrast to some games that require hours of focused attention just to get up to speed, FarmVille is designed to be easy to grasp almost immediately. Of course, every game has experts who make it to higher levels than some, and FarmVille is no different, but anyone — including you! — can become a farming veteran if he or she just keeps playing.

The challenge of self-improvement and competition

How do you beat FarmVille? Easy answer: You don't. Rather than display a final challenge and a "Congratulations, you win!" screen signaling the end of the game, FarmVille features a never-ending cycle of farm-tending for its own sake.

That doesn't mean the game doesn't have any goals, though. The possibilities for self-improvement are nearly endless, depending on what aspects of the game are most important to you. Some farmers might want to gain experience points and reach higher levels as quickly as possible. Others may focus on amassing as many items as they can. Still others may focus on growing and mastering all the crops, or amassing a fortune in Farm Coins, or earning every possible ribbon. What you do with your FarmVille experience is largely up to you. Improving your statistics for their own sake is all well and good, but many farmers also turn FarmVille into a competition with their friends, battling to reach ever-higher accomplishments before their neighbors do. Keeping up with the Joneses applies just as much in the virtual realm as the real world, and many FarmVille players take beating their neighbors to that next goal incredibly seriously.

Social gaming and FarmVille

Although FarmVille can technically be played as a single-player game, it takes advantage of Facebook's social networking framework to encourage interaction with other players. Socializing with other players by visiting their farms, sharing gifts, and participating in cooperative jobs is one of the keys to getting the most out of the game. This focus on social interaction puts FarmVille at the forefront of a new trend called social gaming.

Simply defined, a social game is any game with social interaction. Although social gaming isn't an entirely new concept, it has recently become one of the hottest sectors of the video game industry. Because of the success of games such as FarmVille, many game developers are eager to get a piece of the social gaming pie. And it's not a small pie by any means. Whereas tens of millions of people play traditional video games on consoles and personal computers, simple social games have attracted hundreds of millions of players, many of whom never bothered to keep up with the reflex-heavy and technically complex world of traditional video games.

Creativity

The virtual world of FarmVille isn't just a place to live out your rural fanta-
sies; it can also be a canvas to express your artistic sensibilities. By carefully
setting items down in specific arrangements, you can create anything from
re-creations of famous paintings and cartoon characters to FarmVille-ized
versions of real-world architecture and three-dimensional visual effects.
True, these creations don't serve any larger economic purpose on your farm,
but as any artist can tell you, sometimes creation is its own reward.

One of the most common methods for creating FarmVille art is by stacking
multicolored hay bales next to each other in a massive grid. By treating each
hay bale like a pixel in a digital image, you can make these grids form any
image you can think of. With each hay bale costing 100 to 600 Farm Coins (see
Chapter 5 for more about amassing Farm Coins), it's definitely a pricey hobby,
but one that can generate amazing results, as you can see in Figure 1-1.

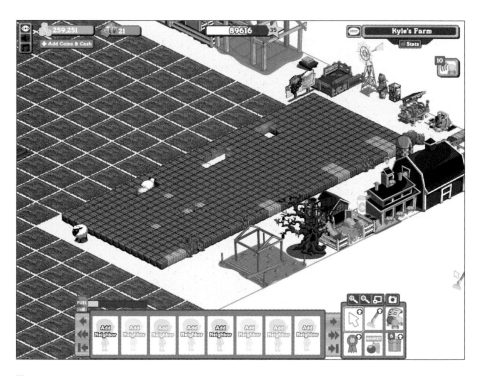

Figure 1-1: An abstract design made using FarmVille hay bales.

Entertainment and escape

Of course, the primary purpose of any game is entertainment, and FarmVille is no different. Most virtual farmers would probably cite entertainment or escape as the main reason they love playing FarmVille, and in today's fast-paced world, who can blame them? For many people, escaping to the virtual world of FarmVille is the next best thing to a real vacation that may be impossible for any number of reasons. The game provides an easy, cheap way to relieve stress, relax, and unwind. There's something about the familiar rhythm of the plowing, seeding, and harvesting cycle that helps make the stresses of everyday life seem just a little less stressful. The camaraderie and companionship generated by interacting with FarmVille neighbors can also provide a sense of community.

Understanding the Key Concepts of FarmVille

Throughout this book, we cover the various facets of FarmVille in great detail, of course, but the following sections give you the basics of how FarmVille works and what you'll actually be doing in the game.

You get your own farm

After you install the FarmVille app on your Facebook account (see how in Chapter 2), you start with a small, mostly empty farm, which we call the *play area*. This farm, and the game itself, aren't actually stored permanently on your computer, but exist on "the cloud" of FarmVille servers maintained by developer Zynga.

Your virtual farmer begins the game owning a few plots of plowed land and a bit of money, denominated in FarmVille's two in-game currencies: *Farm Cash* and *Farm Coins* (discussed in detail in Chapter 5). You can purchase more of this currency using real money, but you can also earn it simply by playing the game, as discussed in the next section.

You can easily customize the look of your farmer (see Chapter 3), but customizing and growing your farm to your desired specifications is a bit more complicated and forms the bulk of the game.

You grow crops, plant trees, and tend animals

That little bit of money you start with won't last very long if you don't invest it in profitable items. Using the mouse, you click around your farm using in-game tools (as discussed in Chapter 3) to plow plots of land, plant crops, and, eventually, harvest those crops for more money than you put in.

These crops grow, ripen, and eventually wither even when you're not actively playing the game, meaning that you have to check in and harvest them on a real-time schedule. You can also purchase trees and animals, and periodically collect coins from them without worrying as much about keeping to a strict play schedule. We tell you about these money-generating items in more detail in Chapter 3 and Chapter 6.

You decorate your farm

FarmVille currency isn't just good for generating more FarmVille currency — it's also good for buying decorations that make your farm uniquely yours. These decorations don't serve any functional gameplay purpose, but many farmers lose hours of their lives choosing and arranging the game's hundreds of in-game decorating options to their particular tastes. Think of this portion of the game as a virtual, farm-themed doll house, with an ever-expanding selection of accessories waiting to fill it up.

You help your neighbors (and they help you)

As a social game, FarmVille is partially focused on helping fellow players, known in the game as neighbors. FarmVille neighbors are a subset of your Facebook friends, so although all your FarmVille neighbors are Facebook friends, not all your Facebook friends are necessarily FarmVille neighbors.

You can help your neighbors by sending them free gifts or by visiting their farms and performing some basic farming tasks daily. After you've been playing for a while, you'll also be qualified to work with neighbors on co-op missions (as discussed in Chapter 12) and buy crafted goods from the Farmers Market (as discussed in Chapter 7). Of course, your neighbors can do all these things for you as well, forming a big, reciprocal cycle of good will.

It's not all sunshine and happiness, though — some players can get pretty competitive about FarmVille, working hard to make their farms that much more spectacular than those of their neighbors. Chapter 4 discusses interacting with neighbors in much more detail.

You upgrade your farm (and yourself)

As you perform various actions and buy various in-game items in FarmVille, you earn *experience points* (XP) to denote your progress. Earning enough experience points grants you a new *level*, which often comes with the ability to buy new items or access new purchasable items, as discussed in Chapter 8.

Avoiding FarmVille "addiction"

In a January 2010 episode of his syndicated talk show, television psychologist Dr. Phil confronted a mother whose love of FarmVille had probably gone too far. She admitted that the game was stopping her from returning phone calls or talking to her family, and generally causing her to neglect her responsibilities. Using his trademark "get real" approach, Dr. Phil pleaded with this woman to end her "ridiculous addiction" and "get out of FarmVille! . . . Reintroduce yourself to your family. Cook a meal. Go on a date. Go to a movie. Go jog. Go sit out in the backyard and watch the grass grow. Do something. Actually, maybe start a garden for real."

Certainly there are many worse things to be addicted to than video games, but getting a bit too engrossed in the virtual world is a very real risk for some people. FarmVille players can be especially susceptible to the effects of addiction for several reasons. The game's time-sensitive crops encourage players to check in frequently to avoid withered crops. A built-in community of fellow players can draw people away from their friends and family in the real world. Weekly updates and limited-edition items keep players coming back to see what's coming next. Random gifts and hidden items have a slot-machine–like effect on some players, keeping them clicking for that next random reward.

If you ever get to the point where you start thinking, "I can't stop watching my crops!" you're not alone. Many people engage in virtual farm life not just for an occasional escape but also as a constant way to avoid real-world problems and responsibilities. It can happen to anyone:

Dimitar Kerin, a Bulgarian politician, made international headlines for tending his virtual crops during budget meetings, even after he was asked to stop by fellow city council members.

Don't let the risk of addiction threaten to ruin the fun you can have farming. Instead, follow these tips for avoiding addiction — not just in FarmVille, but with any video or computer game.

- **Limit the time you spend playing.** Set a strict time limit for how much you'll allow yourself to play each day — a half hour or an hour, perhaps — and stick to it religiously. Use a stopwatch or a kitchen timer to help remind yourself to stop playing when your time is up.

- **Schedule your gameplay.** Set aside a specific time every day to play the game, and don't let yourself log in before or after that time. Use the scheduled play time as something to look forward to throughout the day rather than allow the game to kill productive time.

- **Make a list of your real-world obligations for the day.** Reward yourself with a quick visit to FarmVille after you've completed everything on your list — but not before.

- **Plant crops that fit your lifestyle.** Crops that sprout every four hours demand constant attention and frequent logins to harvest. Planting crops with longer growing times requires less frequent play time to get them harvested; it also gives you a longer margin of error for avoiding withered crops. For more on farming on your own schedule, see Chapter 6.

As you *level up*, as the process of earning new levels is known, you earn the ability to purchase storage buildings (discussed in Chapter 9) and farm expansions (discussed in Chapter 6) to help your farm hold even more items. You also earn access to more advanced features of the game, such as vehicles that help you perform farming tasks more quickly (as discussed in Chapter 6) and the Farmers Market, which lets you craft goods and sell them to neighbors (as discussed in Chapter 7).

Besides experience points and levels, you can also earn more specific *achievements* for certain in-game actions. These include ribbons for performing certain actions a set number of times, collections for finding certain hidden items, and crop mastery levels for harvesting certain crops frequently. These achievements are discussed in more detail in Chapter 11.

As mentioned earlier in the chapter, this continuous process of farming and improvement has no end point. Developer Zynga is constantly adding new features and new items to keep long-time players interested (as discussed in Chapter 10), and players often change which aspect of the game they want to focus on as they continue to play (as discussed in Chapter 15).

Getting Set Up to Play

In This Chapter

▶ Getting what you need to get started with FarmVille

▶ Creating a Facebook account

▶ Installing and playing FarmVille

▶ Playing FarmVille on FarmVille.com and mobile devices

So you're ready to become a virtual farmer, eh? Well, we're happy to help you do that, but first things first: You have to make sure you have what you need to get started. Using a computer with Internet access is the easiest way to play FarmVille, and practically any computer that can handle a graphical Web browser can handle the game. You might need to download a few extra programs and adjust some settings, though, and this chapter tells you how to do that.

After your computer is all set up for FarmVille, you need to get connected to Facebook before you start farming. This chapter tells you how to set up a Facebook account or, if you already have one, how to install the FarmVille app to make it playable from your existing Facebook account.

Don't have a computer? That's okay; you can now play FarmVille on Apple iOS devices, including the iPhone. In this chapter, you also discover how to find and install the mobile version of the game, and you find out how the mobile version differs from the versions on a traditional computer.

Getting Your Computer's Ducks in a Row

In contrast to most games on traditional gaming consoles such as the Nintendo Wii or Sony PlayStation 3, FarmVille is a Web-based game that you can play without inserting a disc or installing any programs to your hard drive. Your farm and the game program required to maintain it exist as part of a series of online data centers maintained by FarmVille's publisher, Zynga.

This means that a user can employ practically any computer with an Internet connection and a graphical Web browser to play FarmVille. We say "practically any computer" because the one you use does need to meet a few basic requirements for you to play FarmVille on it. We describe those requirements in the next few sections.

Getting on the Internet

This book assumes that your computer can connect to the Internet and that you've obtained a connection from an Internet service provider (ISP). If you need help getting set up with an Internet connection and making your way around the Web, check out *The Internet For Dummies*, 12th Edition, by John R. Levine and Margaret Levine Young (Wiley).

Although FarmVille is playable on a dial-up Internet connection, a broadband Internet connection greatly improves the speed and smoothness of your farming experience. Similarly, although you don't need the latest graphics card or expensive hardware to run FarmVille, the game may look smoother and run its animations more quickly on a more powerful machine.

Choosing a compatible Web browser

Because FarmVille is a Web-based game, you obviously need a Web browser to access it. Zynga suggests the following FarmVille-compatible Internet browsers, all of which can be downloaded for free from their associated Web sites.

- **Google Chrome:** `http://www.google.com/chrome`
- **Mozilla Firefox:** `http://www.mozilla.com/ firefox/`
- **Apple Safari:** `http://www.apple.com/safari/download/`
- **Microsoft Internet Explorer:** `http://www.microsoft.com/windows/ internet-explorer/`

Make sure that your browser has been updated to the latest version before going forward.

The Internet browser you're using may affect your FarmVille farming! If you experience lags during game play, try switching browsers. If you're a regular Internet Explorer user, for example, try Google Chrome or another browser and see whether performance improves.

Getting the Adobe Flash Player

In addition to a Web browser, your computer needs the Adobe Flash Player add-on for you to play FarmVille. Adobe Flash is a multimedia platform that allows Web sites to include interactive and animated content, including games and videos.

You may already have the Adobe Flash Player installed on your computer; it comes that way with many systems. Either way, go get the latest version of the player by visiting and following the directions on the official Adobe Flash Player site at `http://get.adobe.com/flashplayer/`.

Adobe offers a certified, virus-free version of its Flash Player for free at the aforementioned Web site. Be wary of downloading the player from other sites that might request payment or include malicious software with your download. Also note that the free Flash Player is different from professional development tools such as Adobe Flash Builder and Flash Professional, which do cost money but aren't required for playing FarmVille.

Enabling JavaScript

To play FarmVille, you need to make sure that your browser has JavaScript enabled. JavaScript lets your browser talk to the FarmVille servers and keep the farm that you see on your screen synced with the version stored in the Internet "cloud" of online servers.

The following sections describe how to enable JavaScript on the various Web browsers that Zynga recommends for the game. You need to follow the directions we provide here only if you've installed Abode Flash Player and the game doesn't load after you install it. In each case, the game should load properly after you complete the steps and reload the page.

Apple Safari

Enable JavaScript in Safari by following these steps:

1. **Click the Gears icon.**

2. **On the drop-down menu that appears, select Preferences.**

3. **When the Preference menu opens, select the Security tab.**

  4. **Select the Enable JavaScript check box.**

  5. **Click the red X in the upper-right corner of the menu.**

  6. **Click the Refresh button in your browser window.**

Mozilla Firefox

Here's how to enable JavaScript in the Firefox browser:

  1. **Choose Tools⇨Options.**

  2. **On the Options menu that appears, click the Content tab.**

  3. **On the menu that appears, select the Enable JavaScript check box.**

  4. **Click OK.**

  5. **Click the Refresh button in your browser window.**

Internet Explorer

Enable JavaScript in Internet Explorer using these steps:

  1. **Choose Tools⇨Internet Options.**

  2. **On the Internet Options menu that appears, select the Security tab.**

  3. **On the Security menu that appears, click the Internet icon (looks like a globe).**

  4. **Click Custom Level.**

  5. **In the Settings list that appears, scroll down to the Scripting section.**

  6. **Select the Enable button under Active Scripting.**

  7. **Click OK on the Settings list and then click OK on the Security menu.**

  8. **Click the Refresh button in your browser window.**

Chrome

Chrome automatically installs with JavaScript enabled, so you don't have to do anything.

Optimizing your performance

For most users, FarmVille should run just fine after you've installed Flash Player and enabled JavaScript. However, if you're running into loading problems or other performance issues such as lags in play or out-of-sync errors, here are a few things you can try to make your farming experience run more smoothly:

✔ **Close other programs and browsers while playing FarmVille.** Although having no other applications running isn't strictly necessary, it can definitely improve the stability of your computer and help prevent frequent crashing.

✔ **Select a lower graphics setting.** Clicking the Eye icon that appears in the top-left corner of the FarmVille game area toggles the game's graphics between high and low quality. Low-quality graphics may look rougher but should also make the game run faster. (For more on using FarmVille's in-game menu, see the section about navigating FarmVille in Chapter 3).

✔ **Clear your cache.** Clearing your cache improves game play by making your system run faster and more smoothly, as well as by making pages load faster.

Creating a Facebook Account So That You Can Play the Game

If you're not already one of the 500 million (and growing) people with a Facebook account, you need to change that fact before jumping into FarmVille. Luckily, signing up for Facebook is a free and easy process that shouldn't take long. Plus, signing up for Facebook can unlock a social journey. Just be careful of "oversharing."

Although it's tempting to post everything about you and your life on your new Facebook account, sharing too much personal information on the Internet, and especially on social networking sites such as Facebook, can be dangerous. Don't include information such as your physical address or home phone number in your profile unless you have a very compelling reason to do so, and strongly consider using Facebook's privacy controls to allow only your confirmed friends to view any updates you make to your profile.

To set up your Facebook account, follow these steps:

1. **In your preferred Web browser, go to** http://www.facebook.com.

   The Facebook sign-up/login page appears, as shown in Figure 2-1.

2. **Sign up for your personal account by providing the following information:**

   • **Your first and last names.**

   • **A valid e-mail address:** You need this address to confirm your account. Don't worry; Facebook doesn't share this address with the wider world if you don't want it to.

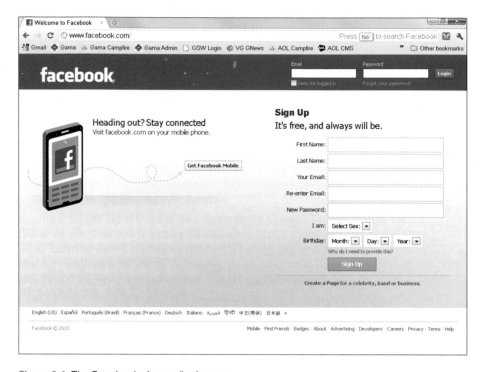

Figure 2-1: The Facebook sign-up/login page.

- **Password:** Choose something memorable but not obvious; "password," for example, is *not* a good choice. Passwords that intersperse capital letters with lowercase ones, as well as with numbers or symbols, are much more secure than a simple series of letters or numbers.

- **Sex:** Fill in your gender here.

- **Your Birthday:** Note that Facebook currently doesn't allow users under 13 years of age.

3. **Click the green Sign Up button.**

   A Security Check page appears, asking you to type in a randomized set of words shown in a security image.

4. **Type the two security words shown in the text box and click the Sign Up button.**

   The Find Friends page appears.

5. **Optional Information:** For each of the options in the following bulleted list, you can enter the requested information or click the Skip button to continue without sharing this information with Facebook.

   - **Find Friends:** Enter your e-mail address and e-mail password; then click Find Friends to have Facebook automatically search for members who are already listed in your e-mail contacts. On the next screen, select the check boxes next to the contacts you want to add as Facebook "friends." Then click Add As Friends.

   - **Profile Information:** Enter the name of your high school, college or university, and employer. As you type, the Facebook network associated with each organization appears in a drop-down list. Select the appropriate network (and your class year, for the schools); then click Save & Continue to move on.

   - **Profile Picture:** Click Upload a Photo and then click Choose File to select a digital photo from your computer, or click Take a Photo and then Save Picture to capture your image via your webcam. Click Save & Continue when you're happy with your digital avatar.

6. **Check your e-mail for a confirmation message from Facebook.** Click the link provided in the e-mail to confirm and validate your e-mail address.

Facebook: A Brief History

Social networking mega-site Facebook.com got its start at Harvard University in 2004. Facebook co-creator Mark Zuckerberg conceived of the site as a MySpace-style social network focused exclusively on letting college students connect and interact (though there's some controversy as to whether he devised the idea on his own or not). Though Harvard students were the first to have access to the site, the network quickly expanded to other colleges and then high schools and employers. Finally, in September 2006, anyone with a valid e-mail address could sign up for the site.

Though the functionality of the site was initially quite basic, features such as tagging, photo-sharing, and the now-ubiquitous wall were introduced at a breakneck pace over the subsequent years. In May 2007, the introduction of the Facebook platform allowed third-party companies to build applications that integrated seamlessly with Facebook's social network, letting users connect with their friends in myriad new ways. This integration included games such as FarmVille, which launched on the network in June 2009.

Although some users may feel that the current incarnation of Facebook has lost sight of the site's initial student-focused purpose, the majority of the 500 million current users would probably disagree. Now worth anywhere from $12 to $100 billion (depending on whose valuation of the private company you believe), the site continues to attract hundreds of thousands of new users daily and doesn't seem poised to stop growing any time soon.

Congratulations! You're now among the newest members of Facebook. The very first thing you should do with your new account is edit your privacy settings. Click the Account button in the upper-right hand corner of the page; then click Privacy settings. From this page, you can control which of your personal details will be viewable by friends, friends of friends, or people on the Internet at large.

For more on protecting your Facebook privacy and getting the most from your new account, we recommend *Facebook For Dummies* by Carolyn Abram and Leah Pearlman (Wiley). For the rest of you, let's get farming!

Installing the FarmVille App

If you've set up your Facebook account (see the preceding section for how to do that), you're almost ready to start enjoying life on your virtual farm! Installing the FarmVille app to your account is the only piece of business left to take care of before you can start the game, and it's an easy one.

Although you can also access the FarmVille app through a Facebook search, an invitation from a Facebook friend, or the game's public-facing Facebook page, here's the most direct way to get the app installed to your Facebook account:

1. **Go to** http://apps.facebook.com/onthefarm.

2. **Log in to your Facebook account and enter the e-mail address and password you used when signing up for your account; then click Login.**

   If you're already logged in to Facebook, you can skip this step. See the "Creating a Facebook Account So That You Can Play the Game," section, earlier in this chapter, if you haven't yet obtained a Facebook account.

   The Request for Permission page appears, as shown in Figure 2-2.

3. **Click the blue Allow button to give FarmVille access to the basic profile information on your Facebook account.**

   This information includes your name, profile picture, gender, networks, user ID, list of friends, and any other information you've shared with everyone via Facebook. FarmVille uses this information primarily to display your name and profile picture to your FarmVille friends, and to tailor advertising opportunities to your expected interests.

   After you click Allow, another Request for Permission page appears, asking for permission to send you e-mail.

Figure 2-2: The Request for Permission page.

4. (Optional) Click the blue Allow button to let FarmVille send you e-mail regarding the game.

By clicking Allow here, you give FarmVille permission to e-mail you directly with reminders to harvest your crops as well as notifications about gifts and special events. If you don't want to receive e-mail from FarmVille, click Don't Allow.

The FarmVille loading page appears after you complete this step.

5. (Optional) Click Install to download and install the FarmVille Game Bar onto your Web browser.

If you choose this option, the FarmVille game bar will appear at the top of your Web browser the next time you restart the browser. This Game Bar will offer reminders about the status of your crops, your pending gift requests, and more. If you want to install the Game Bar later, see the instructions listed in Chapter 5. Note that you need either Internet Explorer 7 or Firefox 3.6 (or higher versions of those) to install the Game Bar. If you use an unsupported browser to install the FarmVille app, you will be prompted to use a different browser to install the Game Bar.

After you complete the preceding steps, FarmVille should load automatically. If it doesn't, make sure that you've both installed the Adobe Flash Player and enabled JavaScript. (See the sections for performing each of these tasks earlier in this chapter.)

We cover details on how to start playing your newly installed game in Chapter 3. The remainder of this chapter discusses how to best integrate FarmVille into your normal Facebook activities and network of online friends.

Bookmarking FarmVille on your Facebook account

Remembering to enter FarmVille's URL into your browser's address box each time you want to play can quickly get annoying. Luckily, playing FarmVille automatically adds the game to a Bookmarks sidebar on the left side of your Facebook home page, as shown in Figure 2-3. The exact position of FarmVille on this bookmarks list may change as you use other apps, but it will jump back to the top every time you play FarmVille.

You can also bookmark FarmVille using your Web browser.

Figure 2-3: How the FarmVille bookmark appears on your Facebook sidebar.

Playing directly from FarmVille.com

If you don't want to go through the Facebook home page every time you play FarmVille, you can also access the game directly through the FarmVille Web site at `http://www.farmville.com`, as shown in Figure 2-4. The game is almost exactly the same in both Web locations — in fact, the same farm you maintain on Facebook is accessible on FarmVille.com, and vice versa.

Figure 2-4: Playing FarmVille through FarmVille.com.

Despite the new location, you still need a Facebook account to play on FarmVille.com, and you'll be prompted to log in with your Facebook account when you visit the site.

So why play at FarmVille.com? Well, playing on the site gives you access to "FarmVille.com Exclusive" gifts, which you can't send through the gift-giving page on Facebook. For more on giving gifts, see Chapter 4.

Additionally, FarmVille.com allows you to control specific settings regarding e-mail notifications sent to you by Zynga. Click the "Click here to update your preferences" message on the FarmVille.com Home page to display a list of different notifications the game can send you via e-mail, as shown in Figure 2-5. Select the radio button under the Yes column for the options you'd like to activate and then click Save to confirm your settings.

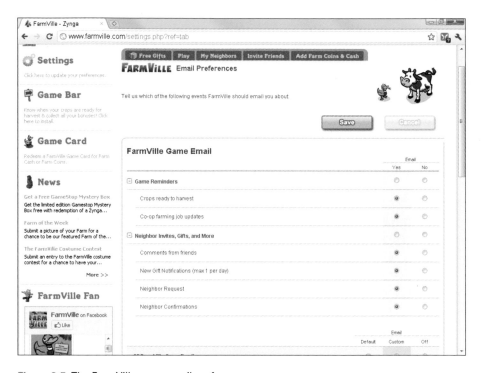

Figure 2-5: The FarmVille.com e-mail preferences menu.

Finally, FarmVille.com features a different site layout surrounding the game than the familiar, minimalist design found on Facebook.com. Some users prefer the FarmVille.com layout over Facebook's because it's chock full of FarmVille news and updates. As an extra bonus, FarmVille.com is also free of Facebook's user-targeted advertising, which some players find bothersome.

Playing FarmVille from your mobile iDevice

In June 2010, Zynga launched the first mobile FarmVille app for the iPhone, iPod Touch, and iPad. The FarmVille app offers access to the same farm you maintain on Facebook.com or FarmVille.com, only now it's literally at your fingertips on the go, wherever you go!

As a perk of using the FarmVille app for your mobile devices, FarmVille offers exclusive in-game items that you can purchase. The only way to access such items is to purchase them through the FarmVille Market when using the FarmVille app on your iOS device.

Another mobile device perk is the ability to send exclusive free gifts to your neighbors. Although anyone can see the exclusive items in the Market or on the Gifting page, they are labeled as locked if you're not using an iOS device. These iOS exclusive gifting items change frequently, so be sure to check your device frequently for new gift opportunities.

You can download the FarmVille app by searching for FarmVille on your device's App Store, or you can download the app to iTunes by visiting `http://itunes.apple.com/us/app/farmville-by-zynga/ id375562663?mt=8`. For more on installing mobile apps on your iDevice, see *iPhone For Dummies*, 4th Edition, by Edward C. Baig and Bob LeVitus (Wiley).

Turning Facebook friends into FarmVille neighbors

Starting a farm can be lonely without anyone to farm with, so the best way to jumpstart your farming frenzy is to add your existing Facebook friends to your FarmVille game as neighbors. Neighbors are integral to the FarmVille experience, as we discuss in more detail in Chapter 4. You can start with people who already play or invite those who don't to join. Asking friends who already play and sending out invitations to those who don't is a great starting point for neighbor acquisition, and as a bonus, you are adding people you actually know! FarmVille neighbors make farming more fun and more productive by increasing your coins and experience points. (Chapter 8 tells you more about experience points.)

Suggesting FarmVille to friends

You can invite your Facebook friends to play FarmVille by accessing the My Neighbors tab found above your FarmVille Home Page. Your friends have to accept your invitation to play and also must add you as a neighbor before they show up on your Neighbors list.

Inviting friends who don't play FarmVille

To invite your Facebook friends who don't play FarmVille, simply click the Invite Friends button located at the top of your FarmVille game's Home page menu. The Invite button triggers a list of all your Facebook friends. Scroll through the list and select the friends you want to invite. You can invite up to 40 friends at one time.

Adding friends as neighbors

Maybe you already have some Facebook friends playing FarmVille but just don't know it. You can find out who is playing and add them as neighbors by clicking the My Neighbors tab located at the top of your FarmVille game's

Home page menu. All your Facebook friends who play FarmVille automatically appear on the My Neighbors page. Now that you can see who is playing, simply click the blue button labeled Add [Friend Name] as Neighbor on the bottom right

You can read all about the importance of neighbors and find out about additional ways to find neighbors in Chapter 4.

3

Getting Around in FarmVille and Starting Your Farm

In This Chapter

▶ Navigating FarmVille

▶ Using the FarmVille menu

▶ Getting your farm off the ground

A ssuming that you've set up your Facebook account and your first FarmVille farm, you're ready to get farming. After reading this chapter, you'll be harvesting your farm like an expert virtual farmer — and you won't even have to break a sweat.

The first sections of this chapter describe all the menus and icons that you use to play the game. If you prefer to get straight to farming, skip to the "Starting Your Farm: Level 1" section and flip back to earlier sections whenever you want to know how to get to a particular area or use a certain tool. Finally, we present a few quick tips that will get you on the road to virtual farming success that much more quickly.

Using the Top Menu to Navigate FarmVille

The top menu consists of six brown tabs and a FarmVille Requests button located above the FarmVille play area (see Figure 3-1). The following sections explain the items on the top menu and what you can access by clicking them.

Top menu

Options menu　　　　Other stats

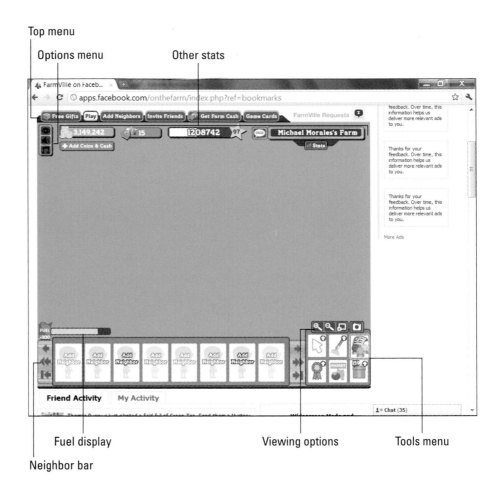

Fuel display　　　　Viewing options　　　　Tools menu

Neighbor bar

Figure 3-1: The major parts of the FarmVille user interface.

The Free Gifts tab: Sending gifts to your neighbors

Clicking the Free Gifts tab redirects you to the FarmVille Gifting page, shown in Figure 3-2, where you can select free gifts to send to your farming neighbors. (For more on meeting and interacting with FarmVille neighbors, see Chapter 4). Though the specific items on the –Gifting page differ for each farmer and occasionally change throughout the year, the page always includes a variety of decorations, trees, animals, and supplies that your friends can use on their farms. (For more details of using each of these items, see Chapter 6.)

Figure 3-2: The FarmVille Gifting page.

To send a gift, follow these steps:

1. **On the top menu, click the Free Gifts tab.**

   The Gifting page appears, showing an array of available gifts.

2. **Select the radio button under the gift you want to give and click Proceed to Send**

   Note that some free gifts may be labeled as "Locked." This label signifies that your farmer isn't at a high enough level to send that gift yet. (For more on attaining higher levels, see Chapter 8.) Also note that some gifts may be labeled as "FarmVille.com exclusive" or "iPhone exclusive." You need to access the game on those platforms to send the gift.

   When you click the Proceed to Send button, the Friend Selection page appears.

3. **Select the check boxes for any number of friends to whom you want to send the gift.**

   Note that you can send only one free gift per friend per day. If you've already sent a specific friend a gift today, that friend does not appear on the Friend Selection page.

On the Friend Selection screen, you can type a name in the Start Typing a Name box to jump straight to a specific Facebook friend. In addition, you can limit the list to fellow FarmVille players among your Facebook friends by clicking the FarmVille Friends tab atop the list.

4. **Click Send FarmVille Gift Request to send your gift.**

The Play tab: Heading down to the farm

Clicking the Play tab always redirects you to the play area for your farm, where you seed your crops, place buildings and decorations, and so on. Clicking Play while you're already on your farm refreshes your page with the latest version from Zynga's servers, but you need to refresh your page only if your connection falls out of sync for some reason. (See Chapter 14 for help with synchronization issues.)

The My Neighbors tab: Keeping in touch with your FarmVille neighbors

Clicking the My Neighbors tab brings up the My Neighbors page. As shown in Figure 3-3, this page displays information about your current Facebook friends who play FarmVille. Each friend is grouped into one of the following three categories:

- Non-neighbors
- Neighbors
- Pending neighbor requests

Each friend's current FarmVille level, number of earned achievements, and number of neighbors are displayed. You can use the buttons on the My Neighbors page to do the following:

- Send a neighbor request to your non-neighbors
- Cancel requests sent to pending neighbors
- Remove active neighbors from your neighbor list

You can also send free gifts to both neighbors and non-neighbors, as described in the section "The Free Gifts tab: Sending gifts to your neighbors," earlier in this chapter. For much more on interacting with neighbors, see Chapter 4.

Figure 3-3: The My Neighbors page.

The My Neighbors page is the only place where you can remove deadbeat neighbors — those who have become inactive farmers — so remember to use it to keep your neighbors list lean and pruned.

The Invite Friends tab: Recruiting more neighbors

Inviting your Facebook friends who don't play FarmVille to join in the fun is easy. Just follow these steps:

1. **Click the Invite Friends tab in the top menu.**

   The Invite Friends page appears with a list and pictures of your Facebook friends.

2. **Click the names of whichever friends you'd like to invite to play the game.**

   You can also use the Filter Friends drop-down menu to filter your Friends list by personal networks, or you can type a name into the box labeled Find Friends to jump to a specific Facebook friend.

3. **Click the blue Send FarmVille Request button.**

   Any Facebook friends who accept your invitation to play FarmVille don't show up as your FarmVille neighbors until they accept your neighbor request. See Chapter 4 for more on sending and accepting neighbor requests.

The Get Farm Cash tab: Increasing your farm's assets

Clicking the Get Farm Cash tab on the top menu displays a page where you buy in-game currency to purchase items and farm upgrades. We tell you all about how to use this menu in Chapter 5.

The Game Card tab: Redeeming your FarmVille Game Cards

Clicking the Game Card tab on the top menu displays a page where you can redeem your FarmVille Game Cards. You can use Game Cards to purchase Farm Cash or Farm Coins. We tell you more about how Game Cards work in Chapter 5.

The FarmVille Requests tab: Taking care of actions awaiting your attention

Clicking the FarmVille Requests tab on the top menu displays the FarmVille section of your Facebook Requests page, as shown in Figure 3-4. This section lists a selection of in-game events that require action on your part, including the following:

- **FarmVille gifts sent to you by other players:** These free items appear in your Gift Box after being accepted.
- **Neighbor invitations:** Requests from fellow Facebook friends who would like to be FarmVille neighbors with you.
- **Neighbor help requests:** Accepting these requests will send the requested item to your neighbor, or help them with an in-game event such as a barn-raising.

Note that this tab appears as inactive (grayed out) if you have no pending FarmVille requests, in which case you should bug your friends to send you some more gifts, already!

To accept a request, you click the Accept and Play button next to it, and a new page appears, asking whether you have more gifts or requests to accept. Clicking Yes returns you to the Facebook Requests page, whereas clicking No takes you directly to the FarmVille game page.

If you accidentally click the wrong button, don't worry; you can just click the Play tab or the FarmVille Requests tab to get where you want to go, and your request will still be accepted.

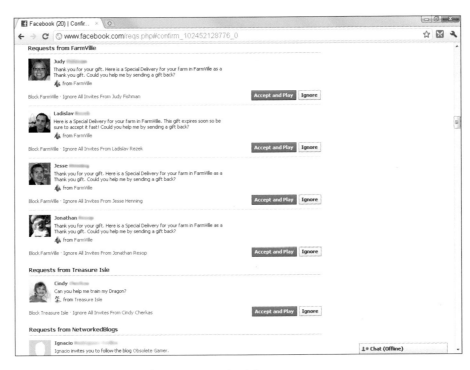

Figure 3-4: The FarmVille section of the Facebook Requests page.

You can also accept your FarmVille requests by clicking the See All link next to Facebook Requests on the right side of your Facebook home page.

FarmVille requests don't last forever — in fact, they expire if you don't answer them within a month. After a gift request has been accepted, however, the item remains in your in-game Gift Box indefinitely, so be sure to click the Accept and Play button as soon as possible, even if you don't plan to use the gift just yet.

Setting Graphics and Sound Preferences through the Options Menu

You find the Options menu in the top left of the FarmVille playing area, right next to your Farm Coin counter. Clicking any of the buttons in this menu toggles them between active (highlighted in white) and inactive (highlighted in dark brown).

The Options menu features the following three options:

✔ **Toggle Graphics Quality:** Clicking the eye icon lets you choose between high- and low-resolution graphics. Although running the game with lower-quality graphics gives in-game items a rougher appearance and more jagged edges, it also may help FarmVille run more smoothly. Try turning down the quality to see whether it helps your playing experience.

✔ **Sound On/Off:** Clicking the speaker icon toggles the sound effects on your farm, including animal noises and vehicle exhaust sounds.

✔ **Music On/Off:** Clicking the music note icon toggles the familiar FarmVille theme music.

Keeping Track of your Farming Stats

The FarmVille interface is loaded with informational icons, but don't feel overwhelmed by all those icons. As you play the game, you'll quickly grow familiar with them. Each of the icons in the following list represents an essential aspect of effective and efficient farming:

✔ **Coin Display:** Displays your current amount of Farm Coins. Note that this number updates in real time as you buy items and harvest crops. For more on obtaining and spending Farm Coins (and Farm Cash, next on the list), see Chapter 5.

✔ **Farm Cash Display:** Displays your current amount of Farm Cash. Note that even when you gain Farm Cash through a purchase or by leveling up, this display may not update until you reload the game.

✔ **XP & Level Meter:** Displays your current amount of accumulated experience points, or XP, which are signified by the white number) and your FarmVille level (shown inside the yellow star). The size of the white bar indicates roughly how much progress you've made toward your next level. Hover over any portion of this display to see exactly how many XP you need to reach your next level. (For more on levels, see Chapter 8.)

✔ **Sign Post:** Clicking this button allows you to place a Sign Post or leave a comment on your farm a farm you're visiting. After clicking the icon, click an empty portion of the farm to bring up the Comments menu, as shown in Figure 3-5. Type your message in the text box and then click the Post button to add your comment to the farm's comments thread. These comments are readable by anyone who visits that farm, so don't write anything you're not comfortable sharing with the wider world.

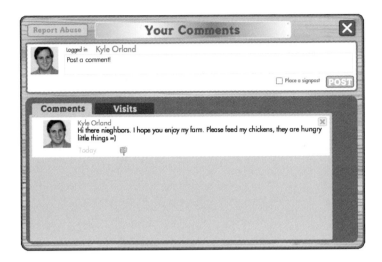

Figure 3-5: The Comments menu.

Note that you can select optional check boxes on the Comments menu to copy the comment to your neighbor's Facebook wall or to leave the comment as a message sign, which then sits on the farm and is permanently readable by anyone who clicks it.

On the Comments menu, you can also click the Visits tab to show which neighbors have recently visited your farm. Click Report Abuse to go to a Zynga Web site where you can report abusive comments. (See Chapter 13 for more on contacting Zynga User Support for this and other issues.)

✔ **Farm Name:** In case you forget, this area displays whose farm you're currently visiting, even if it's your own!

✔ **Stats Bar:** Clicking the Stats icon underneath the Farm Name icon displays a rundown of the number of the various in-game achievements earned by you or your neighbor. From left to right, these numbers represent:

- Level
- Ribbons
- Masteries
- Medals
- Collections
- Constructed Buildings

Note that clicking the Ribbons, Masteries, or Medals icons further expands the menu to show breakdowns for each achievement by color or star level. Click the small white arrow to collapse the Stats menu again. For more on what all these achievements mean, see Chapter 8 for level, Chapter 9 for buildings, and Chapter 11 for the rest.

 ✔ **Comments:** Click the picture of a speaking person in the upper-right corner of the play area to bring up the Comments menu for the current farm, as shown in Figure 3-5 and discussed in the bullet describing the Sign Post, earlier in this list.

 ✔ **Fuel Display:** Located on the bottom-left corner of the game area, this icon displays how much fuel you currently have for vehicles. The number in the green area indicates how many full tanks of fuel you've earned, and the yellow bar indicates how much of the current tank remains. For more on using fuel and vehicles, see Chapter 6.

 For a precise measure of how many plots you can plow, seed, or harvest with your current fuel, hover your mouse over the Fuel Display icon.

✔ **Neighbor bar:** This bar lists all your FarmVille neighbors, organized from left to right according to their total XP. Use the arrows on either side of the bar to scroll the list in that direction. The single arrow moves the list one neighbor at a time; the double arrows move the list one page at a time; and the arrow with a vertical line jumps you to either end of the list.

Clicking a neighbor's name or picture on this bar brings up a menu letting you send gifts, visit and help your neighbors farm, or invite new friends to your neighbors list. For more on interacting with neighbors using these options, see Chapter 4.

Viewing your farm close up or from afar

You use the three brown buttons sitting above the Tools menu in the bottom-right corner of the play area to control how you view the current farm.

 ✔ **Zoom In:** Click the icon of a magnifying glass with a plus sign (+) to zoom in the in-game view for a closer look at the current farm.

 ✔ **Zoom Out:** Click the icon of a magnifying glass with a minus sign (-) to zoom out the in-game view for a view that covers more land.

 You can also use your mouse's scroll wheel to zoom in (flick the scroll wheel up) or out (flick the scroll wheel down). If the scroll wheel is moving the entire Web page rather than just the FarmVille view, try clicking the FarmVille game area to gain control of the viewpoint.

✏ **Toggle Full Screen:** Clicking this icon toggles between Full Screen mode, which makes the game area fill all the available monitor space, and the regular view, which reduces the game area to a small window on a larger Web page.

Note that you can use the Esc key on your keyboard to quickly exit Full Screen mode and return to the regular view. This doesn't work the other way around, however. Also note that certain in-game actions, such as visiting a neighbor's farm, or certain other events on your computer, such as having your antivirus program running a scan, may automatically cause the game to exit Full Screen mode.

✏ **Take a picture:** Click this button to display a menu that allows you to take a picture of your farm. You can then save this picture to your computer or post it on your Facebook wall. For more information on taking pictures of your farm, see Chapter 14.

Controlling the view

When the view is zoomed in to a close-up of some area of your farm, you may want to move the view around to see other areas. To do so, just click and hold the mouse button anywhere on the farm and then move the mouse in the direction you want the view to move. Release the mouse when you're done moving the view to continue farming.

Walking the farm

Clicking any open spot on your farm causes your farmer avatar to walk over to that location. Although this kind of idle movement doesn't serve any specific purpose in the game, it can be useful for positioning your farmer to be included in pictures of your farm.

Getting to Know the Tools Menu

The Tools menu in the bottom-right corner of the FarmVille play area is the heart and soul of the FarmVille experience. You use the tools on this menu to do everything from planting crops and buying seeds to accepting gifts and taking part in co-operative farming missions — and everything in between. The more familiar you become with these tools, the more effective your virtual farming will be.

Here are the options on the Tools menu:

✏ **Multi:** Click the white arrow in the upper-left-hand corner of the Tools menu to select the Multi tool. This white arrow is the default cursor that you use for most basic actions in FarmVille, including planting seeds, harvesting trees and animals, and moving your viewpoint of your farm around. Unless otherwise noted, when we say to click something in this book, we mean to click it with the Multi tool selected.

Hovering the mouse over the Multi tool icon expands the tool to a menu with two additional tools, Recycle and Move (note that these tools may appear on the main Tools menu on new farms). Note that, for the most part, you can access the functions of these tools simply by clicking an item with the Multi tool and choosing the appropriate action from the menu that appears. However, using these more specific tools can let you perform some repetitive tasks more quickly:

- *Recycle:* Click the white recycling symbol to choose the Recycle tool and quickly sell any item on your farm for Farm Coins with a single click. If an item has no coin value — such as a plot for planting — clicking it with the Recycle tool simply deletes it. Note that even when an item does have a resale value, it will usually be much lower than the price you paid to purchase the item.

  The first time you use the Recycle tool after using another tool, a pop-up notification box appears, asking you to confirm the deletion by clicking the Accept or Cancel buttons. Don't just automatically click Accept; you may permanently lose an exclusive item that can be hard or impossible to reacquire. Double-check what you're expecting to delete first.

  You can prevent the notification box from popping up again by selecting the Turn On Quick Delete check box, which suppresses warnings for any recycled item worth fewer than 1,000 Farm Coins. You can also select the check box labeled "Don't warn me about selling of deleting decorations until I switch tools" to suppress warnings about all decorations. These warnings can be useful, however, if you're trying to clear out a whole section of knick-knacks but don't accidentally want to destroy your nearby crops.

- *Move:* Click the white hand icon to select the Move tool, which you can use to move anything on your farm. Clicking an item with the Move tool once picks it up; clicking again drops the item in its new location.

  Note that two objects can't share the exact same location — if the object you're holding appears slightly translucent or has a red box showing underneath it, at least part of it overlaps with another object, as far as the game is concerned. Try dropping the object back into its original location and then clearing out some space in your planned location before moving the item again.

  You can even use the Move tool to pick up and move square planting plots, whether they're fallow, plowed, or seeded. Although moving plots doesn't jibe with real life (we doubt that topsoil

would survive such a move intact), it can be incredibly useful in
FarmVille when you're trying to rearrange an entire field of plots
quickly. That's the beauty of virtual farming!

 ✔ **Plow:** Click the green hoe icon on the top-center section of the Tools
menu to choose the Plow tool. Clicking the Plow tool on any unoccupied
portion of your farm turns that small square into a plowed plot of land,
suitable for planting. You can also use the Plow tool to re-plow a fallow
plot of land after it's been harvested, although you can also use the
Multi tool for this purpose.

Plowing land with the Plow tool doesn't use any fuel, but it does require
many more clicks than using a vehicle such as the Tractor or Combine
to get the job done. It also requires you to wait for your farmer avatar
to slooooowly walk over to the area you want plowed to carry out the
action. (If you block your farmer, you don't have to wait for your avatar
to walk around; see the tip in the "Block your farmer" section, later in
this chapter, for instructions on how to block your farmer.)

Hovering your mouse over the Plow tool expands the menu to include a
variety of FarmVille vehicles (assuming that you've purchased the vehicles from the FarmVille Market). Chapter 6 tells you how to use vehicles
to speed up your planting and harvest.

 ✔ **Co-Op Farming:** After you've reached level 20, an icon showing three
farmers in front of a checklist appears in the top-right corner of the Tools
menu. Click this icon to display the Co-Op Farming menu. This menu and
the co-op farming jobs it describes are discussed in Chapter 12.

✔ **Ribbons:** Click the blue ribbon icon to bring up the Ribbons menu,
which presents the requirements for a variety of ribbon achievements.
We discuss these achievements in detail in Chapter 11.

If you hover the mouse over the blue ribbon icon rather than click it,
the Collections icon appears. Clicking this icon brings up the Collections
menu, which displays how many collectible items you've gathered and
how many more you need to complete each set. Collections are discussed in Chapter 11.

 ✔ **Market:** Click the Market icon in the bottom row of the Tools menu to
buy seeds, decorations, buildings, animals, and any other item for sale in
FarmVille. (We cover the FarmVille Market menu in depth in Chapter 6.)

 ✔ **Gifts:** Click the blue present icon to bring up your Gift inventory. This
menu shows all the gifts that you've collected but not yet placed on your
farm. The number in pink above the icon represents the number of gifts
currently in your box, which can't exceed 500. For more on sending and
receiving gifts, see Chapter 4.

Hover over the Gift icon to bring up the Storage icon, which you can
click for access to the Storage menu and your stored items. For more on
storage, see Chapter 11.

Starting Your Farm: Level 1

Every farmer starts out with the following statistics and in-game currency:

- Level: 1
- XP: 0
- Coins: 240
- Farm Cash: 5
- Plowed plots of land: 6 plots
- Total farm space: Enough for 144 plowed plots (12 along each edge of the square farm space)

The game starts you off with a small interactive tutorial that instructs you on the farming process, but in this section, we walk you through your first harvest, so feel free to click the Skip This Tutorial button and keep reading.

Customizing your farmer

When you load your farm for the first time, a menu pops up to let you customize the look of your farmer avatar. This avatar represents you in the game and "physically" walks around to perform various in-game tasks on different parts of your farm.

You use the Customize My Farmer menu, shown in Figure 3-6, to change various elements of your avatar's appearance, such as skin color, hair, facial features, and clothes.

Here's a quick breakdown of how to use the major portions of this menu:

- **Gender:** Click the Gender button at the top of the menu; then click either the male or female outline to change the gender of your farmer.
- **Facial Features:** Click the Facial Features button at the top of the menu, then choose the facial feature you'd like to edit from the drop-down list. Click the Use button underneath the facial feature you'd like to put on your farmer, and it will immediately appear on the sample farmer on the right. Your changes aren't permanent until you click the Save and Close button at the bottom of the menu, so don't be afraid to try a few options to see which one you prefer. Make sure to click the right and left arrows on the sides of the menu to see all the options for each facial feature.

✔ **Clothing:** Click the Clothing button at the top of the menu; then choose which item of clothing you want to customize from the drop-down list. Clothing is divided into two separate categories: clothing in your inventory and clothing in the FarmVille Market. For the clothing in your inventory, simply click the Use button underneath the item of clothing you'd like to see on the sample farmer on the right. For clothing in the Market, click the Buy button below the item to add it to your inventory, where you can put it on or take it off at your leisure.

You can also click the Try On button below an article of clothing in the Market to see what it will look like on your farmer before purchasing it. After you've tried on a fully assembled ensemble of Market clothing, click the Buy Now button underneath your farmer preview to buy all the items simultaneously. The Total price for all the clothing items is listed in the price tag underneath your farmer, and you can see an itemized list of the items you'll be buying by hovering the mouse over the letter *I* in the upper-right corner of the price tag. You can also click the Reset button to take off any clothes your farmer is currently trying on.

✔ **Save and Close:** When you're happy with the way your farmer looks, click the Save and Close to see your new avatar on the farm.

You can bring up the Customize My Farmer menu at any time later on simply by clicking your farmer.

Figure 3-6: The Customize My Farmer menu.

Plowing, seeding, and harvesting

The majority of your time and effort in FarmVille involves the continuous cycle of plowing, seeding, and harvesting of various crops. The following steps walk you through starting this cycle on your first farm:

1. **On the Tools menu, click the Plow tool and then click any open plot of land on your farm.**

   You can also click existing, fallow plots of land (indicated by their light-brown color) to plow them and make them suitable for planting. A small square of dirt (or *plot)* that you plow turns a darker brown. You can repeat this step multiple times until your field is full of plowed plots, but remember to leave some Farm Coins available to purchase seeds in the next step.

   Plowing a plot of land earns you one XP and costs 15 coins per plot.

2. **Bring up the Market menu by clicking on a plowed plot or by clicking the Market icon (shown here in the margin) in the Tools menu.**

   The Market menu appears. Not all seeds will be available for purchase at first, but you will unlock more as you gain higher levels (as described in Chapter 8).

3. **Click the Buy button underneath the seed you'd like to plant.**

   Each seed on the Market menu is labeled with a preset amount of time before the crop will be ready to harvest. Try to plan ahead so that you'll be available to harvest your crops soon after they're ready. If you don't, your crops may wither to useless husks.

   Also take into account the price of the seed you're purchasing (shown next to the coin symbol) as well as the eventual harvest price and the number of XP gained for each harvest. For more on planning your farming schedule and navigating the Market menu, see Chapter 6. For recommendations of some good seeds to choose, see Chapter 17.

   When you click the Buy button, the Market menu disappears and the chosen seed shows up next to your mouse pointer.

4. **Click a plowed plot to plant the purchased seed.**

   The plowed plot becomes a seeded plot, as indicated by small buds of your planted crop. Coins are removed from your account to purchase the seed at this point, and XP are added to your total (the exact number of each depends on the specific seed you chose).

   You can repeat this step as many times as you'd like to seed multiple plowed plots. If you want to plant a different seed in some plots, click the Market menu icon in the Tools menu and return to Step 3.

5. Wait for your crops to ripen.

Planted seeds can take anywhere from two hours to four days of real time to ripen and be ready to harvest. You can check on your crops during this ripening time by hovering your mouse over a seeded plot to display, as a percentage, how ripe the crop is. When a crop is fully ripened, it changes appearance and displays as "100% grown" when you hover your mouse over it.

If you wait too long to harvest crops after they ripen, they wither into shriveled, brown husks that are not worth any coins. If this happens, you have to go back to Step 1 and re-plow that plot of land. The time it takes a ripened crop to wither is the same as the amount of time it takes for that seed to turn in to a ripened crop.

6. Click the Multi tool and then click a fully ripened crop to harvest it.

Farm Coins are added to your account based on the harvest value of seed planted. The plot of land turns into a light-brown, fallow piece of land. Repeat this step as often as necessary until all ripened crops are harvested. This piece of land can then be plowed and seeded again in a repeat of the cycle that drives much of the FarmVille economy.

Diversifying Your Farm

FarmVille is about more than just harvesting crops. The game also offers animals and pets to tend to, trees to grow, and decorations to place. Although none of these options is strictly necessary for a successful farm, they can help add a personal, lively touch to your farm as well as earn you some coins and XP in the process.

Farm animals

The types of animals available in FarmVille aren't limited to just those traditionally found on farms. Elephants? Check. Penguins? There has to be a Penguin farm somewhere, right? Pink Cows? You bet (isn't that where Strawberry Milk comes from?).

Besides making your farm look cute, animals can also be a profitable part of your farm. Just as you harvest crops for coins, so can you harvest most animals every so often, also for coins. A pink indicator icon above the animal tells you when that animal is ready to harvest. Simply click the animal with the Multi tool to collect your coins. Each animal has a specific gestation time before harvesting and yields a specific number of coins when harvested. Despite the grisly sounding name, *harvesting* an animal doesn't actually harm the beast (see the sidebar "A humane harvest" for more about what harvesting involves). Also note that some animals, such as white owls, butterflies, doves, and squirrels, are considered decorative animals and can't be harvested.

If you're desperate for coins, you can sell your animals for a small sum. Simply click the animal with the Recycle tool, or click the animal with the Multi tool and select Sell from the drop-down menu. Because animals can earn you lots of coins over the long run through harvesting, we don't recommend selling an animal unless you really need coins immediately or desperately need to clear space on your farm. Note that you can't sell animals before reaching level 7. (See Chapter 8 for more on reaching new levels.)

Certain types of animals, such as chickens, horses, and pigs, can be placed in shelters for easy harvesting and a chance at secret items with each harvest. See Chapter 9 for more on getting and using animal shelters.

FarmVille gives you several ways to obtain animals, including the following:

✔ **Adoption:** As you play FarmVille, every so often a pop-up notification appears, asking whether you want to find a home for a lost, lonely animal. You can't keep the animal for yourself, but if you click Share, you can post a message about the lost animal to your Facebook news feed. Your neighbors can then click the link in that message to adopt the animal and place it on their farm. Likewise, if you see a lost animal on your friend's news feed, you can click the link to adopt it for your farm. (It will appear in your Gift Box.)

Note that only the first person to click each news feed link can adopt the animal in question, so keep your eyes peeled and your clicking finger ready. Also note that some types of animals are available exclusively through adoption.

✔ **Receive as a gift:** Animals are often featured on the FarmVille Gifting page, discussed earlier in this chapter. Receiving free animal gifts from your friends is one of the easiest ways to fill your farm with life, so encourage your neighbors to send you animal gifts any way you can.

✔ **Purchase:** Many animals can be purchased from the FarmVille Market directly with either Farm Cash or coins. Usually, limited-edition animals can be purchased only with Farm Cash. See Chapter 6 for more on using the FarmVille Market to purchase animals.

Pets

Pets in FarmVille, including puppies and dogs, are just like regular animals, but with extra features and requirements. They follow you around the farm as you move, ready to help at a moment's notice.

A humane harvest

If you've always wanted to have a farm because of your love of animals, you'll be happy to know that harvesting animals in FarmVille doesn't harm any animals, even virtually. Instead, the lucrative "harvest" from the animal technically comes from some sort of product that the animal produces. You collect milk from cows and feathers from ducks, for instance. Sheep produce wool, and pigs find valuable truffles. The developers at Zynga can get pretty creative when it comes to harvesting animals that don't seem to have a friendly purpose or use. For example, whenever you harvest from a Baby Tiger, it magically produces lucrative "Good Luck." It's enough to warm the heart of even the most strident animal rights activist.

To obtain a pet, follow these steps:

1. **On the Market menu, click the Animals tab and then the Pets tab.**

   A list of various pets appears.

2. **Click the Buy button underneath the pet you want to purchase.**

   The Pet Customization menu, shown in Figure 3-7, appears.

3. **Use the buttons on this menu to choose your new pet's gender, color, and name; then click the Buy button to make your purchase.**

Figure 3-7: The Pet Customization menu.

Note that pets that are purchased as puppies require regular feeding to become full-fledged adult dogs. To feed a puppy, click it with the Multi tool and then choose Feed from the drop-down menu. Feeding your puppy requires Puppy Kibble, which you purchase from the Market (for one Farm Cash each) or receive as a gift from friends. Pets purchased with coins come with one day's worth of kibble, whereas puppies purchased with Farm Cash comes with a full two weeks' worth.

You can tickle your puppy by clicking it and choosing Tickle from the drop-down menu. Your puppy will roll over onto its back and shake its legs as hearts pop up above its tummy. Adorable!

Puppies that are purchased with coins can run away if they're not fed once daily. If a puppy runs away, you can rescue it from the Dog Pound by paying Farm Cash for its return.

After 14 consecutive daily feedings, a puppy grows into an adult dog, which no longer requires daily feedings. You can also teach adult dogs tricks by feeding them Dog Treats purchased from the Market. The kinds of tricks the adult dog can learn depends on the breed. For example, the Border Collie can harvest 20 animals on your farm by "herding" them in a single click.

Dogs will forget their tricks if they're not fed new treats daily, so make sure you're stocked up!

Trees

Growing and harvesting trees is another way to earn coins. As with crops, trees take time to ripen before being ready for harvest. In contrast to crops, however, trees can be harvested many times from one planting. Trees don't wither as crops do, either, so you can harvest them at your leisure.

You can purchase trees directly with Farm Cash or coins in the market, receive them as gifts via the Gifting page, or find them as Mystery Gifts from friends (see Chapter 4 for more on gifts). After you plant a tree on an open patch of soil, it immediately begins ripening. Hover over a tree with the Multi tool to see how ripe it is as a percentage. When a tree reaches the 100% mark and is ready to harvest, click it with the Multi tool to reset the ripeness to 0% and receive a bonus in coins.

Each specific type of tree has its own unique ripening time and coin yield from each harvest. Some trees, such as the Falling Blossom, Dogwood, Birch, Magnolia, and Jacaranda trees, are strictly decorative and can't be harvested for coins.

You can purchase some of the most lucrative trees in FarmVille only with Farm Cash. The Acai tree is the most profitable tree in the game, yielding 158 coins every two days, but it will cost you a whopping 27 Farm Cash to get one.

You can purchase certain other lucrative trees only during the short window when they're available as limited-edition items. The Lychee and Asian Pear trees, which yield 140 coins each harvest, were some of the best of these, but keep your eyes peeled for new limited-edition trees, which can show up at any time.

Then there are the highly-sought-after trees that you have to acquire as gifts from your neighbors. These include the Jackfruit tree, which you can get as a free Mystery Gift, and the Ginkgo tree, which your neighbors can send you as a normal gift.

Although some farmers complain that trees can ruin the look of a farm by blocking the view of items or crops, some farmers place them strategically to hide unsightly objects. Placing trees on the top edge of a farm is a good way to ensure that they won't get in the way of any other items on your farm.

Decorations

Decorations are simply items that don't yield coins or serve any productive purpose on your farm. You purchase them from the Market, receive them as gifts, or find them in Mystery Eggs, Mystery Gifts, or Mystery Boxes.

Even though owning decorations may not seem efficient, you can earn a few ribbon achievements as a reward for owning them (see Chapter 11 for more on earning ribbons). Purchasing decorations from the Market also yields XP, which you can use to build up your farm's level (see Chapter 8 for more on achieving higher levels). Note that decorative items purchased with Farm Cash usually yield more XP than those purchased with coins.

Even though they aren't strictly productive, many farmers enjoy using hundreds of decorative items to customize their farm and make it more aesthetically pleasing. Still other farmers balk at the uselessness of decorations and devote their entire farms to items and crops that can earn XP and coins. Others fall somewhere in between these two extremes. Which type of farm you want to create is entirely up to you.

Tips for New Farmers

Although your new farm might not look so hot compared to your veteran FarmVille neighbors, don't let these humble beginnings get you down. You, too, can become a FarmVille Millionaire in a very short time if you stick to the following tips for new farmers.

Block your farmer

One of the biggest time sinks in all of FarmVille is waiting for your slow farmer to walk all the way across your farm just to collect some chicken eggs or what have you. You can get around this wait, oddly enough, by setting up barriers to block your farmer from getting around your farm.

When you load your farm, take note of where your farmer avatar is initially positioned. This central spot will be the same every time you load your farm. By setting up a small ring of obstacles around this position, as shown in Figure 3-8, your farmer will be trapped and unable to reach any of the various crops, animals, trees, and items littering the rest of your farm. Instead of making the game impossible to play, this actually makes playing much more efficient by letting you perform actions without waiting for your farmer to walk to the appropriate part of the farm. Neat trick, huh?

You can use any solid object to build your square prison — hay bales, fences, ducks. . . Be creative! Be careful not to leave any gaps in the wall where your farmer could squeeze out or the block won't be effective. You can test for gaps by clicking outside the block and seeing whether your farmer can walk to the location you indicated. If he or she stays in the center, congratulations — you've set up an effective prison.

After you upgrade your farm with an expansion, your avatar's starting position will change and you'll have to set up a new blocking pattern.

Wait to decorate

We know it's tempting to buy the most extravagant-looking items from the Market as soon as you can, especially when you've got coins to spare. However, it pays to be frugal at first and to focus on more productive uses for your coins. Because decorations usually don't yield a regular income, buying them in bulk means you could quickly find yourself with an empty pocketbook and a farm full of useless junk.

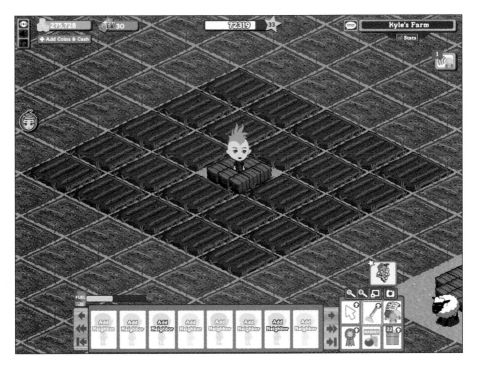

Figure 3-8: An effectively blocked-in farmer.

Add neighbors

The more neighbors you have, the more opportunities you have to receive gifts, earn coins, collect bonuses, and build up your farm. For more on adding and interacting with neighbors, see Chapter 4.

Watch your Facebook news feed

Every farmer could use more coins and animals when starting out, and getting those items for free is a great way to jumpstart your profits. You can collect coin bonus rewards and adoptable animals from your farming friends by clicking the links they share in their news feeds (see Figure 3-9).

Figure 3-9: A lost animal shared via a friend's Facebook newsfeed.

Maximize your crop space

Buying a larger farm means you have more space to plant crops. Having more space to plant crops means you can earn more money in the same amount of time. Earning more money means you can afford to buy a larger farm more quickly. Buying a larger farm means you have more space to plant crops. You can probably see how this cycle can be advantageous. For more on buying farm upgrades, see Chapter 6.

Plant fast-growing crops

The fastest way to earn coins is to keep a steady flow of crops growing on your farm. Berries tend to have the fastest growing times; thus, you can turn over a plot of land with berries more frequently, and therefore more profitably, than you can a plot with another crop. Of course, you also have to check in to harvest your crops more often, but no one said that virtual farming success would come easily. (If we said that earlier in the book, we were lying.) Fast-growing crops also usually come with little to no XP rewards for planting, so they will slow down your progress toward gaining new levels (see Chapter 8 for more on experience points and levels).

4

Won't You Be My Neighbor?

In This Chapter

▶ Finding and adding more neighbors

▶ Helping yourself by helping your neighbors

▶ Being a good neighbor and understanding FarmVille etiquette

▶ Posting gifts and bonuses to your Facebook news feed

lthough you can play FarmVille wholly as a single-player experience, adding some neighbors can substantially enhance your enjoyment of the game. Though a good neighbor can't be purchased for any price, these farming companions provide priceless benefits. Such benefits include tangible ones, such as receiving coins, experience points (XP), and free gifts, as well as intangibles ones: the joy of sharing the FarmVille experience with like-minded friends.

This chapter tells you everything you need to know about finding neighbors, maximizing all the benefits of having them, and treating them right.

Finding and Adding Neighbors

Signing up to play FarmVille is completely free, so anyone with Internet access is a potential neighbor. Some friends and contacts are more likely than others to become neighbors, however, as we explain in the following section.

Sending neighbor requests to Facebook friends

The friends you've already amassed on your Facebook account are the most obvious source of new FarmVille neighbors. In fact, any potential neighbor must first become your Facebook friend before he or she can become your FarmVille neighbor.

For much more on finding and adding Facebook friends, we recommend *Facebook For Dummies,* by Carolyn Abram and Leah Pearlman (Wiley).

Sending neighbor requests to friends who have already installed FarmVille

With more than 50 million players worldwide, chances are good that some of your Facebook friends are already playing FarmVille. Obviously, these friends are the likeliest to accept a request to be your in-game neighbor.

To send a request to these friends, follow these steps:

1. **Click the My Neighbors tab on the top menu, found above the FarmVille play area.**

   The My Neighbors page appears, as shown in Figure 4-1. A list of your current Facebook friends who have already installed FarmVille appears at the top of this page.

Figure 4-1: The My Neighbors page.

2. **Click the blue Add as Neighbor button next to the friend to whom you want to send a neighbor request.**

   A confirmation window appears. You can click the Add Personal Message link on this window to type an optional note to go along with your request.

3. **Click Send.**

   A neighbor request will be posted to your friend's Facebook news feed. That friend will now appear in the Pending Neighbors section of the My Neighbors page.

4. **Repeat Steps 2 and 3 for as many neighbor requests as you want to send.**

Neighbor requests are just that: requests. Your Facebook friend has to click the Accept and Play button on the news feed post you sent before he or she officially becomes your neighbor. Friends who accept then appear in the form of a profile picture and username in the Neighbor bar at the bottom of your FarmVille game.

Just because a Facebook friend has installed FarmVille doesn't mean that he or she is still actively playing the game. Look for friends listed with a high FarmVille level and number of neighbors on the My Neighbors page; these are the most likely to be actively looking for new neighbors.

Also, try not to take it personally if one of your Facebook friends doesn't accept your neighbor request. Most likely, some friends just don't want to get sucked back into the potentially addictive world of virtual farming. It's not you . . . it's them.

Sending FarmVille invitations to Facebook friends who haven't installed FarmVille

One reason for FarmVille's popularity is that many current players convince their Facebook friends to give the game a try. You can join this viral advertising chorus by sending personalized invitations to any of your Facebook friends who have yet to try the game.

To invite unconverted Facebook friends to sign up for FarmVille, follow these steps:

1. **Click the Invite Friends tab above the Farmville play area.**

   The Invite Friends page, shown in Figure 4-2 appears. You can also access this page by clicking an Add Neighbor icon in the Neighbor bar at the bottom of the play area.

Figure 4-2: The Invite Friends page.

2. **Click the name or picture of up to 50 friends you want to invite to play Farmville.**

   You can type all or part of a friend's name in the text box at the top of the list to find a specific friend. You can also click the Filter Friend drop-down menu to show only friends from a specific Facebook group or network.

3. **(Optional) In the Invite by E-mail Address area, type the e-mail addresses of anyone else you want to invite.**

   Be sure to put a comma between each e-mail address if you're sending to multiple recipients.

4. **Click the blue Send FarmVille Request button.**

   A confirmation window appears. You can click the Add Personal Message link on this window to type an optional note to go along with your request.

5. **Click the blue Send button.**

   A post appears on your friend's Facebook news feed, asking him or her to join you in playing FarmVille. Any friends who click the Accept and Play button are asked to install the game and set up their farm.

A newly invited player is not automatically added to your Neighbors list. After your friend installs the game (and shows up on the My Neighbors tab as a friend who has already installed FarmVille), you still have to send that friend a neighbor request, as discussed in the "Sending neighbor requests to friends who have already installed FarmVille" section of this chapter. Your friend then has to accept this request before you can visit his or her farm or take part in other neighbor activities with that player.

At this point in the history of FarmVille, most people who are on Facebook and have not tried the game have done so out of personal choice rather than ignorance. Some of your Facebook friends may be annoyed if you try to get them to install and play a game they have no interest in, especially if you send multiple requests. Of course, you're free to try and convince your friends that they're missing out by not playing FarmVille. Just don't be surprised if your friends don't take to the idea as readily as you might hope.

Finding more neighbors

So you've already sent a neighbor request to every single one of your FarmVille-playing Facebook friends, and yet you *still* want more neighbors? Well, good. This shows that you understand the importance of neighbors in helping you get the most out of your FarmVille farm.

After you've exhausted all your existing Facebook friends as potential FarmVille neighbors, you have only one option for increasing your neighbor count — finding some new friends! Luckily, you have better ways to find potential neighbors than hanging out in a dark bar or posting a personal ad in the paper ("Single white female seeks open-minded partner interested in virtual fertilizer . . ."). Instead, you can try many other places online to find like-minded players looking to find more neighbors.

Zynga's official forums host an entire thread devoted to connecting people who are looking for new neighbors. You can find this thread by visiting `http://forums.zynga.com/showthread.php?t=796991`. There, you can post a link to your Facebook profile page so that people can send you Facebook friend and FarmVille neighbor requests, or you can simply use the existing links to send requests of your own to hundreds of potentially willing neighbors. However, you can post only one friend request per week at the FarmVille forum.

Another way to seek neighbors is through Facebook itself. Simply type "FarmVille neighbor" into the search box on your Facebook home page to see a list of dozens of Facebook groups where like-minded people gather to look for new neighbors (see Figure 4-3). You can post a note in these groups, asking others to add you as a Facebook friend and FarmVille neighbor, or click a poster's name and send that person a friend request directly.

Figure 4-3: A listing of some FarmVille neighbor-finding groups on Facebook.

Before you start adding strangers as friends on your Facebook account, you should consider how doing so may impact the security of your Facebook account and your personal information. By default, these new friends will be able to view any information you post on Facebook — even information you'd like to limit to real friends only — and will be able to send you messages and post on your wall.

Luckily, you can set privacy and security setting for these FarmVille "stranger neighbors" separately from the settings for the rest of your Facebook friends. To do so, follow these steps.

1. **Click the Friends button on the left sidebar of your Facebook home page.**

   The Friends page appears.

2. **Click the Edit Friends button, located at the top-right corner of the Friends page.**

   The Edit Friends page appears, showing a list of all your current friends.

3. **Click the Create a List button located at the top right.**

   The Create New List menu appears.

4. **Type a name for your new list in the text box.**

   Make the name something applicable and memorable, such as "FarmVille-only friends" or "Stranger Neighbors."

5. **(Optional) Click the names of any friends you want to add to this list.**

   If you already have some stranger neighbors as Facebook friends, you can add them to your new list by clicking their profile picture. You can also add them later, if you prefer.

6. **Click the Create List button.**

   A page for your new list appears. You can access this page at any time by returning to the Edit Friends page in Step 2 and clicking the name of the list in the left sidebar.

7. **Type all or part of the name of the stranger neighbor you'd like to add to the list in the text box.**

   A drop-down list of all the Facebook friends who match that name appears as you type.

8. **Click the name of the stranger neighbor you'd like to add to the list.**

   The stranger neighbor is added to the list and appears below the text entry field. Repeat Steps 7 and 8 as often as necessary until all your stranger neighbors have been added to the list

   Alternatively, you can click the Add Multiple button and then click the faces of as many friends as you'd like. Click the Save List button to speed up the process.

   If you add more strangers as Facebook friends later, you will have to actively add them to this list by starting from Step 7. You can also add someone directly to it when you accept a friend request. To do so, accept the request, click the Add to List button, select the stranger neighbor list, and then click the blue Save button.

9. **Click the Account menu in the upper-right corner and choose Privacy Settings.**

   The Facebook Privacy Settings page appears.

10. **Click the Customize Settings button below your current settings.**

    The Facebook Privacy Settings Customization page appears, as shown in Figure 4-4.

Figure 4-4: The Facebook Privacy Settings Customization page.

11. Click the drop-down menu for the specific settings you want to restrict and click Customize.

A pop-up menu appears, asking which people you'd like to make this information visible to or hidden from.

12. In the Hide This From area, type all or part of the name of the stranger neighbor group and then click the name of that group when it appears.

The group appears in the Hide This From area.

13. Click Save Setting.

Repeat Steps 11 and 12 until you've set the privacy settings to your liking. Note that you have to set the privacy for the group only once; from then on, any stranger neighbors you add to the group will automatically be limited to what they can and can't do and see on your Facebook profile.

Removing neighbors

You are allowed a maximum of 300 neighbors at a time, and you should do everything you can to hit that limit. Although managing 300 neighbors might seem tough, keep in mind that having a lot of neighbors increases your ability to receive free gifts and take part in in-game activities that require neighbors, as discussed later in this chapter.

Not all neighbors are created equal, however. Often, a neighbor will agree to your request and then never visit your farm, send a gift, participate in a co-op job, or do anything else to help you out. Or neighbors will stop playing FarmVille after accepting your request, thereby clogging your Neighbors list with static or empty farms.

These inactive neighbors are still minimally useful — you can still visit their farms and receive coin and experience rewards for helping out, even if that help will go unappreciated. Still, as you near your 300-neighbor limit (or if you just want to clean things up), you may want to cull some of the dead weight from your Neighbors list. You can do this from the My Neighbors page by clicking the Remove as Neighbor button next to any current neighbor.

You don't receive confirmation for this kind of neighbor removal, so you'll have to send another neighbor request if you mis-click. Be careful!

Helping Your Neighbors

In FarmVille as in life, being a good neighbor is a two-way street. Certainly, your neighbors can help you out with stuff like free items, farm work, and help with co-op jobs, but you're also expected to do the same things to help those neighbors.

Luckily, FarmVille provides bonuses such as XP, Farm Coins, and even rare Mystery Eggs for being a good neighbor, thereby proving that you can indeed do well by doing good. Read on for a description of all the ways FarmVille neighbors can be helpful to each other and what benefits they get in return.

Reaping what you sow by visiting your neighbors' farms

It might seem silly to go do farm work on your neighbors' farms when you have so much to do on your own farm. But don't be fooled — visiting and helping your neighbors' farms is a great way to earn some extra Farm Coins, XP, and possibly some free items each day.

To visit a neighbor's farm, simply click that neighbor's image in the Neighbor bar at the bottom of the play area and then click Visit/Help Farm from the drop-down menu. The farming screen fades out for a few seconds and your neighbor's farm appears with your farmer avatar standing in the center. To return to your farm at any time, click the Return Home button just above the Tools menu, as shown in Figure 4-5.

Figure 4-5: The Return Home button.

Note that your neighbor's farm can take a few seconds to load completely (or longer, depending on the speed of your Internet connection). Some items on the neighbor's farm may appear as shadows for a while, only to pop suddenly into existence as the data is downloaded from Zynga's server.

Farming on your neighbor's farm isn't exactly like farming on your own — you're actually quite limited in the actions you can take to help your neighbor. Each action comes with its own separate reward as well, as discussed in the upcoming list.

Note that, except for feeding chickens, you can complete only five of these tasks in aggregate per neighbor farm per calendar day. For example, you can harvest two trees, fertilize two plots of land, and unwither one crop before having to move on to another farm for the day. Feeding chickens in chicken coops does not count toward this total, but you can feed each neighbor's chickens only once per day. A new day in FarmVille starts at midnight Eastern time.

Following are the activities you earn benefits for if you perform them on a neighbor's farm:

- ✔ **Fertilize crops:** Click any unfertilized, seeded plot of land on your neighbor's farm to fertilize that plot. You earn ten Farm Coins and one XP for each plot fertilized this way. Because of your good deed, your neighbor will also earn an additional XP when he or she harvests that plot of land.

   If your neighbor has used a Fertilize All item recently, you might not be able to find an unfertilized plot of land to fertilize.

- ✔ **Plow fallow land:** Click any patch of unproductive, light-brown fallow land to plow that land and make it ready for seeding by your neighbor. You receive 10 Farm Coins and one XP per plot plowed in this manner.

- ✔ **Unwither dead crops:** Click a plot of brown, withered crops on a neighbor's farm to unwither that crop and restore it to full, harvestable health. You earn 10 Farm Coins and one experience point per plot plowed in this manner.

If your neighbor has not played FarmVille for 14 days or more, you'll be given the option to unwither *all* of that neighbor's crops for free.

- **Harvest animals:** Just as on your farm, animals that are ready to harvest on a neighbor's farm appear with a pink arrow above their head. Click these animals to harvest the animal and receive up to 50 Farm Coins for your trouble. (For more on harvesting animals, see Chapter 3.)

  Note that some of your neighbors' animals will yield more coins than others when harvested. To receive the maximum 50-coin bounty, look for horses, foals, swans, cats, and goats to harvest. Also, don't worry that you're somehow stealing from your neighbor by harvesting their prized animals — your neighbor will also receive the same coin rewards when they visit next visit their farm.

- **Harvest trees:** If a neighbor's tree is ready to harvest, a sickle icon appears next to your pointer and the word Harvest appears when you hover your mouse over that tree. Click the tree to harvest it and receive up to 50 coins.

  As with animals, some of your neighbors' trees will produce a larger coin bonus than others when harvested. Trees that produce the maximum 50-coin bonus include Olive, Jackfruit, Passion Fruit, Gulmohar, Banana, and Date.

- **Feed chickens:** While visiting a neighbor's farm, click that farm's chicken coop to feed the chickens. A pop-up box notifies you as to whether you've received a Mystery Egg for your trouble. If you have, you can click the Share button to in turn post a Mystery Egg to your Facebook news feed, as discussed in the "Giving and Receiving Gifts" section, later in this chapter.

  Either way, you receive 100 Farm Coins and 10 XP for feeding a coop of chickens, making this one of the most lucrative actions you can perform on a neighbor's farm.

  Fed chickens are also more likely to provide Mystery Eggs when harvested by your neighbor. (See Chapter 9 for more about mystery prizes.)

If a neighbor has helped your farm using any of the preceding methods, that farmer's avatar appears on your farm the next time you log in to play FarmVille. Click that avatar and then click the Accept Help button in the drop-down menu to finalize the help the neighbor has provided. Be sure to do this before doing any other farming tasks; otherwise, your neighbors' help could be rendered moot if you perform the tasks yourself.

Providing more neighborly assistance

Besides helping neighbors directly via farm visits, neighbors can choose among plenty of other in-game tasks to help each other with. These include

- **Participating in co-op jobs:** Neighbors can join together in co-op jobs to receive mutually beneficial bonuses for the planting and harvesting they were going to do anyway. See Chapter 12 for much more on participating in co-op jobs.

- **Collecting items for limited-edition events:** FarmVille occasionally has a themed collection event that requires you to collect items to redeem for exclusive prizes. You can often collect more of these items by clicking themed buildings placed on your neighbors' farms. See Chapter 10 for more details about limited-edition events.

- **Constructing buildings and upgrading vehicles:** Neighbors can send each other building materials and vehicle parts as gifts, saving each other from spending lots of Farm Cash to construct a building or upgrade a vehicle. See this chapter's "Giving and Receiving Gifts" section for more on sending gifts, or Chapter 9 for more on constructing buildings and Chapter 6 for more on upgrading vehicles.

- **Expanding your farm:** Although you can purchase a farm expansion with Farm Cash at any time, the ability to buy those expansions with Farm Coins is only unlocked when you reach various milestone numbers of neighbors. See Chapter 6 for more on buying farm expansions.

- **Collecting bushels and selling crafted goods:** Having more neighbors means having more potential sources of free bushels of goods from the Farmers Market, as well as more potential customers for the crafted goods you make. See Chapter 7 for more on participating in the Farmers Market (which is different from the FarmVille Market that you get to using the Market menu).

- **Earning ribbons:** Many ribbons either require you to have a certain number of neighbors or help neighbors a certain number of times. Having neighbors helps you earn these ribbon achievements and the coin and XP bonuses that go with them. For more on these ribbons, see Chapter 11.

- **Giving and receiving gifts:** Who doesn't love free stuff? Giving and receiving free gifts is one of the most important roles for a good neighbor. See the upcoming section for more on giving and receiving gifts.

- **Sharing items and bonuses through news feed links:** Neighbors can share free items and bonuses by posting links to their Facebook news feed, as we mention throughout this book. See the section later in this chapter for more details on how to post on and take advantage of news feed links.

Giving and Receiving Gifts

Sending free gifts is one of the most rewarding things FarmVille neighbors can do for one another. The animals, trees, decorations, and construction materials available as free gifts are often hard to obtain by other means, and a farmer can save a significant amount of Farm Cash by receiving them rather than purchasing them from the Market.

Even if your neighbor doesn't have an immediate need for a specific gift, he or she can still sell it to gain some Farm Coins. For this reason, you should strive to send something to each of your neighbors as often as possible.

Giving gifts

To send free gifts to your neighbors, follow these steps:

1. **Click the brown Free Gifts tab located above the FarmVille game area.**

   The Free Gifts page appears, as shown in Figure 4-6.

2. **Select the radio button under the gift you'd like to give.**

   Note that you can choose only one distinct gift to give at a time. If you want to give a separate gift to another neighbor, you can come back to the Gifting page later.

Figure 4-6: The Free Gifts page.

3. **Click either of the purple Proceed to Send buttons at the bottom and top of the Free Gifts list.**

   The Friend Selection page appears.

4. **Select the check boxes next to the friends to whom you want to send the gift.**

   Note that you can click the FarmVille Friends tab to limit the list to only people who have installed FarmVille on their Facebook account. You can send gifts to other Facebook friends, but they'll have to install the game before they can accept your gifts.

   You can also type all or part of a friend's name into the text box above the Friends list to find a particular friend quickly. If you add a friend accidentally, click the X next to that person's name in the lower portion of the Friend selection area to remove the person from the list of recipients.

5. **Click the blue Send FarmVille Gift Request button.**

   A pop-up notification asks you to confirm or cancel your gift.

6. **Click the blue Send button.**

   Your farm reappears. A news post detailing your gift shows up on your neighbor's Facebook news feed. The neighbor then has to accept the gift using the method outlined in the next section.

You can send up to a maximum of 50 gifts, in aggregate, to your FarmVille neighbors in a 4-hour period. You are also limited to one gift per neighbor every four hours.

If you're looking for a specific giftable item for yourself, try sending that same item to a few of your neighbors. Chances are, you'll receive multiple thank you gifts of the same type in return.

Accepting and using gifts

Just as in real life, you have to actively accept a gift in FarmVille before you can open and use it. Unfortunately, the process for accepting a gift in FarmVille isn't as straightforward as just taking a wrapped box someone hands you. Recipients of FarmVille gifts have to take action to accept those gifts before using them.

To accept any and all gifts you've been sent, follow these steps:

1. **Click the FarmVille Requests button in the upper-right corner of the FarmVille play area.**

   The number of gifts you have waiting to be accepted appears in a blue square, as shown in Figure 4-7. If no number appears, you currently have no pending gifts to accept, so tell your neighbors to get off their behinds and send you something, darn it!

Figure 4-7: The FarmVille Requests button.

A pop-up notification appears, asking whether you really want to accept your pending gift requests now. Think long and hard about this decision . . . just kidding; there's really nothing to think about. It's free stuff. Free!

2. **Click the Accept button.**

   The Farmville section of your Facebook requests page appears, as shown in Figure 4-8. You can also access your Facebook request page at any time by clicking the See All Requests button on the right sidebar of your Facebook home page.

Figure 4-8: The FarmVille section of your Facebook Requests page.

3. **Click the Accept and Play button next to the gift you want to accept.**

   You can also click the Ignore button to permanently reject a gift, but really, why would you want to do that? It's a free gift. Free! Remember, you can always sell an unwanted gift for Farm Coins.

   The Gift Acceptance confirmation page appears, as shown in Figure 4-9.

Do you have more pending gifts to accept?

Yes   No

Please remember to accept each gift right away.

Figure 4-9: The Gift Acceptance confirmation page.

4. **(Optional) Click the Send a Thank You Gift button and then the Send button on the confirmation window to send a gift back to the sender.**

Although this step isn't strictly necessary, sending gifts back to neighbors who send you gifts is a good way to ensure that you get more gifts in the future.

5. **Click the Yes button under "Do you have more pending gifts to accept?" to accept more gifts, or the No button to return to your farm.**

If you click the Yes button, go back to Step 3 to continue accepting gifts until you have no more to accept.

Don't worry if you accidentally click No when you actually do have more gifts — you can go back to Step 1 and accept your remaining gifts at any time.

6. **Click the Gift Box icon in the Tools menu.**

The Gift Box menu appears, which contains all the gifts you accepted in Steps 1 through 5.

7. **Click the Use, Sell, or Re-Gift buttons that appear under your gifts.**

If you click the Use button, you return to your farm to place the item (if it's a tangible item). Tangible items such as animals and decorations take up physical space on your farm. If it's an intangible item such as a shovel, fuel, or Farm Cash, the item is added to your inventory automatically.

Although a shovel is, in real-world terms, a "tangible" object, our reference to it and other items as "intangible" means that such items don't take up physical (that is, virtual) space on your farm.

If you click the Sell button, a pop-up notification appears, listing the item's sale price and asking whether you're sure you want to sell that gift. Click the Accept button to sell the gift for Farm Coins or the Cancel button if you were just curious. Note that some items sell for zero coins, so selling them is useful only for clearing space in your Gift Box.

If you click the Re-gift button (which is not available for all items), a pop-up notification asks you how many of the gifts you want to give away. Click the Send button to confirm or Cancel to reconsider.

Gifts expire two weeks after they are sent. If you try to accept a gift after this time, you receive nothing but a message urging you to accept your gifts sooner next time. You'd be wise to take that advice.

Other Ways to Be a Good Neighbor: Farming Etiquette

The perfect FarmVille neighbor would visit each friend's farm daily, completing as many neighborly tasks as he or she can and pocketing a whole lot of coins and XP in the process. In practice, visiting every day might not be feasible for farmers who have limited time to play or have reached the maximum of 300 neighbors for their farm.

Even if you can't visit daily, it's still important to do your part to create and maintain a good relationship with each of your neighbors. If you strive to be a thoughtful neighbor, chances are good that your neighbors will return the favor.

Here are a few tips on the etiquette of being a FarmVille neighbor:

- **Feed chickens:** If you have time to do only one task on a neighbor's farm, this is the one to do. Not only do you get a beefy bonus of 100 coins and 10 XP for a single click, but the Mystery Eggs that you and your neighbor could receive from the action can be quite lucrative. (See Chapter 9 to see just how lucrative.)

- **Fertilize and unwither crops:** Although plowing a neighbor's fields and harvesting his or her trees and animals are useful time savers, your neighbor can perform these actions quite easily with a few free clicks. If your neighbors want to fertilize or unwither their own crops, however, they'll probably have to spend some hard-to-get Farm Cash to do it. Give these actions priority over other actions when you visit a neighbor's farm so that they can save a little virtual currency.

✔ **Give and you shall receive:** Sending out free gifts is a great way to encourage your neighbors to send free gifts in return. The game provides a link for someone to return the favor right there on the gift notification pop-up; also, giving gifts makes your neighbors more likely to think positively of you and want to reward you for your help.

✔ **Always send a return gift after you receive a gift:** If you have a reputation for returning gifts when you receive them, your neighbors will be more likely to send you gifts out of the blue, purely out of self-interest if nothing else.

✔ **Do your part to help complete co-op jobs:** Signing up for jobs that you fail to help with is not only rude but also reduces the chance that your neighbors will participate in and help complete co-op jobs that *you* start. See Chapter 12 for more on co-op jobs.

✔ **Block off the center of your farm:** Blocking off the center of your farm by trapping your farmer avatar both saves you time while working on your own farm and keeps visiting neighbors from having to wait for their farmer to walk long distances to help you out. See Chapter 3 for more on blocking off the center of your farm.

✔ **Share the wealth:** Whenever the game asks whether you want to share a free item or bonus on your Facebook news feed, take advantage of the opportunity! Doing so increases your reputation as a generous neighbor while also giving you bragging rights to your in-game accomplishments.

✔ **Re-gift unusable items:** Turn your trash into someone else's treasure by clicking the Re-gift button under unwanted or unusable items in your Gift Box. Those items are then posted to your Facebook news feed, where they have a chance of finding a good home.

Posting Items and Bonuses to a Facebook News Feed

While you're playing FarmVille, many opportunities arise for you to post a message on your Facebook news feed. These news posts can involve everything from opportunities to adopt animals or accept free items to requests for help with building upgrades.

These opportunities are usually indicated by a Share button or something similar that shows up in a pop-up notification window as you play. Clicking such a button brings up the News Feed publishing box, as shown in Figure 4-10.

Figure 4-10: A Facebook News feed publishing box.

Next, follow these steps to post a message:

1. **(Optional) Type a personal message in the text box.**

   This message adds a more personal touch to the default news post written by FarmVille. You can also click the lock next to the Publish button to restrict the news post's visibility to a certain limited group of your Facebook friends. This feature can be especially handy for sharing FarmVille links only with people you know are interested in playing the game.

2. **Click Publish.**

   The link will be shared on your news feed. Note that you can instead click Skip to pass up the opportunity to share with your neighbors if you want.

Your neighbors will be able to click the link that appears in their news feed to accept the item or bonus or provide help with your request. Note that some items shared via news feeds are available for only a limited time, or are available only to the first few neighbors who click the link. Be sure to click news feed links shared by your neighbors as soon as possible to take full advantage of these opportunities.

Part II
Seeking Your FarmVille Fortune

The 5th Wave   By Rich Tennant

"I'm not going to tell you again. No more Farm Coins until you've cleaned up your Pigpen and sent that fence post you promised your sister."

The second part of the book focuses on the financial aspects of FarmVille. We describe the various FarmVille currencies and how to earn them or purchase them directly using real money. Next, we take you on a trip to the FarmVille Market to see how you can spend all that money. We dissect the Market menu and let you in on some ways to maximize your profit. We end this part with a discussion of the Farmers Market, where you sell and exchange your goods and set up your very own crafting building so that you can earn more coins!

5

For the Love of Virtual Money

. . . .

In This Chapter:

▶ Understanding the various types of currency used in FarmVille

▶ Earning Farm Coins and Farm Cash in the game

▶ Learning how to convert real money into FarmVille currency

▶ Earning "free" FarmVille currency using special offers and promotions

. . . .

*P*laying FarmVille effectively requires earning in-game currency constantly. Without currency, you can't purchase the seeds you need to grow crops or any of the other items that drive the FarmVille economy.

Unlike most countries in the real world, the land of FarmVille actually has two separate currencies: Farm Coins and Farm Cash . Each currency has its strengths and weaknesses, and you can buy many items using either currency, but you can't combine currencies in one purchase or exchange one currency for another. Also, even though you technically earn both currencies by playing the game, savvy farmers know that some currency is harder to come by than others.

Confused? Don't worry — this chapter shows you the essential differences between Farm Coins and Farm Cash, and tells you when you should spend one and save the other. We also tell you how to use FarmVille's de facto third currency — real-world money — to make optional purchases of in-game currency. Finally, this chapter provides some tips for how to get free FarmVille currency outside the game, stretching both your virtual and your real wallets as far as they'll go.

Acquiring Farm Coins for Essentials

Farm Coins are the basic currency used in FarmVille, and every new FarmVille player starts with 240 coins. You can use Farm Coins to purchase everything from seeds and animals to storage buildings, decorations, vehicles, and land expansions. Although you must use Farm Cash to obtain many premium items, the items that you absolutely *need* to play the game tend to be available for purchase with Farm Coins.

You can use these coins however you wish, but keep in mind that although money *does* grow on trees (and crops and animals) in FarmVille, you have to purchase those trees (and crops and animals) before you can reap their rewards. If you spend all your early money on frivolous items, you'll have to break out your wallet and use real money to replenish your virtual coin purse, as we explain in "Spending Real Money on Virtual Goods," later in this chapter.

If you run out of coins, try visiting neighbors' farms, where you can get paid for actions such as fertilizing their crops, harvesting their trees, feeding their chickens, or collecting from animals. See Chapter 4 for more on interacting with neighbors. Totally broke farmers can also keep an eye on bonus links in their Facebook news feed to score some free coins.

Earning Farm Coins

As mentioned at the start of the chapter, a major aspect of playing FarmVille is to earn FarmVille coins continuously. Without coins, you can't purchase the seeds you need to grow crops or any of the other items that drive the FarmVille economy.

Although you can spend real money on Farm Coins, you can also earn them quite easily in the game. Earning coins can be hard at first, because new farmers have fewer resources and opportunities to drive their engine of economic growth. If you're a diligent farmer, however, you'll soon be earning coins as an easy and natural part of your life in FarmVille.

You have a wide variety of methods for earning Farm Coins, including:

- **Harvesting crops, trees, and animals:** This is by far the most common method for generating coins. Through regular harvesting, these items all provide predictable, reliable income that, over time, far outstrips the initial investment you put into them. For more on how to acquire and harvest all these items, see Chapter 3.

  Crops need to be harvested promptly when they're fully grown or they wither and lose all value. Trees and animals don't wither but should be harvested frequently to maximize returns. See Chapter 6 for more on keeping to an efficient farming schedule.

- **Earning ribbons:** You earn ribbons by completing various FarmVille tasks, and each new ribbon comes with a reward in the form of Farm Coins and experience points (XP). For more on how to earn ribbons and the specific rewards associated with them, see Chapter 11.

- **Selling crafted goods:** By setting up a crafting building, you can turn bushels of crops into crafted goods, which your neighbors can then purchase using their coins. Eighty percent of the purchase price for these goods goes directly into your Farm Coins account. For a much more detailed account of the entire crafting and selling process, see Chapter 7.

- **Visiting neighbors and completing friend missions:** When you visit a neighbor's farm, you can earn Farm Coins and XP by performing helpful actions such as fertilizing crops, harvesting trees, collecting from animals, and feeding chickens. It's doing well by doing good. For more on visiting other farms and helping neighbors, see Chapter 4.

- **Celebrating your neighbors' achievements:** When your FarmVille friends achieve certain goals in FarmVille, the game gives them the option to share a bonus with their friends by posting a message on their Facebook wall. If you see such a message on a friend's wall, click the Get a Bonus From [Friend's Name] link to earn free coins and XP. Note that these bonuses last for only 24 hours, and only the first few neighbors who click the link get the bonus, so keep your eyes peeled and click those links promptly.

Earning Farm Coins quickly

Everybody wants to get rich quickly, and FarmVille players are no exception. Many new farmers want to know the quickest ways to earn coins in the game. Accumulating coins happens naturally when you persistently grow crops, limit your unnecessary spending, and consider some of the following suggestions for earning coins:

- **Know your crops:** Each FarmVille crop has a specific growing time, seed price, and harvest yield associated with it. You can use these numbers to figure out which available crops provide the most daily profit per plot of land. For a fuller discussion of maximizing the profit you earn from each plot of plowed land, see Chapter 6. Also, see Chapter 17 to find out about some of the most lucrative crops in the game.

- **Know your animals:** As with crops, some animals generate more daily harvestable profits than others. In contrast to crops, though, different animals take up a different amount of space on your farm, meaning that you have to also consider whether having an animal is the most efficient use of your land. Look for animals such as calves, which leave a relatively small footprint on your farm and can be harvested for a relatively high 80 coins each day.

✔ **Grow a tree:** Trees are some of the most efficient sources of income in FarmVille. They require no maintenance and automatically generate harvestable profits 24 hours a day, seven days a week. Plus, because trees don't wither, you can harvest them on your own schedule. As with calves, trees leave a relatively small footprint on your farm, meaning that you can also fit lots of trees in a relatively small space. Over time, the coins you earn from a single tree will return your initial investment in them many times over.

✔ **Expand your farm:** When you can afford to expand your farm, do it as soon as possible. Expanding your farm gives you more land, which means more crops, which means more coins, which means more expansions, which means . . . more land! For more on purchasing farm expansions, see Chapter 6.

Acquiring Farm Cash for Premium Items

Farm Cash — also known as FarmVille Dollars or Farm Bucks, or is abbreviated as FV$ — is the more exclusive of the two virtual currencies in FarmVille. You can use Farm Cash to purchase many exclusive items that you can't buy with Farm Coins, or use it as an alternative method of payment for some items that you can also purchase with Farm Coins.

You can also often use Farm Cash to speed up processes that would usually require time, help from neighbors, or extra work on your farm to complete.

Earning Farm Cash

Although Farm Cash is very difficult to obtain just by playing FarmVille, you do have a few ways to earn it in the game itself:

✔ **Start a new farm:** Each new FarmVille player receives five Farm Cash to start with. Before you get any big ideas, you can't start multiple farms and merge them together to create one big pile of free Farm Cash, so don't even think about it.

✔ **Level up:** Every time you reach a new level (up to level 100), you earn one Farm Cash in your account. For more on reaching new levels, see Chapter 8.

✔ **Open mystery items:** Occasionally, you'll find Farm Cash hidden inside Mystery Gifts, Mystery Eggs, and Gift Boxes. For more on how to get these items, see Chapter 4.

Aside from these limited methods, the only way to earn Farm Cash is by purchasing it with real money or participating in special advertising offers. See the next section in this chapter for more on both of these Farm Cash acquisition methods.

Knowing when to use Farm Cash

Although both Farm Cash and Farm Coins can be obtained simply by playing FarmVille, Farm Cash is much more difficult to earn in the normal course of the game. Therefore, in general you want to be much more careful when using Farm Cash to make a purchase.

That said, some reasons to use Farm Cash rather than Farm Coins are the following:

- **Buying Farm Cash exclusives:** Some items simply aren't available for any amount of Farm Coins. These Farm Cash exclusives are usually limited-edition items that are exceedingly rare or otherwise distinct from the kinds of items you can get with Farm Coins. If you want to differentiate your farms or show off your rarefied taste, you may have to break out the Farm Cash.

- **Bypassing construction phases:** Although you can purchase most buildings using either Farm Coins or Farm Cash, if you choose to do so using coins, you have to rely on donations of materials from friends before you can complete the building. If you use Farm Cash, you can bypass this annoying, time-consuming process and set up your completed building in one fell swoop. For more on buildings, see Chapter 9.

- **Buying land expansions:** Although you can use Farm Coins to expand your farm (see Chapter 6), the largest farms can require a truly obscene amount of coins to purchase. If you don't have enough coins, you can use Farm Cash to upgrade your farm more quickly. Remember that bigger farms provide more space to place crops, trees, and animals and therefore can generate more Farm Coins more quickly.

- **Buying Hot Rod vehicles:** You can purchase regular vehicles with either Farm Cash or coins, but the only way to get Hot Rod vehicles is by shelling out Farm Cash. These vehicles can plow, seed, or harvest nine plots of land in a single click, helping you get your farming done faster than by using any of the other vehicles. For more on buying and using vehicles, see Chapter 6.

- **Buying fuel:** Although you can earn fuel several ways in FarmVille, the only way to purchase it directly is by spending Farm Cash. If your vehicles are sitting idle and you need to harvest immediately, the price might be worth it.

✔ **Earning more experience points:** Buying exclusive items with Farm Cash generally earns more experience points than purchasing similar items with coins. If you're willing to shell out the cash, this can be an efficient method for earning higher levels. For more on levels, see Chapter 8.

Spending Real Money on Virtual Goods

Although you can play FarmVille without spending a dime on the game, you can also spend real money to give yourself a leg up over the competition. You have several ways to convert your real, legal tender into FarmVille currency, including making an in-game credit card purchase and buying a Game Card from a local retailer. If you don't want to spend real money, you can also earn Farm Cash by participating in advertising offers from third-party vendors.

To spend or not to spend real money?

The idea of exchanging legal tender for FarmVille's entirely fake currencies is somewhat controversial. Although many players enjoy FarmVille without shelling out one shiny red cent for the privilege, Zynga makes hundreds of millions of dollars every year from players who voluntarily use their hard-earned money to buy items that exist only as pixels on a screen and bits in a server.

Many of these paying players spend just a few dollars a month to buy the occasional limited-edition item or to hurry along an especially slow in-game process. But some players take their FarmVille spending seriously. One pre-teen in the United Kingdom made headlines when he used his mom's credit card (without her permission, needless to say) to purchase almost $1,400 worth of FarmVille virtual goods. There are reports of FarmVille V.I.Ps (Very Important Players) who purchase every special limited-edition item that FarmVille offers and a "Platinum Purchase Program" that accepts wire transfers of $500 and up from those truly obsessive players.

As with all decisions regarding your money (except for taxes), what you spend on FarmVille is entirely up to you. Everyone has different priorities and tolerances for spending money. Some people like saving their money for a rainy day; others prefer burning through it like there's a hole in their pocket. Whatever decision you make regarding your FarmVille spending, you can still have a great time playing the game.

Some food for thought, though: Although a spendthrift player can always decide to buy more FarmVille currency later, a player who invests in a lot of FarmVille currency will never be able to convert that currency back to real, legal tender. As the ancient Romans used to say, caveat agricola — let the farmer beware. Okay, they probably never said that, but they would have if they'd have had FarmVille back then. Trust us.

Buying Farm Coins and Cash through FarmVille

The FarmVille developers at Zynga have made buying FarmVille currency so easy that you don't even have to leave the game to do it. Click the Get Farm Cash tab above the FarmVille play area to display the Buy Farm Cash & Coins menu, as shown in Figure 5-1. Then follow these steps to add more in-game currency to your account:

1. **Select the amount of Farm Cash or Farm Coins that you want to purchase and click Continue.**

   Note that spending more money gets you a better in-game exchange rate. Whereas spending $1 earns only four Farm Cash, for example, spending $50 earns 310 Farm Cash, or more than six Farm Cash per real dollar. That in-game money doesn't go bad, either, so plan ahead and buy in bulk to save.

Figure 5-1: The Buy Farm Coins & Cash menu.

2. **Select the appropriate radio button to choose whether to pay with a new credit card, a previously used credit card, or a PayPal account and click Continue.**

FarmVille accepts any valid Visa, Mastercard, American Express, Discover, or JCB card. You can also use a PayPal account; for more on using this option, visit http://www.paypal.com or check out *PayPal For Dummies,* by Victoria Rosenborg and Marsha Collier(Wiley).

If you've purchased or earned any of Facebook's Credits currency, you can select the Apply Existing Balance check box to put those Credits toward your purchase at a rate of 10 cents per Facebook Credit.

Facebook automatically stores any new credit card information you enter, so you won't have to type it in again the next time you want to buy FarmVille currency. If you'd like to delete this information from Facebook for security reasons, go to the Facebook Account Settings page (under the accounts menu in the upper-right of your Facebook home page) and click the Payments tab.

3. **Enter your credit card information and click Complete Purchase, or log in to your PayPal account and click Agree and Pay.**

   Note that this step is skipped if you use an existing credit card already stored by Facebook.

Farm Cash and Farm Coins are not refundable, meaning you can't convert in-game currency back into cold, hard cash. After you click the Complete Payment or Agree and Pay button, your money is usable only in FarmVille, so make sure you don't actually need that cash to pay your mortgage or gas bill or something before continuing.

After your payment is processed, your Farm Cash or Farm Coins are added to your current total. The purchased currency usually appears in your FarmVille account pretty promptly, but note that it can take a few hours or even a few days for your currency purchase to show up. If your purchased currency doesn't show up after a few days, see Chapter 13 for details on contacting Zynga support for help.

Using a nontraditional payment provider

Just below the Buy Farm Cash & Coins menu, Zynga provides links to buy FarmVille currency through a number of less traditional payment methods, as shown in Figure 5-2. These options let you pay for your currency using a debit card, cell phone, home phone, existing online payment account, or a variety of prepaid cards purchased from retail locations.

To use any of these services, click the appropriate link, choose the amount of Farm Cash you want from the menu, click the Get Farm Cash button, and then enter the required login or payment information in the browser window that pops up. As happens when you pay using a traditional payment method, your currency should appear in your FarmVille account in a few days at most.

Figure 5-2: Nontraditional payment options for purchasing FarmVille currency.

An alternative to paying online: FarmVille Game Cards

If you're unwilling or unable to use any of the online payment methods discussed in the last section, you can purchase FarmVille Game Cards at many brick-and-mortar retailers. You can then redeem these cards online for FarmVille currency. Although using Game Cards to get FarmVille currency is decidedly less convenient than using the online payment methods, there are a few reasons you might want to consider it, as discussed in the "Why use Game Cards?" sidebar.

Where to buy FarmVille Game Cards

As of this writing, FarmVille Game Cards are stocked at the following retailers:

- 7-Eleven
- Best Buy
- GameStop
- Target
- Walmart
- Walgreens

Why use Game Cards?

There are several reasons that you might want to trek to a local store and purchase a Game Card rather than pay for your FarmVille currency online. The first is obvious: Many people are still not comfortable sharing their financial information online. Although Facebook and FarmVille use encryption technology to secure your online payments, no online payment method is foolproof, and there's always a chance that hackers could somehow obtain your payment and billing information through an online transaction. Buying a Game Card in a brick-and-mortar store is anonymous and lets you keep your personal information personal.

Game Cards are also a convenient option for people who don't have access to a credit card or other online payment account. This applies especially to children, who usually don't have

credit cards, and whereas Mom is likely to be wary of handing her credit card over to the kids, a prepaid Game Card removes the risk of an unauthorized shopping spree.

Which brings us to the final advantage Game Cards have over online payments: gifts. Currently, FarmVille lets you use online payments only to add in-game currency to your personal account. If you want to give some Farm Cash or Farm Coins to a friend, your only options are to buy a physical Game Card to give them or to purchase a Zynga Game Card online (see the "Sending Zynga Game Cards as online gifts" section in this chapter). Just as retail gift cards do, Game Cards make great presents for FarmVille-lovers. Hey, you know what other present they might enjoy? This book! Why not buy another copy (or 12!)?

Redeeming FarmVille Game Cards

When you purchase your FarmVille Game Card, you need to have it activated at checkout. You then need to redeem it for FarmVille currency online. To do so, click the Game Cards tab above the FarmVille play area and scroll down the page a bit. Just under the Buy Farm Cash & Coins menu, you see a message reading "Have a FarmVille Game Card? Click here to redeem."

Click that link to bring up the Redeem Your Game Card menu, as shown in Figure 5-3, and then follow these steps to redeem your card:

1. **Enter the PIN code from the card in the box labeled Enter PIN Code.**

   You find this code on the back of your Game Card.

2. **Click Next Step.**

   A confirmation screen appears. Your Farm Cash is automatically e added to your existing Farm Cash bank.

Figure 5-3: The Redeem Your Game Card menu.

Sending Zynga Game Cards as online gifts

In addition to buying a FarmVille Game Card at a brick-and-mortar retailer, you can purchase a Zynga Game Card online as a gift. These virtual cards technically work for any Zynga game but can be personalized to feature FarmVille.

To give a Zynga Game Card as an online gift:

1. **Enter** http://www.zynga.com/gamecards **in the address box of your Web browser and press the Enter key.**

2. **On the Zynga page that appears, click the Give a Card link on the left sidebar.**

   The Give a Game Card menu opens, as shown in Figure 5-4.

3. **Choose your preferred Game Card amount from the drop-down menu.**

   Zynga Game Cards are currently available in denominations of $10, $15, $25, and $50. You can also use the drop-down menu to choose Canadian dollars (CAD) and British pounds (GBP).

4. **Click the Game Card design you'd like to give.**

   Click the left and right arrows to scroll through the available designs. You can also use the drop-down menu to limit the choices to designs for a certain occasion, such as a birthday or thank you gift.

Figure 5-4: The Give a Game Card menu on Zynga.com.

5. **Fill out the Game Card information and click Continue.**

   Note that you can choose for the Game Card to be delivered at a future date, which is convenient if you're planning ahead for a special event. Also note that the personal message can't be more than 400 characters, including spaces.

6. **Fill in your credit card information or click the PayPal button to pay with your PayPal account; then click the Purchase button.**

   If you're not comfortable using these payment options, consider getting a FarmVille Game Card from a local retailer (see the previous section, "An alternative to paying online: FarmVille Game Cards").

Your Game Card gift will appear in the recipient's e-mail box on the date you chose in Step 5. Redeeming an e-mailed Zynga Game Card works the same as redeeming a physical FarmVille Game Card, except that you find the PIN number in the e-mail message rather than on the back of the card. See the previous section for more details on redeeming Game Cards.

Earning "free" Farm Cash through offers and promotions

For farmers who don't want to buy Farm Cash directly or wait for it to slowly accrue through playing the game, there is a third option. Zynga provides various offers and promotions for you to use to earn bonus Farm Cash. These offers might require you to buy a product, install a program, sign up for a free trial, or watch an advertisement to earn your in-game currency.

Offers

If you scroll to the bottom of the Get Farm Cash page, you see a table with dozens of Farm Cash offers from Zynga's advertising partners, as shown in Figure 5-5. These can include anything from a movie rental service or magazine subscriptions to credit card applications and products.

Each offer consists of a description of the product or service being offered, the specific requirements to earn the Farm Cash, and a button highlighting how much the offer is worth in Farm Cash.

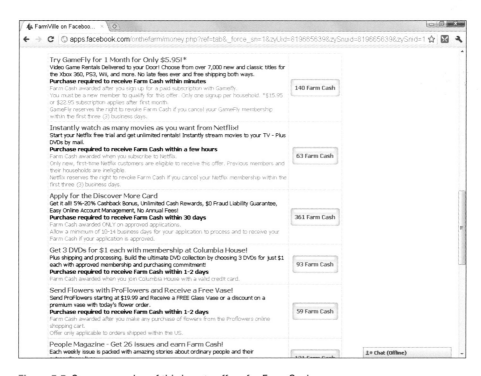

Figure 5-5: Some examples of third-party offers for Farm Cash.

To complete an offer, simply click the Farm Cash button and follow the directions on the page that pops up. Your Farm Cash will appear in your account after the period of time indicated in the offer's description (this time period is highlighted in bold). If your Farm Cash doesn't appear, click the Missing Farm Cash button just below the Buy Farm Cash & Coins menu and click the Contact links there to report a problem. If you still need help, see Chapter 14 for more on contacting Zynga support.

Before you click the Farm Cash link, be sure to read the light gray "requirements" text associated with each offer. This fine print, which highlights in red when you hover the mouse over the offer area, lays out exactly what you need to do to qualify for the free Farm Cash, and it can differ significantly from what the link text might suggest.

For instance, some free trial offers reserve the right to revoke your Farm Cash if you cancel the new subscription within three days. Other subscriptions may increase their monthly rate after a brief trial period if you don't cancel, so watch out!

Also note that most of these offers require submitting personal information such as your mailing address and phone number in addition to your credit card information. Even if you cancel your subscriptions to these services, your information may be sold or given to spammers and junk mailers. Look for the privacy policy at the bottom of the offer page to make sure your information will be protected.

Sponsored links

In addition to the advertising offers on the Get Farm Cash page, Zynga also offers a rotating set of sponsored links from third-party vendors below the FarmVille play area, as shown in Figure 5-6. These always-changing links can offer free Farm Cash for everything from watching a movie trailer to purchasing a Halloween costume, and they often promote new, seasonally appropriate products or services. Simply click the link and follow the directions on the page that pops up to receive your Farm Cash.

Although you can trust the offers and promotions listed in this section, other Web sites offering free Farm Cash may be scams. See Chapter 13 for more on recognizing and avoiding some common FarmVille scams.

Install the FarmVille Game Bar

Zynga currently offers 10 Farm Cash for installing the FarmVille Game Bar on your browser. This toolbar, which stays at the top of your browser even when you're surfing other Web sites, helps you manage common FarmVille tasks with a single click.

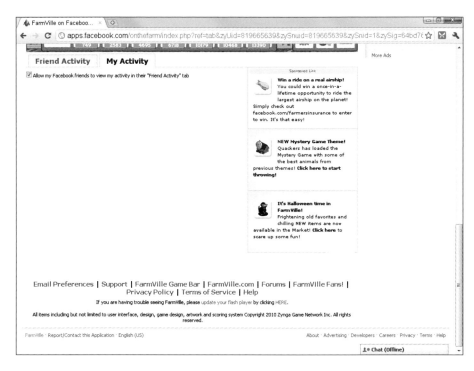

Figure 5-6: Examples of FarmVille sponsored links.

The FarmVille Game Bar works only with Firefox version 3.6 or higher or Internet Explorer version 7 or higher. If you're using a different browser, switch to one of these before performing the following steps.

To install the FarmVille Game Bar:

1. **Enter** http://toolbar.zynga.com/install/farmville/ **into your Web browser's address bar and press Enter.**

   The FarmVille Game Bar Installation page appears, as shown in Figure 5-7.

2. **Click the Facebook Connect button to connect with your Facebook account.**

   If you're not already logged in to Facebook, enter your e-mail address and password in the window that pops up and then click Login.

3. **Click the Install button.**

   If your browser is set to stop the automatic installation of add-ons, you need to click the Allow button that appears in the top-right corner of your browser to continue.

Figure 5-7: The FarmVille Game Bar Installation page.

4. **Click Install Now.**

   The FarmVille Game Bar add-on downloads and installs on your system automatically.

5. **Restart your browser.**

   The FarmVille Game Bar should appear just below the address bar in your browser.

After the FarmVille Game Bar is installed, the 10 Farm Cash you earned for installing it will appear in your FarmVille Gift Box the next time you log in to the game.

Register for a Zynga account

Zynga also offers free Farm Cash to players who register for a new Zynga account when paying for Farm Cash with a PayPal account. Having a Zynga account lets you purchase FarmVille currency without logging in to your PayPal account.

To register for a Zynga account and earn this bonus, follow these steps:

1. **Enter** `http://www.farmville.com` **into your Web browser's address bar and press the Enter key.**

   The Farmville.com page appears in your browser. Note that as of this writing, you can't sign up for a Zynga account when playing on Facebook.

2. **Click the Get Farm Cash tab on the top menu.**

   If you need help navigating FarmVille's menus, see Chapter 3.

2. **Purchase any amount of Farm Cash using a PayPal account.**

   See the "Buying Farm Coins and Cash through FarmVille" section, earlier in this chapter, for more on purchasing Farm Cash from within the game. Note that this step requires having an active PayPal account; for information about what's involved in having a PayPal account, go to `http://www.paypal.com` or check out _PayPal For Dummies,_ by Victoria Rosenborg and Marsha Collier (Wiley).

3. **Complete your transaction.**

   A pop-up notification appears, asking whether you'd like to sign up for a Zynga account.

4. **Enter an e-mail address and password and click Create an Account.**

   A page appears to confirm that your Zynga account has been created.

5. **Check your e-mail account for a confirmation e-mail from Zynga and click the link provided to redeem your free Farm Cash.**

   Your Farm Cash will automatically appear in your accumulated Farm Cash bank the next time you log in to the game.

Agricultural Economics 101: Mastering the FarmVille Market

In This Chapter

▶ Navigating the FarmVille Market

▶ Farming more efficiently

▶ Maximizing your farming profit

*A*t its core, FarmVille is primarily a game about making and spending money to continually expand the size of your farm and increase its assets. The previous chapter explains the types of currency used in FarmVille and how to gain more by purchasing it with real money or by other means, such as receiving gifts. In this chapter, you find out to how to go about spending your FarmVille currency on necessary purchases: the seeds, vehicles, fuel, and other essential items for running and expanding your farm. You buy all these essentials through the Market menu, which is thoroughly described in this chapter.

Also in this chapter are tips for making the best economical use of your most precious nonrenewable resource — time — by using vehicles and other items to speed up your farming. Finally, we lay out a few basic tips for keeping to a set farming schedule and managing your money wisely.

Browsing the FarmVille Market

The Market menu, as seen in Figure 6-1, is the hub for all your purchases in FarmVille. You can access this menu by clicking the Market icon in the Tools menu, which you find in the lower-right corner of the play area.

You can also bring up the Market menu by clicking a plowed plot of land with the Multi tool (Chapter 3 covers the Tools menu) or selecting the Seeder or Combine vehicles from the Tools menu (see the "Vehicles" section, later in this chapter).

To view the various product sections of the FarmVille Market, click the tabs at the top of the Market menu or click the right and left arrows on either side of the menu to scroll through the pages of the current product section.

Figure 6-1: The Seeds section of the Market menu.

Each item listing on the Market menu contains the item's name, a small picture of the item, the time until harvest, and the item's cost, which is displayed in either Farm Coins or Farm Cash, depending on the item. Many item listings also contain additional information about that purchase, such as the item's selling price and the number of experience points (XP) you earn with your purchase. There is also a nifty Preview button for decorations and buildings that you can click to see how the item looks on a farm. To get a sense of the item's size, you can compare it to a farmer avatar and hay bale.

Not all items in the Market are available at all times; many are locked until you achieve a certain level, attract a certain number of neighbors, or master a certain crop. Other items are available only when playing the iOS (mobile device) version of the game, as discussed in Chapter 2. These requirements are clearly marked on the item information box, as shown in Figure 6-2. Click the More Info button, where applicable, to get more details about the requirements for that item's purchase. (See Chapter 8 for more on how to unlock specific items.)

Figure 6-2: Examples of locked items in the Market menu.

Items in the FarmVille Market fall into two general categories:

- **Tangible:** Items that can be physically placed on your farm
- **Consumable:** Items that are used immediately after purchase and don't take up room on your farm

When you click the Buy button under the picture of a tangible Market item, the Market menu disappears and you return to your farm, where you can place that item (or plant that seed) with a click of the mouse. Note that the purchase price for these tangible items isn't deducted from your account until you actively place that item on your farm. Don't worry too much about placement — you can always move these items later using the Move tool.

If you change your mind about a tangible purchase after clicking the Buy button, or simply can't find an open place to put your item, don't panic — just click any button in the Tools menu (such as the Multi tool button) to cancel your pending purchase without spending any in-game currency.

Consumable items that you don't have to actively place on your farm — such as clothing, animal feed, and shovels — are automatically added to your account as soon as you click the Buy button, so be careful where you click the Market menu.

In addition to the Buy button, some Market items also feature a Send button that you click to purchase that item for one of your neighbors. It's important to realize that, in contrast to the free gifts discussed in Chapter 4, sending items this way actually deducts Farm Cash from your account.

Although you can purchase most decorations, animals and vehicles from the Market, FarmVille has some items that you can earn only as free gifts.

Seeds

Click the seeds tab in the Market menu to display a listing of all the available seeds you can plant on your farm, as shown in Figure 6-1. Each seed listing shows the following:

- The per-plot cost of planting the seed
- The selling price for the harvested crop
- The amount of time the plant needs to ripen
- The number of XP you gain for planting each seed

You can click the various tabs underneath the Seeds tab to show only crops of certain types, or click the All tab to show all available seeds.

You need to plow your plots of land before buying the seed — you can't plant on light-brown, unplowed plots. After you click the Buy button, though, you can plant as many plots of that seed as you want without going back to the Market menu in between each seeding.

After you reach level 10, the Market menu also shows the current mastery status of each available crop, displayed as a set of three stars and a green progress bar below the seed's picture. See Chapter 11 for more on mastering crops.

Trees

Click the Trees tab in the Market menu to see a list of all the trees you can purchase for your farm, as shown in Figure 6-3. Each tree listing shows the following information:

- The purchase price
- The sale price if you decide to sell the tree later
- The time required between tree harvests.

Figure 6-3: The Trees section of the Market menu.

The Trees section of the Market is also where you can purchase Arborists to help harvest trees quickly, as discussed later in the "Arborists and Farmhands" section, later in this chapter, and watering cans for mystery seedlings from your orchard.

Animals

Click the Animals tab in the Market menu to see a list of all the animals you can purchase for your farm, as shown in Figure 6-4. Each animal listing shows the following:

- ✔ The purchase price for that animal.
- ✔ The sale price if you decide to sell the animal later.
- ✔ The time required between harvests. If an animal does not have a harvest time listed, it is either a pet or a decorative animal that can't be regularly harvested for coins. (See Chapter 3 for more on the differences between pets and other animals.)

The Animals section of the Market is also the place to buy items for your pets, including kibble, treats, and pet-related decorative items. This section of the Market also includes animal feed for your animal trough and bees for your beehive (see Chapter 9 for more information on how these animal housing buildings work).

Click the Pets tab to show only pets and pet-related items, or the All tab to show all the items in the animals section.

Most animals require a good deal of hard-to-acquire Farm Cash to purchase from the Market. Money-conscious farmers should encourage their friends to send animals as free gifts. They should also watch for opportunities to adopt animals from news feeds. Yet another strategy is to use buildings such as Horse Stables, Dairy Farms, and Nursery Barns, which all have the potential to produce new animals.

Figure 6-4: The Animals sections of the Market menu.

Buildings

Click the Buildings tab in the Market menu to display a list of decorative and functional buildings that you can place on your farm, as shown in Figure 6-5. Each listed building shows the following:

- ✓ The purchase price for that building
- ✓ The sale price if you decide to sell the building later
- ✓ The XP gained for placing that building on your farm

For buildings purchased with Farm Coins, the number of XP you earn for the purchase is equal to one percent of the purchase price.

You can click the various tabs that appear under the Buildings tab to show only buildings of certain types, or you can click the All tab to show all available buildings. Most of the buildings listed in the Buildings section — including all those listed by clicking the Homes and Other tabs — are purely decorative and provide no functional purpose on your farm. Others, such as those listed as a result of clicking the Storage, For Animals, and Crafting tabs, can be used to store items and animals or to craft and sell various goods.

Figure 6-5: The Buildings section of the Market menu.

Some storage buildings and animal shelters can be purchased as frames, which require building materials to be completed into functional buildings, as discussed in Chapter 7. Also note that you can purchase only a limited number of certain functional buildings. After you reach this limit, the Buy button under that building is grayed out, and red "Locked" and "Limit" messages appear under the building's picture in the Market menu.

Decorations

Click the Decorations tab in the Market menu to see a list of purely decorative items that you can purchase to spruce up your farm, as shown in Figure 6-6. As with the other lists of product types on the Market menu, each decoration list shows the decoration's purchase price, its sale price if you decide to sell it later, and the XP gained for placing that decoration on your farm. You can click the various tabs underneath the Decorations tab to show only decorations of certain types, or you can click the All tab to show all available decorations.

Farm Aides

Click the Farm Aides tab in the Market menu to display a list of general improvements that you can purchase for your farm, as shown in Figure 6-7.

Figure 6-6: The Decorations section of the Market menu.

These upgrades fall into two main categories, as described in the following sections.

Figure 6-7: The Farm Aides section of the Market menu.

Land expansions

You can view available land expansions by clicking the Expand tab on the Farm Aides section of the Market menu. Purchasing a land expansion increases the available amount of space on your farm.

When you first create a FarmVille account, your farm is big enough to fit 12 plots of plowed land on each edge of the square farming area, or 144 plots total (if you have no other items or decorations on the farm). Each expansion stretches each edge of your square farm by the length of two plots of land. Existing items and plowed plots remain on your farm after expansion, but they may look off-center because of the new, unspoiled area.

You can purchase land expansions at any time using Farm Cash or, if you have the requisite number of neighbors, with Farm Coins, as detailed in Table 6-1. Note that before purchasing a given land expansion, you must first purchase all smaller land expansions in sequence — you can't save cash by just hoarding your money and leapfrogging up to a higher expansion level.

Table 6-1	Costs and Requirements for Farm Expansions			
Expansion Name	Size (in Plowed Plots)	Cost in Farm Cash	Cost In Farm Coins	Neighbors Needed for Farm Coin Purchase
Homestead	14 x 14 (196 plots)	20	10,000	8
Family Farm	16 x 16 (256 plots)	20	25,000	10
Big Family Farm	18 x 18 (324 plots)	20	50,000	13
Plantation	20 x 20 (400 plots)	20	75,000	16
Big Ole Plantation	22 x 22 (484 plots)	30	250,000	20
Mighty Plantation	24 x 24 (576 plots)	60	500,000	30
Grand Plantation	26 x 26 (676 plots)	80	2,000,000	35

Landscape

Tired of that boring green grass covering your farm? Click the Landscape tab in the Farm Aides section of the Market menu to display a list of new, decorative landscapes, which you can purchase for 1,000 coins each. Click the Buy button, and your farm will be instantly transformed: blanketed by snow, covered with desert sand, or something else of your choosing. Don't worry — these landscapes are purely decorative and don't affect your farm's production.

Changing your farm landscape costs 1,000 coins every time, even if you're changing back to the default Green Pastures landscape or to a landscape you've previously purchased. Although it's not a crippling expense, you should plan to stick with a landscape for a while before making the switch.

You can also find Unwithers and Fertilize All items under this tab of the Market. We discuss these items further in the "Obtaining and Using Vehicles and Tools to Speed Up Your Harvest" section, later in this chapter.

Vehicles

Click the Vehicles tab in the Market menu to purchase vehicles and vehicle-related items, such as chassis, fuel, and vehicle parts. These items can help speed up your planting and harvesting, as discussed in much more detail in the "Obtaining and Using Vehicles and Tools to Speed Up Your Harvest" section, later in this chapter.

Clothing

Click the Clothing tab to bring up a listing of all the avatar clothing available for purchase, as shown in Figure 6-8. Click the Buy button to immediately purchase and dress your avatar in any of the clothing shown in this section.

Note that you don't receive a confirmation for clothing purchases, so be careful what you click in this section. If you'd rather try before you buy, you can click the Try It On? button under any clothing picture to bring up the Customize My Farmer menu, as discussed in Chapter 3.

Limited-edition items

Click the Click for Specials button on the left side of the Market menu to view all the limited-edition items currently available for purchase, as shown in Figure 6-9. These items also appear in the applicable sections of the FarmVille Market discussed earlier in this chapter, with the word *Limited* under the item's picture and an icon indicating the current limited-edition item theme (for example, a pumpkin to represent Halloween items).

Figure 6-8: The Clothes section of the Market menu.

These primarily decorative items are available in the Market for only a short time but can stay on your farm permanently after being purchased. When a limited-edition item is about to leave the Market, the remaining availability time is listed in red text in the item description box, as shown in Figure 6-9.

Figure 6-9: The limited-edition items section of the Market menu.

Obtaining and Using Vehicles and Tools to Speed Up Your Harvest

Although a single click with the Multi tool can do everything from planting seeds to harvesting crops, trees, and animals, all that constant clicking can get pretty tiresome when your farm starts to get big and crowded. Luckily, FarmVille provides a variety of tools and vehicles to reduce the number of clicks required for a variety of common farming tasks.

Animal shelters also speed up your farming by letting you harvest a number of animals with a single click. See Chapter 9 for more on purchasing and using animal shelters.

Vehicles

Much as real-world farming vehicles do, vehicles in FarmVille help speed up farming by decreasing the amount of manual labor you have to invest in common tasks.

Vehicles can be purchased with either Farm Cash or Farm Coins. After you've purchased a vehicle, you can use it by following these steps:

1. **Hover your mouse over the Plow tool in the Tools menu and, from the menu that appears, click the vehicle you want to use.**

   You can also click the vehicle itself and click the appropriate action (plow, seed, or harvest) from the drop-down menu that appears.

   If you've chosen the Seeder or Combine, the Market menu appears. Choose the seed you want to plant and click the Buy button underneath it.

2. **Move your mouse pointer to the area you want to affect with the vehicle.**

   A larger-than-normal effect area appears underneath your mouse pointer, as shown in Figure 6-10. Just how large this area is depends on the type of vehicle, as shown in Table 6-2.

3. **Click the mouse to use the vehicle on the selected area.**

   Clicking an open area with a basic tractor, for instance, plows four plots of land instead of the usual one. Note that each click uses some fuel from your inventory — and if you're out of fuel, this process won't work. (See the "Getting fuel to run your vehicles" section, later in this chapter, for more on obtaining fuel.)

Besides the spent fuel, the costs and benefits of farming with vehicles — including Farm Coin costs, accumulated XP, crop mastery, and the like — are the same as farming those same plots without vehicles.

Note that your plots have to be arranged in a precise grid for your vehicle to cover the area efficiently. As shown in Figure 6-11, plots arranged haphazardly might require more clicks than normal to cover with a vehicle. If your plots are currently misaligned, use the Move tool to rearrange them. (See Chapter 3 for more about the tools available in the Tools menu.)

Also note that you can still use vehicles even if part of the area you're clicking doesn't currently need that vehicle. For instance, you can use the Seeder even if some of the plots under your mouse pointer's effect area are already seeded. The vehicle will just ignore those plots without spending fuel or Farm Coins on them.

Figure 6-10: Preparing to seed four strawberry plots with the Seeder.

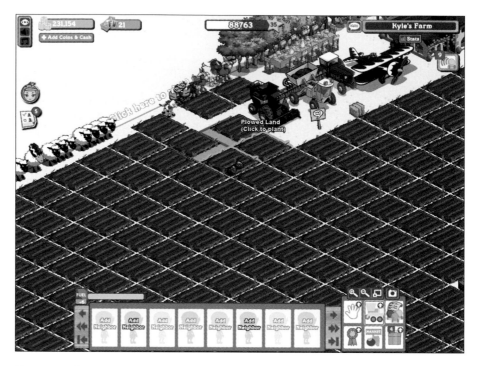

Figure 6-11: Clicking here with the Seeder will seed the plots highlighted in yellow but not the ones highlighted in red.

The types of vehicles that you purchase from the Vehicles section of the Market menu are outlined in Table 6-2 and discussed in more detail in the following sections.

Table 6-2			Types of Vehicles		
Vehicle	*Function*	*How to Obtain*	*Area Covered per Click*	*Fuel Use*	*Level Required to Purchase*
Basic Vehicles					
Tractor	Plowing	5,000 Farm Coins	2 x 2 area of 4 plots	4	12
Seeder	Seeding	30,000 Farm Coins	2 x 2 area of 4 plots	4	14
Harvester	Harvesting	30,000 Farm Coins	2 x 2 area of 4 plots	4	13

Vehicle	Function	How to Obtain	Area Covered per Click	Fuel Use	Level Required to Purchase
Hot Rod Vehicles					
Tractor	Plowing	45,000 Farm Coins or 55 Farm Cash	3 x 3 area of 9 plots	9	10 in Mafia Wars to unlock the coin option
Seeder	Seeding	45,000 Farm Coins or 55 Farm Cash	3 x 3 area of 9 plots	9	15 in FarmVille and level up 5 times in Mafia Wars to unlock for coins
Harvester	Harvesting	45,000 Farm Coins or 55 Farm Cash	3 x 3 area of 9 plots	9	18 in FarmVille and travel to Bangkok in Mafia Wars
Combine	Harvests. Plows, and Seeds simultaneously	500,000 Farm Coins	2 x 2 area of 4 plots	12	31
Hot Rod Combine	Harvests, Plows, and Seeds simultaneously	110 Farm Cash or buy chassis for 500,000 Farm Coins and build using vehicle parts	3 x 4 area of 12 plots or upgraded to a maximum of 4 x 4 area of 16 plots	36 (48 after upgrade)	12 to purchase and 41 to upgrade
Biplane	Instantly grows all seeded plots	30,000 Farm Coins or Reward for Co-op	All plots on your farm	First flight is free, subsequent flights cost Farm Cash	12
Upgraded Vehicles	Same as the vehicle being upgraded	Obtain a garage and vehicle parts as discussed in Chapter 9.	Up to 4 x 4 area of 16 plots after full upgrade.	9 (16 after two upgrades)	Level 26 (to obtain a garage); level 41 to upgrade a Combine

Basic vehicles

The Tractors, Seeder, and Harvester are the most basic vehicles in the game. Each one helps speed up a distinct portion of the planting cycle — plowing, seeding and harvesting, respectively. You can purchase all three using Farm Coins, and with one click, each basic vehicle performs its function over a 2 plot x 2 plot area of 4 plots.

You can use a garage to upgrade your basic vehicles to cover more land with each click. After obtaining a garage, you need to obtain vehicle parts as gifts or as a purchase from the FarmVille market to upgrade each vehicle. Upgrading your vehicle is optional, but many farmers find it useful and time saving because more area of land can be covered per click. The entire upgrade process is discussed in more detail in Chapter 9.

Hot Rod vehicles

All three basic vehicles are also available in hot rod varieties that you can purchase from the Market with Farm Cash. Besides sporting a spiffy paint job over their normal counterparts, Hot Rod vehicles let you plow a 3 plot x 3 plot area of 9 plots with a single click. Hot Rod vehicles still require fuel and properly aligned plots to use correctly, as discussed in the beginning of this section, but can reduce your farming time even further.

Combine

The Combine is the ultimate FarmVille vehicle. With a single click of the Combine, you can quickly harvest, plow, and reseed a 2x2 area of 4 plots your farm. After you've tried it, you'll wonder how you ever farmed any other way.

You can get a Combine in two ways. The first is to purchase a Hot Rod Combine wholesale from the Market menu for a whopping 110 Farm Cash. The other is to purchase a Combine chassis for 500,000 Farm Coins and then use 40 Vehicle Part items to turn that chassis into a full-fledged Combine. Vehicle parts can be purchased from the Market for one Farm Cash each or received as gifts from friends.

Note that a Combine consumes three times as much fuel as a single vehicle would use for that land, but because it's doing three times as much work, it's no less fuel-efficient than a normal vehicle.

Biplane

The biplane is a unique vehicle that lets you skip the wait for your crops to grow to maturity, ripening your entire field with a single click. You can purchase a biplane from the Market for 30,000 Farm Coins, and that purchase includes one free use of the plane's field-growing power.

After that first use, however, the biplane's powerful ability doesn't come so cheaply. Whenever you click the biplane, a pop-up notification asks whether you want to spend a certain amount of Farm Cash to grow all your crops instantly. Although the precise cost for each use depends on the number and current growth status of your crops, growing a full field of long-gestation crops can easily run you more than 100 in Farm Cash. Think carefully about whether you really can't afford to wait out the current growing cycle before spending all that in-game dough.

If you seed an entire field of high-profit, long-gestation crops such as artichokes, potatoes, or yellow melon before using your biplane for the first time, the instant profit from those crops can effectively pay for the purchase immediately.

Getting fuel to run your vehicles

Except for the biplane, all vehicles need fuel to operate. Your current fuel reserves are shown as a gauge in the bottom-left corner of your farm, as shown in Figure 6-12. This fuel is shared among all your FarmVille vehicles and automatically deducted as you use those vehicles. The number under the word *Fuel* indicates how many full tanks you currently have in reserve, whereas the yellow gauge shows the portion of the current tank that remains. Each full fuel tank holds enough fuel to use one basic vehicle on 150 plots of land or a Combine on 50 plots of land. You can hover your mouse over the fuel gauge to see how many plots your current fuel reserves can accommodate.

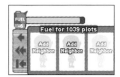

Figure 6-12: The fuel gauge.

After you've purchased your first vehicle, you can use Farm Cash to purchase fuel directly from the Vehicles section of the Market menu or obtain it any of the following ways:

- ✔ Find fuel randomly when plowing land on your own farm.
- ✔ Find fuel randomly when fertilizing plots on neighbors' farms.

- Find fuel randomly in Mystery Gifts, Mystery Eggs, and Gift Boxes; or obtain fuel directly as a gift from a neighbor.

- Click a link offering free fuel in a neighbor's Facebook news feed.

- Trade crafted goods for fuel.

- Complete a collection to receive a fuel bonus.

- Click the Bonus button on the FarmVille Game Bar once a day for that day's free fuel reward. (If you need to install the Game Bar, see Chapter 5 to find out how.)

- Click the link in the Daily Fuel Boost e-mail sent by Zynga, if you've elected to receive such e-mails.

- Allow your fuel to regenerate slowly over time. The precise rate at which your fuel tanks refill depends on the size of your farm. At most, this natural regeneration fills one tank of fuel over a 24-hour period.

- During occasional Free Fuel Week promotions, you can gain fuel bonuses simply for visiting your farm daily. If you visit your farm every day during these promotions, your fuel rewards will increase each day.

Arborists and Farmhands

Using Arborists and Farmhands is a wonderful way to improve the efficiency of your farming. With a single click, Arborists can harvest fruit or nuts from every ripened tree on your farm, and Farmhands can harvest every animal that's ready for harvesting. On a farm with dozens of trees or animals, the time savings from using these helpers can be substantial.

Unfortunately, in contrast to vehicles, these helpers are not permanent fixtures on your farm. Instead, they exist as one-use items that reside in your gift box. You can purchase both Arborists and Farmhands for five Farm Cash per use from the trees and animals sections of the Market menu, respectively. You also have a chance of finding these helpers when harvesting your Horse Stable (see Chapter 9) or opening Mystery Gifts and Mystery Eggs (see Chapter 4).

You can also occasionally send and receive these helpers as free gifts from the Gifting page. Be sure to take advantage of these gift periods by sending Arborists and Farmhands to all your neighbors and requesting that they send ones back in return. Your clicking finger will thank you later.

To get the most economical use out of your Arborists and Farmhands, wait until all your trees or animals are ready for harvest.

Maximizing Your Profit

Although not making money in FarmVille is almost impossible, you can learn some tricks to maximizing your profit while minimizing the time spent with tedious busy work. Read on for the details.

Farming on your schedule: Time is virtual money

Keeping your growing and harvesting cycle going continuously is key to gaining lots of experience points and Farm Coins. Because the FarmVille growing cycle operates in real time — even when you're not playing the game — you need to plan your planting so that you'll be available to harvest crops after they've ripened but before they've withered.

Early in your farming career, you have access to only a few types of crops (as explained in Chapter 3), but even these crops grow over varying time ranges, from four hours to four days. When choosing what type of seed to plant, take a look at the clock and try to predict whether you'll be busy, asleep, or otherwise occupied when that crop will be ready to harvest. If so, pick another crop that will be ready at a more convenient time.

Of course, you don't have to be waiting by the computer for the very moment your crops are ready to harvest. The amount of time a ripened crop takes to wither is equal to the amount of time it takes to ripen after planting. So if you plant a strawberry seed at noon, it will be ready for harvest at 4 p.m. and dead and withered by 8 p.m. Withered crops aren't worth any money, so make sure you make plans to check in on your crops during this time range.

When planting your crops, you should also consider how often you'd like to play FarmVille. Although quick-ripening crops such as raspberries are good at generating lots of coins in a short amount of time, they require checking in every two hours for a harvest, which can quickly get tiresome. Longer-lead crops may be slightly less profitable in the long run, but require less direct attention.

For a quick reference to some of the best crops for each planting situation and level, see Chapter 17.

Another important note: A full harvest "day" in FarmVille actually spans only 23 hours, so crops listed in the Market with harvest times in multiples of "days" may actually be ready quicker than expected. If you plant soybeans at noon on Sunday, for instance, they'll actually be ready for harvest at 11 a.m. on Monday. This also means that a 2-day crop such as eggplant will be ready 46 hours after planting, and so on.

Hover your mouse over any planted crop to see what percentage of that plot has ripened.

Expand on demand

Expanding your farm, as discussed in the "Farm Aides" section, earlier in the chapter, is one of the best ways to supercharge your FarmVille profits. More land means more precious space to grow crops, which means that each growing cycle can bring in more Farm Coins.

Impatient farmers can use their precious Farm Cash on these expansions, whereas cheapskates should make saving up enough Farm Coins for an expansion one of their first goals. Remember to keep a stockpile of coins free after your expansion, though, so that you can plant some crops on your newly expanded land.

Frugal farming

In FarmVille as in life, a penny saved is a penny earned. Although buying lots of fancy decorations early on may seem enticing, you should initially focus on seeds, animals, and trees that will generate steady income and XP long into the future. These items quickly pay for themselves and, with a little patience on your part, leave you with extra money in the long run to buy those decorations you want.

Don't forget that unwanted gifts and items can be sold for extra coins as well. Selling these items both cleans up your inventory and lets you plow the coins you gain into more profitable avenues (pun intended).

The Farmers Market

In This Chapter

▶ Setting up a market stall

▶ Finding, sharing, and using bushels

▶ Crafting goods

▶ Buying and selling crafted goods

▶ Mastering crafts

*R*eceiving money directly for harvesting ripe crops is all well and good, but it's only a part of the benefit you can derive from those crops. By finding and sharing bushels during your harvest, and assembling those bushels into sellable crafted goods, you can get rewards including experience points (XP), Farm Coins, and, most usefully, fuel for farming vehicles.

To be clear, the *Farmers* Market is totally separate from the *FarmVille* Market, the latter being where you purchase seeds, trees, animals, and various other items for your farm. (We tell you all about how to use the FarmVille Market in Chapter 6.)

have:
8 of 1

The trip from bushel to fuel is a bit involved, but this chapter takes you through the entire process, from sharing bushels in your market stall and collecting more bushels from friends to building a crafting building and completing recipes for crafted goods. Pretty soon, the whole process will be a natural part of your everyday farming routine.

Carrot Bushel
You have:
1 of 3

Collecting, Sharing, and Using Bushels

Bushels are the core of the Farmers Market. Bushels are simply a special type of item that you can use to improve your harvests, share with friends to collect bonuses, or collect to help craft goods.

Setting up market stalls

Before you can start collecting bushels, you first need to set up at least one market stall. These special buildings allow you to store and share bushels you find while harvesting crops.

The first time you find a bushel of crops while harvesting your land, a pop-up notification tells you that you've earned a free market stall. Click the Okay button and then place the market stall anywhere on your farm as you normally do (see Chapter 3 for the details on placing items on your farm). An instructional pop-up screen appears after you place the stall, but this book provides a far more in-depth reference, so just click Okay.

You can purchase up to four additional market stalls — for a total of five — from the buildings section of the Market menu. The additional stalls cost 20 Farm Cash or, if you have reached level 15, you can purchase additional stalls for 50,000 Farm Coins each. Note that for every market stall you purchase with Farm Coins, you need a minimum of two additional neighbors before you can purchase the next market stall.

Why would you want more than one market stall? To answer that question, we need to explain a bit more about bushels and how they're collected, shared, and used. The next sections do just that.

Collecting bushels

FarmVille gives you a number of different ways to collect bushels, as follows:

- From harvesting crops
- From your neighbors' market stalls
- From your Facebook news feed
- From co-op jobs
- From making a Farm Cash purchase

We describe these one at a time in the following sections.

Collecting bushels from harvesting crops

Whenever you harvest any nonlimited-edition crop, you have a chance of finding a bushel of that crop. The game lets you know about these found bushels with small pop-up notifications at the bottom of the screen as you harvest. You also receive a summary notification about all the bushels you've found when you finish harvesting your entire field, as shown in Figure 7-1. Click the Share button on this notification to share a free bushel with your neighbors via a news feed post, as discussed in Chapter 4.

Figure 7-1: A summary of bushels found during a harvest.

Whenever you find a bushel while harvesting crops, you receive an extra bushel for every mastery star you've earned for that crop. (We tell you all about crop mastery in Chapter 11.)

When you find bushels through a harvest, you can also share copies of those bushel in your market stall, as discussed in the next section.

Collecting bushels from your neighbors' market stalls

You can also collect bushels that your neighbors are sharing in their market stalls. To collect bushels in this way, follow these steps:

1. **Click any of your market stalls and choose Look Inside from the drop-down menu.**

   The Get Bushels section of the Farmers Market menu appears, as shown in Figure 7-2. (If you leave this section, you can click the Get Bushels tab at the top of the menu to return.)

   Click the up and down arrows on the right side of the menu to see what kinds of bushels are currently being offered in your neighbors' market stalls, as indicated by that neighbor's picture next to the bushel.

2. **Click the green Get button under a neighbor's picture next to the bushel you want.**

   The Shop for Bushels section of the Friend's Market menu appears, as shown in Figure 7-3. Note that this menu may actually show multiple crops on offer from the applicable neighbor, not just the one you're looking for.

Figure 7-2: The Get Bushels section of the Farmers Market menu.

Figure 7-3: The Shop for Bushels section of the Friend's Market menu.

3. **Click the Take One button underneath the bushel you want.**

   You can collect up to three total bushels from each neighbor each calendar day. Note that, for the purposes of the Farmers Market, new days
   start at midnight U.S. Eastern Time.

Although the game calls collecting bushels from friends in this way "purchasing," this process doesn't cost you any Farm Coins or Farm Cash. Also note that the bushels you "purchase" from your neighbors do not reduce the inventory of bushels that those neighbors can use for other purposes.

4. **(Optional) Click the Share button to post a free bushel to your Facebook news feed.**

We discuss this process in more detail in Chapter 4.

5. **Click the Leave button.**

Clicking this button returns you to the Farmer's Market menu, where you began in Step 1. You can keep collecting bushels, or click the red X button in the upper right-hand corner of the menu to return to farming.

You can also collect shared bushels from your neighbors market stalls via the crafting building menu, as discussed in the "Making a crafted good" section, later in this chapter.

Collecting bushels from your Facebook news feed

You can collect bushels by clicking bushel-sharing links in Facebook news feed posts placed by your neighbors. We discuss this process in Chapter 4.

Collecting bushels from co-op jobs

When you complete certain Farmers Market co-op jobs, you can earn sets of bushels required to craft specific goods. See Chapter 12 for the details about co-op jobs.

Collecting bushels from a Farm Cash purchase

You can use Farm Cash to buy the bushels you needs for crafted goods directly, as discussed in the "Making a crafted good" section, later in this chapter.

You can store only 100 bushels in your inventory at a time, regardless of how many market stalls you have. You can see how much of this capacity you're currently using by looking in the upper-left corner of the Get Bushels sections of the Farmers Market menu (refer to Figure 7-2).

If you already have 100 bushels in your inventory, you can't collect further bushels using any of the aforementioned methods. To clear out your inventory, try sharing bushels, as discussed in the next section, or use some bushels to improve your harvest, make pig slop, or create crafted goods, as discussed later in the chapter.

Sharing bushels

Hoarding bushels of crops to yourself would be a good idea if you expected a drought or a long winter, but because neither of those conditions occurs in FarmVille, you should feel free to share bushels with your neighbors using these methods:

- Through market stalls
- Through the Facebook news feed

Keep reading for more on these sharing methods.

Sharing bushels through market stalls

When you find a bushel through a crop harvest, additional copies of that bushel are also automatically placed for sharing in an open market stall. Your neighbors can collect these bushels through the Farmers Market menu, as discussed in the previous section.

As Figure 7-1 indicates, these bushels are available to your neighbors only for a limited time before disappearing from your stall. Market stall bushels are typically available for 24 hours after the initial harvest, but this number increases by eight hours for each mastery star you've earned in the applicable crop. (Chapter 11 tells you all about mastering crops.) If you find more bushels of the same crop later, the availability timer resets.

We want to emphasize here that the bushels shared automatically through your market stall are *not* the same bushels that are stored in your bushel inventory. So, when a neighbor collects a bushel from your market stall, doing so does not reduce the number of that type of bushel in your inventory (or the number of bushels available to be shared with other neighbors before the time limit runs out, for that matter).

Even though you risk nothing from sharing bushels through market stalls, you do gain some reward from sharing. For every neighbor who collects a bushel from your market stall, you can collect a bonus of either 400 Farm Coins, 15 units of fuel, or 10 experience points. When such a bonus is available, a bouncing arrow appears above your market stalls. Click any market stall with such an arrow to display the market stall reward menu, shown in Figure 7-4, and then click the appropriate Select button to claim your reward.

One final note on sharing bushels through market stalls: Each stall can share only one type of bushel. If you find a crop bushel while different types of bushels are currently being offered in all your market stalls, you won't be able to share the newly harvested bushels with your neighbors. Purchasing more market stalls from the Farmer's Market, as discussed in the "Setting up market stalls" section, earlier in this chapter, allows you to share a wider variety of bushels with your neighbors and gives you a better chance of collecting those bushel-sharing bonuses.

Figure 7-4: A market stall crop-sharing reward notification.

Sharing bushels through the Facebook news feed

You can also share bushels directly from your inventory by posting them to your Facebook news feed. This method of bushel sharing doesn't offer any direct rewards, though it can be handy for clearing out your bushel inventory when it gets full. And, hey, generosity is its own reward, isn't it?

To share bushels from your inventory, follow these steps:

1. **Click any of your market stalls and choose Look Inside from the drop-down menu.**

   The Farmers Market menu (refer to Figure 7-2) appears.

2. **Click the Use Bushels tab at the top of the menu.**

   A listing of all the bushels currently in your inventory appears, as shown in Figure 7-5. Click the tabs above the bushels to filter the list by type, or use the left and right arrows on the side of the menu to navigate multiple pages of bushels.

3. **Click the blue Share button under the bushel you want to share with your friends**

   A menu appears, asking how many of the applicable bushels you want to share.

4. **Set the quantity of bushels you want to share using the up and down arrows; then click the green Share button.**

   A notification window appears, asking you to post a notice to your Facebook wall (see Chapter 4 to find out how to post such a notice).

Figure 7-5: The Use Bushels section of the Farmers Market menu.

5. **Click the Publish button.**

   A post is published to your Facebook wall with a link allowing your neighbors to collect those bushels. Note that the shared bushels are removed from your inventory immediately, even if no neighbors have yet used this link.

Using bushels

So what's the point of collecting all these bushels — besides sharing them with hungry neighbors, that is? Well, bushels have a variety of uses on your farm, as we describe in the following sections.

Using bushels for planting and harvest bonuses

You can use bushels to access temporary bonus effects for your usual planting and harvest cycle. The specific bushel harvest bonus depends on the status of that crop, as follows:

✔ **For crops locked in the FarmVille Market menu:** Using a bushel for a crop that is currently locked in the FarmVille Market because of level restrictions gives you a temporary license to plant that crop. For the next two hours, you can purchase and plant that crop as normal. Note that you can still harvest these crops even after the two-hour bonus has worn off.

✔ **For crops you've already mastered:** If you've already achieved all three mastery stars for a crop, using a bushel of that crop activates a bonus of XP for each plot of that crop you harvest in the next two hours. Note that this bonus comes in addition to any experience point bonuses for fertilized crops.

✔ **For all other crops:** For crops that are unlocked in the FarmVille Market menu but not yet fully mastered, using a bushel activates a bonus that gives you an additional mastery point for each plot of that crop you harvest for the next two hours. This bonus is a great way to earn mastery stars much more quickly.

For crops that are already unlocked in the market, you should use your bushels after the seeds of that crop have ripened but before you start harvesting. For maximum efficiency, use a bushel before harvesting an entire field of a single ripe crop.

You can get the bonuses described in the preceding list by following these steps:

1. **Click any of your market stalls and choose Look Inside from the drop-down menu.**

   The Farmers Market menu (refer to Figure 7-2) appears.

2. **Click the Use Bushels tab at the top of the menu.**

   A display of all the bushels currently in your inventory appears (refer to Figure 7-5 to see what an inventory looks like). Click the tabs above the bushels to filter the list by types of crops, or use the left and right arrows on the side of the menu to navigate multiple pages of bushels.

3. **Click the green Use button underneath the bushel you want to use.**

   A pop-up notification appears.

4. **Click the green Accept button.**

   The bushel is removed from your inventory. Click the red X button in the upper-right corner of the Farmers Market menu to return to your farm. A small icon of the bushel appears in the bottom-right corner of the play area, indicating that the bushel's bonus is in effect. This effect lasts for two hours.

You can have only one bushel bonus in effect at any time. If you try to activate a new bushel bonus when another bushel bonus is already in effect, the new bushel bonus cancels out the old one.

Using bushels to make pig slop

If you have a Pigpen on your farm, you can turn your excess bushels into slop that will allow your pigs to hunts for truffles. This is a great way to clear out some space in your bushel inventory and get use out of bushels that you have no other immediate use for. For more on using Pigpens and creating slop from bushels, see Chapter 9.

Using bushels to craft goods

If you've set up a crafting building, you can use your accumulated bushels to create crafted goods, which can be exchanged for fuel and sold for a profit to neighbors. See the remainder of the chapter for a detailed description of how this process works.

Crafting Goods to Increase Profits

Using bushels to improve your harvest is effective, but converting those bushels into crafted goods can be much more lucrative in the long term. You can not only trade the goods crafted from bushels in for an easy source of fuel for vehicles but also sell those goods to other farmers and make a tidy profit in the process.

Converting bushels into goods and then converting goods into fuel and money is a bit of a complicated process, but we lay it all out for you in upcoming pages.

Setting up a crafting building

When you reach level 25, a pop-up notification box says that you now have the ability to set up your first crafting building. This notification gives you a choice to place one of three different types of buildings for different types of goods on your farm, as follows:

- **Bakery:** For pastries and other sweets
- **Spa:** For perfumes and candles
- **Winery:** For mixed drinks and wines

All three are largely similar from a gameplay perspective, so feel free to pick the one that suits your tastes best. Click the Yes, Place button under the building you want; then click any open space on your farm to place the building.

After you place your crafting building, the Crafting Building menu appears (Figure 7-6 shows this menu for a Winery). You can use this menu to make and buy goods, convert goods into fuel, collect bushels from neighbors, and more, as discussed in the following sections.

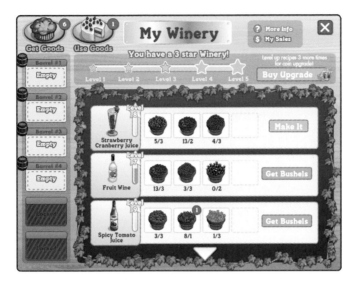

Figure 7-6: The Crafting Building menu for a Winery.

To gain the ability to craft more kinds of goods, you can purchase and place further crafting buildings from the Buildings section of the FarmVille Market menu for 80 Farm Cash each. Note that you can have a maximum of only one of each type of crafting building.

You need at least one market stall before you can start making crafted goods. If you haven't yet earned a free market stall by finding a bushel, you have to purchase one from the Market, as discussed in "Setting up market stalls," earlier in this chapter.

Making a crafted good

The main purpose of a crafting building is to convert bushels into goods, which you can then sell for coins and use for fuel.

Follow these steps to make a crafted good:

1. **Click your crafting building and choose Look Inside from the drop-down menu.**

   The menu for your crafting building appears (refer to Figure 7-6 for an example). Each row in this menu represents a recipe for a different craftable good. (You can click the up and down arrows above and below the visible rows to see more recipes.)

2. **Determine whether you have the required number of bushels for a given crafting recipe, and go on to Step 4 if you do. If you don't, follow any of the methods described in Steps 3a through 3d.**

   Each recipe requires a set number of up to four different bushels, as indicated by the number after the slash under the bushel's picture. The number before the slash under each bushel indicates how many of that bushel you actually have.

3a. **Collect more bushels, if necessary, by using any of the methods for collecting bushels discussed in "Collecting bushels," earlier in this chapter.**

3b. **Click the Get Bushels button to display the Shopping List menu, shown in Figure 7-7.**

   This handy menu shows which ingredients for a specific recipe are currently being offered in your neighbors' market stalls, as indicated by that neighbor's picture in the appropriate row. Click the Get button under any neighbor to bring up your neighbor's Farmers Market Sharing menu; then collect up to three bushels.

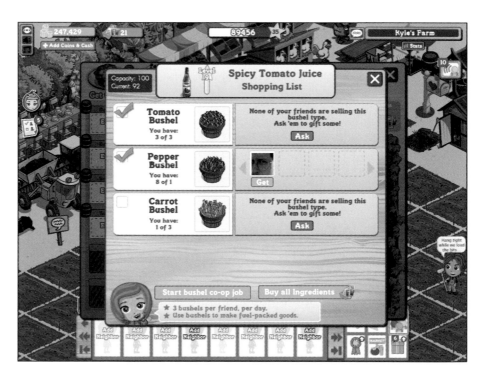

Figure 7-7: The Shopping List menu for a crafting building recipe.

If a neighbor is offering the bushels you need for a recipe from his or her market stall, a small number in a circle appears above that bushel's picture on the crafting building menu. This indicator provides a great shortcut to quickly see which needed bushels are available from neighbors and which you might have to plant and find for yourself.

You can collect only three bushels from each neighbor each calendar day. If you've recently collected bushels from a neighbor, you may have to wait until tomorrow before you can collect more.

3c. Post a request for bushels to your Facebook news feed.

Even if none of your neighbors is offering the necessary bushels, you can post a request for bushels to your Facebook news feed, as discussed in Chapter 4. From the Farmers Market Sharing menu (discussed in Step 3b) click the Ask button and then the Share button and then the Publish button to post a link that your neighbors can click to send you extra bushels.

3d. Buy the bushels necessary for a recipe.

You can also buy bushels needed for a recipe by clicking the Buy All Ingredients link at the bottom of the shopping list menu. Use the arrows on the menu that pops up to choose how many sets of bushels you want to purchase. Then click the Buy button to complete your purchase. Each set of bushels costs three Farm Cash.

4. Click the Make It button for the recipe you want to start crafting.

FarmVille moves the recipe over to an open crafting area on the left side of the crafting building menu, as shown in Figure 7-8, and you earn 50 XP. (The specific crafting area used varies by the type of crafting building.) Note that if all the crafting areas in your crafting building are full, you have to wait or finish some recipes before you can make more. You can earn more crafting areas by upgrading your crafting building, as discussed in the "Upgrading your crafting building" section, later in this chapter.

A pop-up notification asks whether you want to share another copy of the good you're making on your Facebook news feed. Click the Share button to post, as discussed in Chapter 4.

Another pop-up notification asks whether you want to start a co-op job for the current good to get more bushels. Clicking the Okay button takes you to the Co-op Jobs menu. If you prefer to stay on your crafting building menu, click the red X in the corner of the notification instead.

Figure 7-8: Goods sitting in barrels. In six hours, they will be ready to be completed.

5. **Wait for the good to be ready to be finished.**

   After you've put a recipe in a crafting area, you have to wait six hours before you can finish it (except for the first few goods you make, which are ready in a few minutes to give you an idea of how the process works). A message and yellow gauge above the picture of that recipe crafting area shows approximately how much time is left before the good is ready to be finished (refer to Figure 7-8).

6. **After the timer indicates that the good is complete, click the Finish It button above the appropriate crafting area.**

   Congratulations, you've crafted a good. One copy of the good goes in your inventory for personal use, and further copies are placed for sale to your neighbors, as discussed in the "Selling crafted goods" section, later in the chapter.

Leveling up and mastering crafted goods

Each time you make or sell a crafted good, you earn experience toward increasing the level of that recipe. The level of a crafting recipe corresponds directly to the level of the goods that recipe creates, and higher-level goods command a higher price — and therefore more profit — when sold to neighbors. They also yield more fuel when used, as discussed later in the chapter.

The current level of each recipe, as well as the relative progress you've made toward earning the next level, appears as a blue gauge with a star atop it (refer to Figure 7-8). Hover your mouse over this gauge to see exactly how many more times you need to craft a recipe to earn another level for that recipe.

The pattern for leveling up with recipes works like this: Every three levels, you need to make the previous level, plus one additional to level up that recipe. This pattern continues until you have 20 recipes, at which point it caps off. There is no limit to how many times you can level up a recipe. For example, if you had a Level 100 recipe, you'd have to make or sell 20 crafted goods to level it up to 101.

In addition to earning levels for your crafted goods, you can also earn mastery stars for crafting a good frequently. Just as you can earn mastery stars for planting crops (as Chapter 11 explains), so can you earn Farm Coin and XP bonuses for mastering crafted goods. Table 7-1 lists these bonuses. You also earn a mastery sign item, which you can place on your farm, when you earn the first mastery star for an item.

Table 7-1	Crafted Goods Mastery Level Bonuses	
Crafted Good Mastery Level	*Farm Coin Bonus*	*XP Bonus*
1	1,000	500
2	2,500	1,000
3	5,000	1,500
4	10,000	3,000
5	25,000	4,500

You can earn up to five mastery stars for each recipe in your crafting building. The specific level you need to reach to earn a mastery star for that recipe depends on what level your crafting building was at when that recipe was unlocked, as shown in Table 7-2. For example, a recipe such as the Patty Pan Tart, which is unlocked when you upgrade the Bakery to level 2, would need to be increased to level 26 before you could earn its first mastery star. See the "Upgrading your crafting building" section, later in the chapter, for more on leveling up your crafting building.

Table 7-2	Level Requirements to Earn Mastery Stars for Crafted Goods				
Building Level When Recipe Was Unlocked	1-Star Mastery Level	2-Star Mastery Level	3-Star Mastery Level	4-Star Mastery Level	5-Star Mastery Level
1	20	30	50	75	100
2	23	33	50	75	100
3	26	36	50	75	100
4	29	39	50	75	100
5	32	42	50	75	100

Buying crafted goods from neighbors

Besides making crafted goods yourself, you can buy them from your neighbors by using Farm Cash. To make such a purchase, follow these steps:

1. **Click your crafting building and choose Look Inside from the drop-down menu.**

   The menu for your crafting building appears (refer to Figure 7-6 for an example).

2. **Click the Get Goods button located on the top left of the menu.**

   The Available Goods menu appears, as shown in Figure 7-9. You can also access this menu by clicking a neighbor's crafting building when visiting his or her farm, as discussed in Chapter 4, or by clicking the Get Goods button in the Farmers Market menu of your market stall (refer to Figure 7-2).

   Note that the Get Goods button in your Crafting Building menu features a number in a pink circle showing how many neighbors are currently offering items for purchase. If this number does not appear, no goods are currently available for purchase. Try coming back tomorrow to purchase more goods, or encourage your neighbors to craft more goods.

3. **Click the up and down arrows on the right side of the Available Goods menu to scroll through the neighbors offering goods. Click the left and right arrows on each neighbor's item listing to see more available items.**

   Each neighbor's offered items are listed in increasing order of price and level from left to right. You can hover your mouse over a specific good to see exactly how many plots' worth of fuel that good can be traded in for.

Figure 7-9: The Available Goods menu.

4. **Click the green Buy button under the good you want to purchase.**

   The listed price in Farm Coins is deducted from your account and the purchased good is added to your inventory. Note that you can store a maximum of 200 goods in your inventory, as listed in the upper-left corner of the Available Goods menu. If your inventory is full, use some goods to clear space, as discussed in the next section.

You may purchase only one crafted good per neighbor each calendar day. For the purposes of the Farmers Market, days start at midnight Eastern Standard Time.

After your purchase is complete, you can click the Share a Bonus! button to bring up the a Facebook news feed posting menu, as discussed in Chapter 4. If you use this menu to post a message on your news feed, up to three neighbors who click the link in that post can receive a free copy of the same type of good that you just purchased.

Trading crafted goods for fuel

Although collecting all these goods in your inventory is mildly diverting, the real reason for making and buying crafted goods is much more practical — namely, trading the goods in for the fuel needed to power your vehicles. To trade in the goods in your inventory, follow these steps:

1. **Click your crafting building and choose Look Inside from the drop-down menu.**

   The menu screen for your crafting building appears (refer to Figure 7-6).

2. **Click the Use Goods button located on the top left of the menu.**

   The Use Goods menu, shown in Figure 7-10, appears. You can also access this menu by clicking the Use Goods button in the Farmers Market menu of your market stall (refer to Figure 7-2). Use the left and right arrows to scroll through your available goods. Hover your mouse over a particular good to find out exactly how many plots of fuel that good is worth.

Figure 7-10: The Use Goods menu.

3. **Click the green Use button under the good you want to trade in.**

   Fuel is added to your account, as shown in the fuel gauge, which you can see on the left side of the Use Goods menu.

The remaining goods on the Use Goods menu automatically shift to the left when you click the Use button. You can therefore repeatedly click the Use button on the good in the upper-left corner of the menu to quickly use all the goods in your inventory with a minimum of effort.

Selling crafted goods

When you finish making a crafted good, you not only get one copy of that good in your inventory but also automatically offer additional copies of that good for sale to your neighbors. Crafting from higher-level recipes creates more goods for sale.

You can see what crafts are currently available for sale to your neighbors by clicking the My Sales button in the upper-right corner of your crafting building menu. Clicking this button brings up the My Sales menu, shown in Figure 7-11. Use the left and right arrows to scroll through the list of goods currently for sale. You can also see a listing of recent sales and recipe levels at the bottom of this menu.

Figure 7-11: The My Sales menu.

Your neighbors can buy these goods using the method outlined in the "Buying crafted goods from neighbors" section, earlier in this chapter. When you make such a sale, a white arrow appears above your crafting building to let you know you've made a sale. Click the building when this arrow appears to display a sales report notification that tells you which crafted goods were sold and how many Farm Coins you made from those sales.

When you sell a good, 90 percent of the sale price goes directly to your inventory of Farm Coins. (The rest is absorbed by Zynga.) Selling goods also helps earn experience toward leveling up that recipe, as discussed in the "Leveling up and mastering crafted goods" section, earlier in this chapter.

Upgrading your crafting building

Each crafting building starts with three available recipes and two crafting areas in which to make crafted goods. You can improve these numbers by purchasing new levels for your crafting building.

You can purchase crafting building levels with Farm Cash at any time by clicking the Buy Upgrade button in the upper-right corner of your Crafting Building menu, shown in Figure 7-6. You can also earn the right to purchase a crafting building upgrade with Farm Coins by leveling up your recipes a set number of times.

We show you the specific costs and recipe leveling requirements for each new level of your crafting building in Table 7-3. You can also see how many more recipe levels you need to earn a Farm Coin crafting building upgrade by hovering your mouse over the yellow star gauge located in the top-center of your crafting building menu (refer to Figure 7-6).

Note that you have to purchase all previous level upgrades for a building before purchasing the next level upgrade, so you can't save up to skip ahead.

Table 7-3	Requirements and Costs to Level Up Crafting Buildings with Farm Coins		
To Upgrade Your Crafting Building to Level . . .	You Can Spend . . .	Or Level Up Your Recipes . . .	And Then Spend . . .
2	15 Farm Cash	6 times	50,000 Farm Coins
3	25 Farm Cash	18 times	100,000 Farm Coins
4	40 Farm Cash	27 times	400,000 Farm Coins
5	60 Farm Cash	36 times	1,000,000 Farm Coins

With each new level you purchase for your crafting building, you earn three additional recipes and an extra crafting area to make crafted goods. Also, the physical appearance of the crafting building on your farm will improve as you purchase new levels. You can currently upgrade each crafting building only four times — that is, after your crafting building has reached level 5, you can no longer purchase crafting building upgrades.

You can see what recipes will be unlocked by your next crafting building upgrade by scrolling all the way down to the bottom of the recipes list in your crafting building menu (refer to Figure 7-6). If you plan to upgrade your crafting building soon, you may want to take a peek ahead to see what bushels you will need to stock up on ahead of time.

Part III
Expanding Your Reach

The 5th Wave   By Rich Tennant

"That's the problem-on Facebook, everyone knows you're a dog."

*1*n this part, you move on from the fundamentals of FarmVille to more advanced topics that interest invested players. We discuss the levels of FarmVille and some common methods used for leveling up quickly. Then we cover storage facilities and animal housing, both of which are useful to farmers who need more room on their farms. This part ends with a chapter on limited-edition items and special events in FarmVille. We tell you how you can participate in these special events as well as find out the secrets of FarmVille's mystery items, including Mystery Eggs, Boxes, Games, and Gifts.

Reaching New FarmVille Levels

In This Chapter

▶ Understanding experience points

▶ Discovering how levels work in FarmVille

▶ Using common methods for leveling up quickly

What good is building an awesome farm if no one knows just how awesome a farmer you are? Sure, your neighbors can look at your accumulated virtual stuff and see that you've got mad farming skills. Sometimes, though, you want a single number to quantify just how much better your farm is than everyone else's.

Enter experience points and levels, FarmVille's way of measuring your in-game progress. Pretty much every action you take in FarmVille earns you experience points, which in turn earn you new levels, which in turn unlock new items and gameplay features and prove that you are better than all your friends (at FarmVille, at least).

This chapter tells you everything you need to know about FarmVille's experience and leveling systems and how they work. It also shows you some ways to exploit these systems to gain new levels as quickly as possible, with a minimum of all that pesky farming. Hey, no one said virtual farming was a strictly honorable profession.

YEEHAW!

You just won the 100 Fr
Your prize can be four
our gift box. Play aga
'n other great priz

Understanding Levels

Every new farmer starts out at level 1 (a "Field Hand" in the game's parlance), but with a little hard work (and tons of clicking) you, too, can reach the elite FarmVille levels reserved for veteran farmers. To attain such status, you need do only one thing: Earn experience points. Lots of them.

What are experience points (XP)?

Experience points, also known as XP, are a numerical measurement of your progress in FarmVille. Unlike in-game currency such as Farm Cash and Coins, experience points can be gained but not spent. This means that XP is the best method for telling, at a glance, just how much a farmer has actually done in the game. When you reach certain XP targets, FarmVille grants you a new level. (See Table 8-1 and the XP requirements discussion later in the chapter.)

 The total number of XP you've earned so far is displayed as a white number in your XP status bar, located centrally in the top row of the FarmVille play area. The white bar behind this number shows how close you are to reaching the next level, and the accompanying number inside the gold star shows your current level.

 You can compare your XP and level to that of your neighbors by looking at the similar numbers listed along with their name and picture on your neighbor bar at the bottom of the play area. (See Chapter 4 for more on interacting with neighbors.)

How to Earn XP

You can earn XP for everything from working your farm and buying items from the market to helping out your neighbors, selling goods, or clicking bonus links on a Facebook news feed.

Here's a detailed list of all the ways you can gain XP in FarmVille, and how much you can expect from each action.

✓ **Farming:**

- Plowing a plot of land: 1 XP

- Planting seeds: 1–3 XP (depending on the seed)

  For more on maximizing your rate of XP gain through crops, see the section on maximizing profits in Chapter 6.

- Harvesting premium crops: 1–8 XP

  Although harvesting normal crops doesn't earn any XP, after a crop has been mastered, it will grant up to 8 XP per plot harvested. (See Chapter 11 for more on mastering crops and the benefits associated with it.)

- Harvesting fertilized crops: 1 XP

  Crops can be fertilized by a neighbor or a Fertilize All item. For more on fertilizing crops, see Chapter 4.

- Collecting from your horse stable: 100 XP

  Note that you receive this XP bonus only as an occasional gift for collecting from a stable. For more on building and maintaining horse stables and other buildings, see Chapter 9.

✔ **Buying items:**

- Buildings: Up to 50,000 XP

- Decorations: Up to 15,000 XP

- Animals: Up to 10,000 XP

- Vehicles: Up to 5,000 XP

- Pets: 50–500 XP

- Trees: Up to 332 XP

- Limited Edition Theme Items = 0–3,500 XP

- Crafting a good in a crafting building: 50 XP

  For more on crafting and crafting buildings, see Chapter 7.

For more on which items provide the most XP bang for the buck, see the Big Spender leveling method discussed later in this chapter.

✔ **Helping neighbors:**

- Fertilizing or unwithering neighbors' crops or plowing neighbors' plots: 1 XP

  Note that you can perform these combined only five times per neighbor per day. (For more on visiting and helping neighbors' farms, see Chapter 4.)

- Feeding neighbors' chicken coops: 10 XP

  Note that you can feed each neighbor's chicken coop only once a day.

✔ **Earning XP as rewards:**

- Completing a collection set: 250 XP

  For more on collections, see Chapter 11.

- Completing a co-op farming challenge: 260–1035 XP

  For more on co-op farming, see Chapter 12.

- Mastering crops: 25–250 XP

  Level 1 mastery is worth 25 XP, level 2 mastery 50 XP, and level 3 250 XP. For more on mastering crops, see Chapter 11.

- Earning ribbons: 10–1,000 XP

  This includes 10–50 XP for a yellow ribbon, 20–50 XP for a white ribbon, 50–100 XP for a red ribbon, and 100–1,000 XP for a blue ribbon. For more on earning ribbons, see Chapter 11.

- Receiving XP in gifts: 20–1,520 XP

  This includes 20 XP bonuses found in mystery gifts, up to 500 XP bonuses found in mystery eggs (shown in Figure 8-1) and bonuses of up to 2,000 XP found in mystery boxes. For more on giving and receiving gifts, see Chapter 4.

Figure 8-1: An example of an XP bonus gained from a mystery egg.

What are levels?

In FarmVille, levels are simply the game's way of acknowledging when you attain certain amounts of experience points. Each level, starting with the beginning level 1 (Farm Hand), is noted with a number and a unique name. Your current level is always displayed within the gold star in the middle of the top row of the FarmVille play area, next to your experience points.

When you reach a new level, the game informs you with a pop-up notification like the one shown in Figure 8-2. Click the Share button to bring up the Facebook news post menu and share your accomplishment with your Facebook friends, or click Cancel to get back to your farm.

FarmVille's leveling system currently maxes out at levels 999, although this wasn't always the case, as you can read in the "Reaching the highest levels" sidebar. Note that you can continue playing FarmVille and gaining XP after reaching level 999, but your level will no longer increase.

Reaching the highest levels

When FarmVille was first released, farmers couldn't advance past level 70. Farmers who reached this highest level continued to accumulate XP but didn't have any new levels to show for it. As more and more diligent farmers reached level 70, many started demanding a more expansive level system to recognize their continued progress.

FarmVille maker Zynga finally expanded the leveling system a bit in June 2010, raising the level caps from 70 to 90. Just a few weeks later, Zynga increased the cap to level 100 and then increased it further, finally settling on the current cap of 999. The new level caps also brought new incentives for high-level players, including exclusive crops, items, and gifts that can be unlocked only at higher levels (see Table 8-2, later in this chapter, for a list of what gifts you unlock at each level).

Figure 8-2: A level up notification.

Unlocking new items and features by leveling up

Earning new levels isn't just about vanity, though. Many new levels come with the keys to previously locked parts of the FarmVille experience, including new items for purchase and gifting and even previously inaccessible gameplay features.

We lay out these specific rewards, along with the XP and level requirements to obtain them, in Tables 8-1 and 8-2. Note that Zynga occasionally tweaks the XP requirements for each level and the unlock schedule for certain items, so this list might not be entirely accurate in the future.

Table 8-1		Level XP Requirements and Unlocked Features for Levels 1–40			
Level	*Total XP Needed*	*Level Name*	*Buyable Items*	*Giftable Items*	*Gameplay Features*
1	0	Field Hand	See Chapter 3		
2	15	Kinderfarmer	Plum Tree, Hay Bale	Plum Tree	
3	30	Amateur Farmer	Barrel, Colored Hay Bales	Fig Tree, Green Hay Bale	
4	70	Able Farmer	Squash and Lilac Seeds, Chickens, Peach Trees, Rest Tent, Crate	Chicken, Peach Tree	Fertilize neighbors' farms (See Chapter 4)
5	140	Handy Farmer	Pumpkin Seeds, White and Brown Stools	Avocado Trees	
6	250	Nimble Farmer	Artichoke and Spinach Seeds, Mailbox		Storage features (see Chapter 9)
7	400	Savvy Farmer	Rice Seeds, Sheep, Lemon Tree, Butter Churn, Well	Sheep, Lemon Tree	Sell items (see Chapter 3)
8	600	Fancy Farmer	Raspberry and Daffodil Seeds, Wood Pile, Tool Shed	Apricot Tree	
9	850	Sophisticated Farmer	Cotton Seeds, Bike, Wagon		
10	1,150	Splendid Farmer	Cranberry and Chickpea* Seeds, Lime Tree, Fruit Stand, Wood Fence, Picnic Set	Pig, Lime Tree	Crop Mastery and Collections (see Chapter 11)
11	1,500	Farming Magician	Bell Pepper and Rhubarb Seeds, Stone Mailbox	Grapefruit Tree	

Level	Total XP Needed	Level Name	Buyable Items	Giftable Items	Gameplay Features
12	1,900	Farming Wizard	Pepper Seeds, Wheelbarrow, Red and Pink Tractors	Rabbit	
13	2,400	Jolly Rancher	Morning Glory Seeds, Grain Silo, Pink Fence, Wood Bench, Harvester		
14	3,000	Produce Professional	Aloe Vera Seeds, Black, Blue, and Green Fences, Seeder	Banana Tree	
15	3,700	Professor of Agriculture	Pineapple and Red Tulip Seeds, Workshop, Covered Wagon	Duck	
16	4,500	Hot Shot Farmer	Pattypan Squash Seeds, Lil Red Wagon		
17	5,400	Super Shoveler	Blueberry Seeds, BBQ	Passion Fruit Tree	
18	6,400	Super Grower	Watermelon Seeds, Hay Wagon	Goat	
19	7,500	Professional Plower	Grape Seeds; Normal, Black and Pink Cottages; Bird House; Hedge		
20	8,700	Green Giant	Tomato and Pink Rose Seeds, General Store, Hedge Arch, Barrel Wagon	Date Tree	Co-op farming jobs (see Chapter 11)
21	10,000	Rockstar Farmer	Potato and Rye Seeds, Sandbox, Lawnmower	Horse	

(continued)

Table 8-1 *(continued)*

Level	Total XP Needed	Level Name	Buyable Items	Giftable Items	Gameplay Features
22	11,500	Barnyard Behemoth	Carrot Seeds, Baby Bunny Rescue, Windmill, Duck Topiary, Wagon Wheel, Axe and Block		
23	13,500	Magnificent Farmer	Coffee Seeds, Water Pump	Pomegranate Tree	
24	16,000	Cream of the Crop	Corn Seeds, Log Cabin, Telephone Pole		
25	19,000	Sensational Sower	Sunflower Seeds, Elephant Topiary, Hedge Gate, Light Post		Build Crafting Buildings (see Chapter 7)
26	22,500	Sultan of Soil	Ghost Chili Seeds, Farm House		
27	26,500	Thrill of the Till	Cabbage and Zucchini* Seeds, Iron Bench		
28	31,000	Master of Pasture	Green Tea and Gladiolus* Seeds, Goose Topiary		
29	36,000	Sensation of the Plantation	White Grape and Blackberry Seeds, Estate		
30	42,000	Lord of the Plow	Red Wheat and Lavender Seeds, Greenhouse		
31	49,000	Bastillion of the Barn	Sugar Cane Seeds, Lodge, Combine		
32	57,000	Ace of Acreage	Pea Seeds	Olive Tree	

Level	Total XP Needed	Level Name	Buyable Items	Giftable Items	Gameplay Features
33	65,000	Livestock Lord	Yellow Melon Seeds		
34	74,000	Practiced Farmer	Onion Seeds, Villa		
35	83,000	Skilled Farmer	Broccoli and Lily Seeds, Saddleback Pig, Male Ostrich Topiary		
36	93,000	Green Ribbon Farmer	Acorn Squash Seeds		
37	103,000	Clever Farmer	Asparagus Seeds		
38	113,000	Great Farmer	Purple Poppy Seeds		
39	123,000	Smart Farmer	Elderberry Seeds		
40	133,000	Model Farmer	Purple Pod Pea* Seeds, Buffalo Topiary	Mango Tree	

After level 40, the rate of newly unlocked items and gifts slows down a bit. New purchasable items and gifts unlocked at higher levels are shown in Table 8-2.

Having a Villa on your farm is seen by many FarmVille players as a sign of high status. A Villa demonstrates that you've not only put in the time and effort to reach the reasonably lofty level 34, but also managed to save up the 1,000,000 coin asking price. Good job!

Table 8-2	Items Unlocked at Higher Levels	
Level	**Buyable Items**	**Giftable Items**
42	Ginger Seeds	
43	Cucumber Seeds	
44	Columbine Seeds	
45	Iris Seeds, Wind Turbine	
48	Basil Seeds	

(continued)

Level	Buyable Items	Giftable Items
	Table 8-2 *(continued)*	
50	Lemon Balm Seeds	Azaleas
52	Square Melon Seeds	
53	Oat Seeds	
54	Posole Corn Seeds	
55	Arapawa Goat	
57	Heirloom Carrot* Seeds	
59	Orange Daisy Seeds	
60	Bamboo Seeds	Ginko Tree
63	Carnival Squash Seeds	
64	Saffron Seeds	
65	Silo Home	
70	Clover Seeds, Mansion	Floral Container
75	Belted Cow	
76	Amaranth Seeds	
80	White Rose Seeds	Mangrove Tree
85	Pheasant	
90	Forget Me Not Seeds	Dutch Rabbit
95	Cattail Pond	
100		Jacaranda Tree

XP requirements for higher levels

From level 35 to level 70, each new level requires 10,000 more total XP than the previous one. After that, the XP distance between levels starts increasing at faster and faster rates, to the point at which 1,500,000 total XP are required to reach level 101. After that, you need 100,000 more total XP to reach each new level. This means you have to earn a whopping 91,300,000 XP to reach the game's current top level of 999. Good luck!

After level 100, you no longer earn Farm Cash for new levels. There are also no longer new items or names associated with levels after level 100.

Leveling Up Quickly

Leveling up is an important goal for many FarmVille players. Although regular farming with no particular strategy in mind eventually gets you to higher levels, some players just can't wait to see a shiny new number next to their name. FarmVille provides many ways to quickly acquire the XP needed to reach new levels. Here are just a few of the methods that some of FarmVille's best power-levelers rely on.

The hay bale method

Buying decorative items such as hay bales isn't just good for sprucing up your farm — it can also be your ticket to quick XP. Hay bales are particularly efficient for generating experience, earning you 5 XP for each 100-coin purchase.

Requirements

Before starting the hay bale method, you need the following:

- **Cleared farm space:** A wide expanse on which to place your hay bales. Although technically you can perform this method with space for only one hay bale, more space makes the entire process more efficient.
- **Farm Coins:** As many as you can gather and afford to spend — the more the better.
- **Free time and patience:** Lots of it.

How it works

Follow these steps to level up quickly using the hay bale method:

1. **Click the Market button in the Tools menu.**

   The Market menu (which we thoroughly discuss in Chapter 6) appears.

2. **Click the Decorations button.**

   A list of all purchasable decorations appears.

3. **Click the Hay Bales button.**

   A list of all purchasable hay bales appears.

4. **Click the right arrow until you see the regular hay bale.**

   The Market menu should now look like the one shown in Figure 8-3. This straw-colored hay bale costs only 100 Farm Coins.

5. **Click the Buy button underneath the regular hay bale.**

   The Market menu disappears, and a hay bale appears attached to your mouse pointer.

6. **Click open areas on your farm to place as many hay bales as you have room and budget for.**

   Each hay bale you place earns 5 XP and subtracts 100 coins from your balance.

7. **Click the Multi tool on the Tools menu.**

8. **Click each hay bale and then click Sell.**

   This clears space on your farm, allowing you to place more hay bales, and also earns back 5 coins. You get to keep the XP you earned for the purchase!

   You can click the Recycle tool from the Tools menu and use it to sell items much more quickly. See Chapter 3 for more on tools in the Tools menu.

9. **Repeat Steps 1 through 8 as often as desired.**

   Be careful not to deplete your coin balance too much — you still might need money to buy seeds and generate more coins.

Figure 8-3: The Hay Bales purchasing menu.

Costs and benefits

Now that you know how the hay bale method works, let's do some math:

- **Buying a hay bale:** ×100 Farm Coins; +5 XP
- **Selling a hay bale:** +5 Farm Coins
- **Total:** ×95 Farm Coins, +5 XP — 19 Farm Coins/XP

Note that you can also tweak the Hay Bale method by using the same general concept with other items on the Market menu, such as Whitewash Fences. Hay bales provide the best coin-to-XP ratio, however, and their small footprint means you can place more of them in the same space.

Buying lots of hay bales also helps you to earn the Baled Out and Pack Rat ribbons, which in turn reward you with additional coins and XP. See Chapter 11 for more on earning ribbons.

The soybean method

Usually when you plant seeds, you leave your work to sit and ripen before a lucrative harvest. With the soybean method, however, you'll be deleting all your hard work almost immediately but still reaping the XP rewards!

Requirements

The requirements for the soybean method are as follows:

- **Cleared farm space:** On which to plant your soybeans. You can technically perform this method with as little as one plot, but more space will make the entire process more efficient.
- **Farm Coins:** As many as you can gather and afford to spend — the more the better.
- **Free time and patience:** Lots of it.

How it works

Follow these steps to level up quickly using the soybean method.

1. **Plow as many plots of land as possible.**

   This costs 15 coins and earns 1 XP per plot of land. You can plow soybeans using either the Plow tool (the Tools menu is described in Chapter 3) or a vehicle such as the tractor. The tractor can cover more plots of land per click than the Plow tool.

2. **Click the Market button on the Tools menu.**

   The Market menu appears.

3. **Click the Seeds button.**

   A list of all the seeds you can currently buy, shown in Figure 8-4, appears.

4. **Click the Buy button underneath the soybeans.**

   The Market menu disappears and a soybean icon appears next to your mouse pointer.

5. **Click the plowed plots to plant soybeans.**

   Planting soybeans costs 15 coins and earns 2 XP per plot. Note that vehicles such as the seeder can perform this process more quickly because of their ability to seed multiple plots of land in one click.

6. **Hover over the Multi tool on the Tools Menu and click the Recycle tool in the pop-up menu that appears.**

7. **Click the seeded plots to delete them.**

   Even though the plot is gone, you still keep the experience points for the planting.

8. **Repeat Steps 1–7 as often as desired.**

Save a little bit of money to buy seeds that you actually intend to harvest so that you can replenish your Farm Coin account.

Figure 8-4: The Seed Purchasing menu.

Costs and benefits

Here's how the coin and XP breakdown works out for one plot under the soybean method.

- **Plowing a plot of land:** ×15 Farm Coins, + 1 XP
- **Planting a plot of soybeans:** ×15 Coins, + 2 XP
- **Deleting a seeded plot:** ×0 coins, +0 XP
- **Totals:** ×30 Farm Coins, +3 XP — 10 Farm Coins/XP

Soybeans are the cheapest seeds available in the FarmVille Market that also yield XP. The one-day ripening time before harvest is irrelevant when you use the soybean method because the plots are deleted before they can mature.

The soybean method requires fewer coins than the hay bale method to generate the same amount of XP, but it does require significantly more clicking of the mouse, as well as more cleared space on your farm.

The news feed method

One method for gaining XP and levels in FarmVille doesn't actually involve playing the game. By stalking your friends' news feeds for posted XP and coin bonuses, you can level up without planting a single crop or buying a single item. What could be simpler?

Requirements

To gain XP via the news feed method, you need:

- **Neighbors:** As many as you can get. For more on adding and interacting with neighbors, see Chapter 4.
- **Time and attention:** To invest in watching your Facebook news feed for bonus links.

How it works

Follow these steps to gain XP using the news feed method:

1. **Scan your Facebook news feed for FarmVille achievement bonuses posted by your neighbors, as shown in Figure 8-5.**

   Be sure to click the Most Recent tab at the top of your news feed to make sure you see all your friends' updates, not just the ones that Facebook offers as the most relevant.

2. **Click the Get a Bonus from Them link in the news feed post.**

   Coins and experience points are added to your FarmVille account. Note that bonus links expire 24 hours after they're posted, so be sure to scour your news feed frequently.

3. **Click Accept.**

   The game returns you to your farm, and your XP bonus is noted in your account.

Click this link . . .

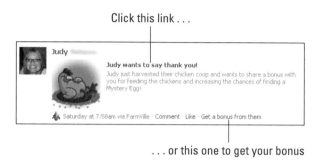

. . . or this one to get your bonus

Figure 8-5: A bonus XP link as seen in a FarmVille news feed.

Costs and benefits

Because collecting news feed bonuses doesn't actually involve playing FarmVille, you pay no in-game cost to this method to gain XP. Only your time and a keen eye for skimming through Facebook updates quickly are required. Therefore, the method is especially useful for new farmers who might not have disposable in-game currency to spend on other methods.

The trick to making the news feed method work for you is having a lot of FarmVille neighbors, and thus more potential bonuses to collect. See Chapter 4 for more on finding and inviting new neighbors to join your FarmVille network. After you've gained those neighbors, be sure to encourage them to click the Share button whenever the game asks whether they want to post a bonus to their wall. Remember, their gain is your gain.

In addition to posting about XP and coin bonuses to celebrate achievements, your neighbors can also post about items such as lost pets, bushels, collectibles, and other bonuses to your newsfeeds. Although these bonuses don't generate XP directly, they can generate coins and other benefits that can lead to increased experience and leveling. You can also occasionally gain free XP from mystery eggs found by feeding your neighbor's chickens — see Chapter 4 for more on how helping your neighbors helps you.

The big-spender method

Because purchasing items from the FarmVille Market grants an XP bonus, farmers who have no qualms about spending loads of Farm Cash or Farm Coins can spend their way right to the upper echelons of FarmVille's leveling system.

Requirements

To gain XP via the big-spender method, you need:

✔ **Disposable income:** The more money you can afford to spend, the more XP you can gain.

✔ **A high level:** Many of the most lucrative XP-boosting items are available only after you've reached a high level. See Table 8-3 for some examples.

How it works

Gaining XP using this method is as simple as spending money in the Market (see Chapter 6 for the details on using the FarmVille Market). Although the specific size of the XP bonus depends on the purchased item, as a general rule items purchased with Farm Cash earn more XP than items purchased with Farm Coins. Generally, the more expensive the item, the more XP you earn. Limited-edition items that rotate in and out of the Market on a schedule usually offer high XP rewards as well. (Chapter 12 covers limited-edition items.)

Farmers who want to level up using Farm Coin purchases alone are probably best off saving up massive amounts of coins for big-ticket items. Some of the most lucrative XP bonuses come attached to some of the most expensive items in the game, as shown in Table 8-3. Items such as the Villa and Mansion can advance you multiple levels in a single purchase.

When purchasing expensive items, remember to keep some coins in reserve so that you can continue to purchase the seeds you'll need to generate more money!

Table 8-3	Big-Ticket Items and Their XP Bonuses		
Item	*Level Unlocked*	*Cost (in Farm Coins)*	*XP bonus*
Grain Silo	13	20,000	200
Estate	29	600,000	6,000
Saddleback Pig	35	300,000	3,000
Villa	34	1,000,000	10,000
Silo Home	65	1,000,000	10,000
Mansion	70	5,000,000	50,000

Costs and benefits

Purchasing single big-ticket items is much less time consuming than purchasing (and deleting) thousands of hay bales or soybeans. On the other hand, earning the Farm Coins or Farm Cash necessary to make these purchases can be an onerous process. Big-ticket items are usually less efficient at converting coins into XP as well. Consider that a Villa purchase earns one XP for every 100 coins spent, whereas planting soybeans earns the same single XP every 10 coins.

That said, players willing to break out their wallets and purchase virtual currency themselves can find themselves on the bullet train to level 999 (see Chapter 5 for more on purchasing in-game currency).

9

Adding Storage Facilities and Animal Shelters

In This Chapter

▶ Understanding how to store and retrieve items and animals

▶ Knowing what to store where

▶ Building and expanding storage facilities

▶ Sheltering and breeding animals

One of the most common requests from virtual farmers is for more storage! After playing FarmVille for a while, the panoply of adorable decorations, designer homes, and priceless animals you've collected can quickly turn your farm from a verdant paradise to a hoarder's nightmare.

Having lots of clutter on your farm not only slows down your game play but also reduces space for profitable crop planting. You can always sell off your excess items and animals to take back your space, of course, but chances are good that you've grown attached to at least a few of the things that make your farm uniquely yours.

For many farmers, storing their extra items and animals using storage buildings is a much more agreeable option. This chapter tells you everything you need to know about FarmVille's storage options.

Understanding Storage and Retrieval of Items and Animals

Two major types of storage are available in FarmVille: animal shelters that hold specific types of animals, and storage facilities that hold all sorts of decorations. Also, some storage facilities, such as Garages and Garden Sheds, can store only specific types of decorations and items.

Stored items can't be seen by neighbors who visit your farm, but they also don't take up any of your valuable farm space (aside from the space needed for the storage facility, that is). Of course, you can place stored items back on your farm if you want, as discussed later in this chapter.

Building storage facilities from frames

You can purchase animal shelters (and some limited-edition buildings) directly with Farm Cash or you can build them using a combination of Farm Coins (to purchase a frame) and building supplies, which can you can receive as gifts from neighbors or purchase using Farm Cash.

Although each building frame requires different quantities and types of building materials to complete (Figure 9-1 shows an example), the construction process is similar for each building type.

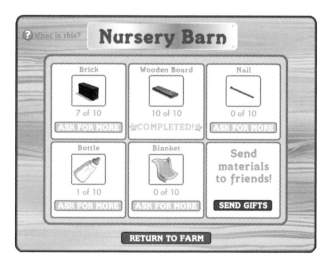

Figure 9-1: The building materials menu for an incomplete nursery barn frame.

The following steps cover the basics of the construction process:

1. **Purchase the frame from the Buildings tab of the FarmVille Market.**

   For more on using the Market menu, see Chapter 6.

2. **Place the frame on your farm.**

   Any open space will do, and you can always move the frame later.

3. **Request building materials from your friends or purchase them with Farm Cash.**

   When you first place a frame, a pop-up notification asks whether you want to post a note to your news feed asking your friends for help with your new construction. Click the Share button to post a request for building materials to your news feed.

   You can post further requests for building materials by clicking any building and then clicking Look Inside on the pop-up menu to display the Building Materials menu, shown in Figure 9-1. Click the Ask for More button under the desired building item to send out another news feed request.

   Alternatively, you can access building materials you need and buy them directly from the Market by clicking Buildings⇨For Animals. One construction material costs one Farm Cash.

4. **After you receive building materials, open your Gift Box by clicking the Gift Box icon on the Tools menu; then click Use underneath the building material you want to use.**

   If you have multiple applicable frames on your farm, you have to choose which building to use the material on.

After you've obtained every building supply needed for your building, the frame is automatically replaced with a functional building that you can use for storage, as discussed in the "Storing items and sheltering animals" section, later in the chapter.

A good ol' fashioned barn raising: Expanding storage facilities

Expanding the capacity for most existing buildings — including Barns, Tool Sheds, Chicken Coops, Dairy Farms, and Nursery Barns — is done via what the game calls a "good ol' fashioned barn raising."

Horse Stables are not expanded using a barn raising, but rather with building materials — just as a building is created from a frame. To expand a Horse Stable, click and then click Look Inside. On the Horse Stable menu that appears, click the Expand tab to see what materials you need for your stable expansion and find buttons to ask for more.

Follow these steps to expand the storage capacity of storage buildings other than the Horse Stable and Pigpen:

1. **Click the building you want to expand and click Expand Storage in the pop-up menu that appears.**

   The Expand Storage menu, shown in Figure 9-2, appears. You can also access this menu by clicking the Expand Storage tab on the Storage Inventory menu on the Tools menu (see the "Retrieving items and animals from storage" section, later in this chapter).

   Note that you can expand only completed buildings. To build frames into completed buildings, see the previous section on building storage facilities from frames.

2. **Click the Expand button under the building you want to try to expand.**

   A pop-up notification asks you to spread the word for a "good ol' fashioned barn raising!"

3. **Click Share.**

   A Facebook news feed post dialog box appears.

4. **Type an optional message and then click Publish.**

   See Chapter 4 for more on making Facebook news feed requests.

Your barn-raising request is now posted on your news feed. Ten of your neighbors need to click the link in this news post over the next three days to complete your barn raising and expand your building's storage, so be sure to bug all your neighbors to click, click, click!

You can have only one barn raising in progress at a time. To cancel your current expansion attempt, return to the Expand Storage menu and click the Give Up button under the building you're trying to expand.

You can also click the Buy button on the Expand Storage menu to skip the barn raising and purchase expanded storage for ten Farm Cash. If you have a barn raising expansion in progress, you can also use the Buy button to finish off the expansion — one Farm Cash is as good as a single click from a neighbor in this case.

Having more neighbors actively playing FarmVille increases the number of people who can send you building supplies as gifts. See Chapter 4 for more on acquiring neighbors.

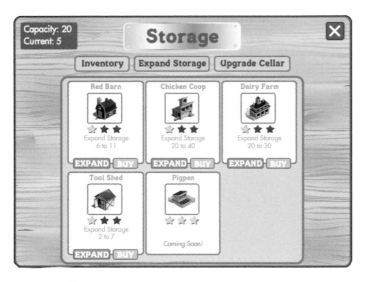

Figure 9-2: The Expand Storage menu.

Storing items and sheltering animals

After you've purchased some storage, storing your excess items and animals is easy. Simply use the Move tool or the Multi tool to move the animal or item over to the appropriate shelter or storage facility; then click again to drop it into its new home (for more on using these tools, see Chapter 3). To store decorations, you can also simply click the item and choose the Store Item option from the pop-up menu.

You can't store a storage building itself. You also can't store any item that is part of a collection event, such as the Tuscan Wedding Tent or Holiday Tree.

Retrieving items from storage

Although your stored items (excluding animals) might reside in different facilities, you access them all through the same Storage Inventory menu, shown in Figure 9-3. To access this menu, click any storage facility and then click the Look Inside option on the menu that pops up. You can also access this menu by hovering over the Gifts icon in the Tools menu and clicking the Storage icon in the menu that pops up.

To take an item out of storage, click the Use button underneath the item and then click an open space on your farm where you want to place it. If you can't find an open spot, or you change your mind, simply click any tool in the Tools menu and your item will go back into storage.

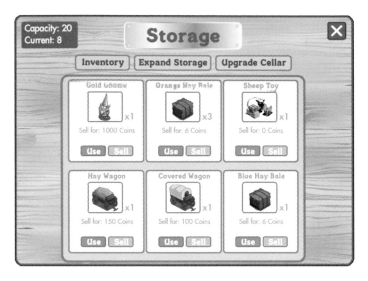

Figure 9-3: The Storage Inventory menu.

You can also click the Sell button under any item on the Storage Inventory menu to exchange the item for Farm Coins. Be sure to think carefully before confirming this choice with the Accept button because the only way to get back items you've sold is to buy them again.

Removing animals from storage

To remove an animal from a shelter, click the shelter and click the Look Inside option on the menu that pops up to bring up the Animal Storage menu for that building. Click the Remove button underneath the animal you want to put on your farm; then click any open area on the farm to place your animal. Note that with a Pigpen, you may have to click the curtain where the pigs are sleeping before you see the Remove button.

Animals are much more lucrative when they're in an animal shelter, as discussed in the "Sheltering Your Animals" section, later in this chapter, so you usually want to keep your shelters as packed as possible. If you find yourself removing some animals to make room for more profitable ones, consider expanding your storage.

A Brief History of FarmVille Storage

When FarmVille first launched in June 2009, barns and tool sheds were the only storage options available. These buildings could be purchased with Farm Cash or constructed and expanded with the help of neighbors, just as they can be today. However, even with expansion, early FarmVille players quickly found themselves bumping up against the small maximum limit for items in their tool sheds and barns.

In August 2010, Zynga introduced the Storage Cellar to fix this problem. This revamped storage solution allows for a maximum storage capacity of 500 items per farm. If you had existing barns or tool sheds before underground storage was introduced, they can still contribute to your storage capacity. However, there's no getting around the 500 maximum capacity per farm, no matter how many grandfathered storage facilities you have.

Choosing the Right Kind of Storage Facilities

Some storage facilities are more efficient than others; some serve more specific purposes than others. You can play the game more effectively when you develop a good grasp of what to put where, why, and when.

Following are the storage facilities used for decorations and vehicles:

- **Storage Cellar:** Stores up to 500 decorations
- **Barns and Tool Sheds:** Older storage options that can still be used to expand your general decoration storage capacity
- **Garage:** Stores your vehicles
- **Garden Shed:** Stores perfect bunches of flowers

The next sections explain each of these facilities in more detail.

Storage Cellar

The Storage Cellar is by far the most efficient storage facility in FarmVille, taking up very little space on your farm while potentially holding hundreds of decorations. You unlock the ability to buy a storage cellar at level 16, and there's really no reason not to purchase the 1-coin Cellar from the Market as soon as you can.

After you purchase your cellar, find a small, out-of-the-way place on your farm and dig there with a click. The Storage Cellar menu, shown in Figure 9-4, appears. (You can display this menu up at any time by clicking your Storage Cellar and then clicking the Look Inside menu option that pops up, or by clicking the Upgrade Cellar tab on from the Storage Inventory menu; refer to Figure 9-3 to see that menu.)

After you place a Storage Cellar on your farm, you can't sell or delete it. You can, however, move it, so don't worry that your Storage Cellar will ruin a pristine section of your farm.

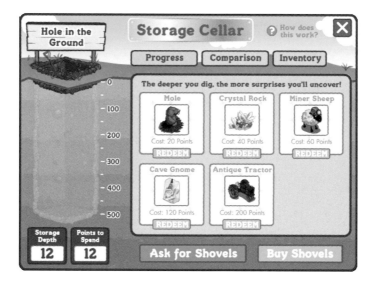

Figure 9-4: The Storage Cellar menu.

The Storage Depth section of the Storage Cellar menu displays how many decorations you can currently store in your cellar. Note that Barns and Tool Sheds can also contribute to the total storage capacity on your farm, but that total can never exceed 500 decorations.

Your Storage Cellar starts at a storage depth of zero, but you can increase this number by collecting shovels. You can collect shovels in a few ways:

  ✔ **Receive them as gifts:** Neighbors can send you two shovels as a free gift from their Gifting page (see Chapter 4 for more on neighbors and gifts). Click the Ask for Shovels button on the Storage Cellar menu to let your friends know you're on the lookout for more storage capacity.

✔ **Purchase them:** You can purchase 10 shovels for 5 Farm Cash on the FarmVille Market menu. (See Chapter 6 for more on the Market.) Or if you're already on the Storage Cellar menu, just click the Buy Shovels button to go directly to the Shovel section of the Market menu.

✔ **Gather them from news feed links:** You can collect shovels by clicking shared shovel links in your friends' Facebook news feeds. (See Chapter 4 for more on collecting items and bonuses from news feed links.)

Every shovel you obtain automatically increases your Cellar's storage capacity by one. Each shovel you collect also gives you a point, which you can spend on exclusive decorations, as shown next to your storage capacity in the Storage Cellar menu. Click the Redeem button under any of the available exclusive decorations on the Storage Cellar menu to add that item to your Gift Box. Don't worry — spending your accumulated points on these decorations does not decrease your storage capacity!

From the Storage Cellar menu, you can also click the Comparison tab to see how your cellar's depth compares to that of your friends, or click the Inventory button to go to the Storage Inventory menu (refer to Figure 9-3).

Barns and Tool Sheds

Ever since FarmVille's much more expandable Storage Cellar became available, farmers have come to use Barns and Tool Sheds for decoration more than storage. However, you can still purchase both of these building types from the Market menu, and both of them add to your total storage capacity. Barns and Tool Sheds also provide a good storage option for players who haven't yet reached level 16 and therefore can't yet purchase a Storage Cellar.

You can purchase the basic Red Barn and Tool Shed from the Market menu for 40,000 and 14,000 Farm Coins, respectively. Each provides the following storage space:

Red Barn: Six decorations

Tool shed: Two decorations (initially)

For a quicker storage boost, you can use Farm Cash to purchase colored Barns that hold 20 items initially, or colored Tool Sheds that hold 15 items (specific prices vary). Although these special buildings can add a touch of class to your farm, storage-minded farmers should probably invest their Farm Cash in shovels for their Storage Cellars instead (see previous section).

No matter how many Tool Sheds or Barns you buy, your total storage capacity can never exceed 500 items.

Garage

Although Cellars, Tool Sheds, and Barns are great for storing most decorations found on your farm, you can't use them to store those bulky but useful vehicles. To store vehicles, you need a Garage.

To purchase a Garage, you first have to reach level 22. At that level, you can purchase a Garage frame from the Market menu for 50,000 Farm Coins. Note that you still need some to obtain building materials before your Garage is functional (see the "Building storage facilities from frames" section, earlier in the chapter).

When your Garage is complete, however, you can use it to store up to 20 vehicles. You store a vehicle in the same way as any other item (or animal): Moving it using the Move tool or Multi tool.

You can't store the Biplane in a Garage.

Besides storing vehicles, you can also use your Garage to upgrade the vehicles inside after you reach level 26. Upgraded vehicles can cover more plots of land with a single click — 9 plots after a single upgrade or 16 plots after two upgrades.

The process for upgrading a vehicle is just about the same as the process of building a storage facility from a frame. You need a certain number of special Vehicle Part items to complete the upgrade. You can obtain these as gifts from friends or purchase them from the Market menu — same as for building materials.

Although you can purchase and receive vehicle parts even if you don't have a Garage, a Garage is required to upgrade your vehicles.

If you own only one version of each of the three basic vehicles — the Tractor, Seeder, and Harvester — you may want to consider selling your Garage after you've upgraded your vehicles. Garages take up a considerable amount of space on your farm — more space than your three vehicles take up unstored, actually. Your vehicle upgrades stay intact even if you choose to sell your garage, so don't worry about wasting your effort on upgrades. If you own more than three vehicles, however, by all means use your Garage as a way to keep them from taking up all your precious land.

Garden Shed

A Garden Shed is a special type of storage building used to store perfect bunches of flowers, which you sometimes find when harvesting flower crops on your farm. You can then share these bunches with friends or place them temporarily on your farm as decorations. Without a Garden Shed, however, you can't keep the perfect bunches for your own use.

Although no minimum level is necessary to purchase a Garden Shed with coins, you need to obtain at least ten neighbors before you can purchase one. (For more on gaining neighbors, see Chapter 4.) When you have enough neighbors, you can purchase a Shed from the Market menu by clicking Buildings⇨ Other and paying 30,000 Farm Coins. Even if you don't have ten neighbors, you can also purchase a garden shed with 30 Farm Cash if you've reached level 8.

Your new garden shed comes with ten free perfect bunches — five Pink Roses and five Lavender. You can access these bunches by clicking the Garden Shed and then clicking Look Inside to bring up the Garden Shed menu, shown in Figure 9-5. From here, you can choose to place any of your currently stored perfect bunches by clicking the Use button and then clicking an empty plot of land on the farm. Note that perfect bunches turn droopy anywhere from 14 to 20 days after you place them (depending on the type of flower). To remove a droopy bunch, click it and then click Delete, or click the Recycle tool on the Tools menu and then click the bunch you want to remove.

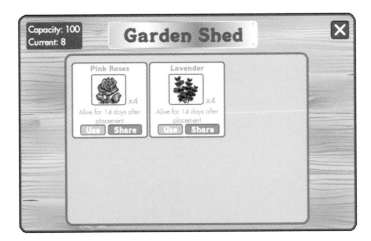

Figure 9-5: The Garden Shed menu.

You can also share your perfect bunches with friends. To share one, follow these steps:

1. **On the Garden Shed menu, click the Share button.**

   The Flower Sharing dialog box appears.

2. **Click the up and down arrows next to the number to choose a quantity of flowers to share.**

3. **Click the Share button to display the Facebook news feed dialog box and enter an optional personal message.**

4. **Click Publish.**

You can store up to 100 perfect bunches of flowers in your Garden Shed at any time. To clear out space for new bunches, place your current bunches on your farm or share them with friends. You can also adopt perfect bunches that friends post on their news feeds by clicking the links in those posts, but note that those bunches will be stored in your Gift Box, not your Shed.

Sheltering Your Animals

In addition to storage for decorations and vehicles, you can also use specific buildings to house the various animals on your farm. Storing animals in these buildings not only makes collecting coins from multiple animals faster and easier but can also provide bonus items and coins for each collection.

The following buildings can be used to store specific types of animals:

- **Chicken Coop:** Stores your chickens and allows you to collect mystery eggs
- **Dairy Farm:** Stores your cows and lets you create baby calves
- **Horse Stable:** Stores your horses and lets you create foals
- **Nursery Farm:** Stores baby calves and foals and lets them grow into full-grown animals
- **Beehive:** Stores honeybees and lets you collect coins and items
- **Pigpen:** Stores pigs and lets you find lucrative truffles

The next sections explain each of these facilities in more detail.

Chicken Coop

The Chicken Coop is a building that provides a compact home for all types of chickens in FarmVille. You can purchase a basic Coop, which can hold up to 20 chickens, for 5,000 Farm Coins. Note that your new Coop doesn't come preloaded with chickens — you have to provide those yourself.

You can view the contents of your Chicken Coop and more detailed information on how many of each type of chicken are in the Coop by clicking the Coop and then clicking Look Inside to display the Chicken Coop menu, shown in Figure 9-6.

Storing your chickens in a coop allows you to harvest them all when they're ready with a single click of the Coop (see Chapter 2 for more on harvesting animals). Harvesting chickens from a Coop also gives you a chance at finding Mystery Eggs (which we tell you more about in Chapter 10).

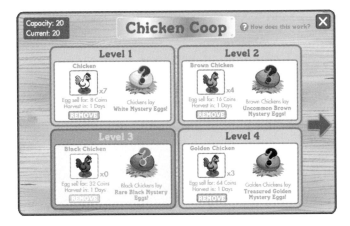

Figure 9-6: The Chicken Coop menu.

Although you can't keep the Mystery Eggs you find in your own Chicken Coop, you can share them with your neighbors by clicking the Share button to post the egg to your Facebook news feed. Even if you don't find any Mystery Eggs during a Coop harvest, you receive a coin bonus from the Coop. The size of this bonus depends on the rarity of the chickens inside; it ranges from two to five times the normal value of the eggs harvested from your chickens.

Each farm can have only one Chicken Coop, so if you want to store more than 20 chickens, you have to expand your coop (see the "Expanding storage facilities" section, earlier in this chapter). The basic Coop expands to four more sizes, with all five as follows:

- ✓ **Chicken Coop:** Stores 20 chickens
- ✓ **Big Coop:** Stores 40 chickens
- ✓ **Huge Coop:** Stores 60 chickens
- ✓ **Giant Coop:** Stores 80 chickens
- ✓ **Super Coop:** Stores 100 chickens

Besides providing more space to store your chickens, upgrading to a Huge Coop also increases your chances of finding Mystery Eggs during a harvest by 30 percent.

Neighbors visiting your farm can feed your chickens by clicking your Coop. Likewise, you can visit up to 50 of your neighbors' farms each day and feed their chickens, too! You can find Mystery Eggs when feeding chickens, and fed chickens also have a higher chance of delivering a Mystery Egg when they're harvested. The more your neighbors feed your chickens, the better the chance that they'll produce Mystery Eggs, so encourage your neighbors to come by and help every day.

If you don't have a Chicken Coop, you'll receive one in your Gift Box when you open any Mystery Egg. This free Chicken Coop is stocked with one free white chicken and a few white Mystery Eggs that you can share with friends.

Dairy Farm

The Dairy Farm is a building for housing FarmVille cows. You can purchase this building at any time with 20 Farm Cash, or you can buy one for 10,000 coins after you've reached level 8 and obtained at least five neighbors. Note that you can have only five Dairy Farms that you've purchased with coins, but you have no limit on the number of Farm Cash–funded Dairy Farms on your farm.

Initially, a Dairy Farm can hold up to 20 cows at a time, but each dairy farm can be expanded to hold more cows (To find out how to expand it, see the "Expanding storage facilities" section, earlier in this chapter.)

The basic Dairy Farm expands to two more sizes, with all three as follows:

- **Dairy Farm:** Stores 20 cows
- **Big Dairy Farm:** Stores 30 cows
- **Huge Dairy Farm:** Stores 40 cows

As with other animal shelters, Dairy Farms allow you to harvest all the animals inside with a single click. You can also use the Dairy Farm to create baby calves; Each time you harvest a Dairy Farm that contains a bull, you have the chance to receive a baby calf. Bulls can't be purchased from the Market menu; the only way to obtain a bull is by adopting it from a link on a neighbor's Facebook news feed. For more on adopting animals from a news feed, see Chapter 4.

The type of calf produced by a Dairy Farm harvest depends on the type of cow housed in that specific Dairy Farm. For example, a Dairy Farm with a limited-edition Groovy Cow and a bull has a chance of producing a Groovy Calf when you harvest it. You can also share a copy of your new baby calf via a news feed post; up to ten of your neighbors can accept this gift.

Harvesting a Dairy Farm also gives you a chance of finding a bag of fertilizer. You can't use this fertilizer yourself, but you can share it with your neighbors through your Facebook news feed. Any neighbor who claims the fertilizer from your feed can fertilize ten plots of land — rather than the normal five — the next time he or she visits your farm.

Horse Stable

The Horse Stable is, unsurprisingly, a building used to house your FarmVille horses. You can purchase a frame for your Horse Stable at any time for 5,000 farm coins, but you need to obtain building items before your stable is functional (see the "Building storage facilities from frames" section, earlier in this chapter).

After it's complete, your Horse Stable can initially hold up to 10 horses. You can have only one Horse Stable on your farm, so if you want to store more horses, you need to expand your Stable (see the "Expanding a storage facility" section, earlier in this chapter, for how to do that). Stables can be expanded in increments of five horses at a time to hold a maximum of 40 horses for a fully upgraded stable.

As with other animal shelters, the Horse Stable lets you harvest all the animals inside with just a single click. As an added bonus, you can harvest horses stored in a stable every day rather than wait three days to harvest horses out in the open. When you harvest horses from a Stable, you also have a chance at finding bonuses, which include 100 free XP or consumables such as Farmhands and Arborists.

You can also get baby animals — in this case, foals — when you harvest your Horse Stable. To have a chance at generating a foal from your harvest, you first need to find a Stallion to put in your Stable, which is easier said than done. You can't purchase Stallions from the Market menu; they can be found only as prizes in Mystery Boxes or Mystery Games (see Chapter 10 for more on mystery prizes) or via links from posts on your neighbors' Facebook news feeds.

Occasionally, you find wandering Stallions via a pop-up notification as you play FarmVille, but in contrast to other adoptable animals, these Stallions won't live on your farm permanently. Instead, they stay in your Stable for a single harvest before leaving.

If and when you find a foal in your Stable harvest, you can share the blessed event via by giving foals to neighbors. You do so via a news feed post, and five of your neighbors can accept a foal.

Nursery Barn

The Nursery Barn houses all your adorable baby calves and foals. As with Horse Stables, you can purchase the frame to a Nursery Barn for 5,000 Farm Coins at any point, but you must collect building materials before the Varn is functional (see the "Building storage facilities from frames" section, earlier in this chapter). A basic Nursery Barn can house up to 20 baby calves or foals, but you can upgrade that capacity to 30 and then a maximum of 40 baby animals.

Besides providing one-click harvesting for all your baby animals, Nursery Barns also provide a chance to transform your baby animals into adult horses or cows every time the Barn is harvested. These adult animals will appear in your Gift Box for placement on your farm. You can also share a copy of your new adult animal via a news feed post that can be accepted by up to five of your neighbors.

Note that your animal may actually change breeds when it transforms from baby to adult. For example, the Pink Patch Calf will transform into an adult Chocolate Cow. Basically, game publisher Zynga uses this method to prevent farmers from obtaining limited-edition adult animals without spending the required Farm Cash. Therefore, you may want to leave certain baby animals *out* of your nursery barn if you are trying to collect every different type of distinct animal.

In contrast to other types of animal housing, a Nursery Barn full of baby calves actually takes up *more* space on your farm than those same baby animals would occupy unstored. If you're simply looking to use your farm space most efficiently, consider stuffing your nursery barn with larger foals rather than small baby calves.

Beehive

The Beehive is a special type of animal housing that can store up to 200 Honeybees and one Queen Bee. You can purchase the Beehive frame from the Market menu for 5,000 Farm Coins, but you need to collect building supplies from neighbors or purchase them with Farm Cash before it's functional.

You can have other types of animals on you farm before you have storage facilities for them, but with bees, you need the Beehive first. Additionally, you need to acquire a Queen Bee before you can acquire any plain old honeybees. You can purchase a Queen Bee in the Market for 10 Farm Cash or try your luck at finding one by planting and harvesting flowers or fertilizing your neighbors' flower crops. Honeybees can also be purchased from the Market menu with Farm Cash, or you can receive them as free gifts from your friends. You can request Honeybees using the Ask for Honeybees button in the Beehive menu, shown in Figure 9-7. You find this menu by clicking the Beehive and then clicking the Look Inside button on the pop-up menu.

As with other animal shelters, Beehives can be regularly harvested for coins with a single click, generating up to 600 coins a day for a full Beehive. In contrast to other animals, however, bees will begin to flee your Beehive and leave your farm if you do not check in every 48 hours, so be sure to stay on top of your harvesting schedule.

The more Honeybees you own, the greater your chances of finding pollinated seed and Fertilize All items when harvesting crops on your farm. Finding a pollinated seed item while harvesting allows you to purchase pollinated seeds of the harvested crop from the Market menu for the next two days. These crops have a 50 percent higher chance of generating bushels when harvested. See Chapter 7 for more on collecting and using bushels.

Figure 9-7: The Beehive menu.

Pigpen

The Pigpen is a storage building for all types of FarmVille pigs — and FarmVille has lots of different kinds of pigs! As with other animal shelters, you can purchase the frame for 5,000 Farm Coins, but you need to obtain building items before it is functional (see the "Building storage facilities from frames" section, earlier in the chapter). You can have only one Pigpen on your farm, and the basic Pigpen can hold up to 20 pigs. Pigpens can be expanded to hold up to 40 pigs.

If you place a Pregnant Sow into your Pigpen, it will turn into a normal pig and not produce any piglets, so watch out!

Pigpens allow you to harvest all your pigs with a single click. They also decrease the time between harvest from two days for an unpenned pig to one day for all the pigs inside your pen.

Clicking your Pigpen and then clicking the Look Inside button on the pop-up menu brings up the Pigpen menu, shown in Figure 9-8. To use this menu, you first need to obtain some pig slop, which you can do in the following ways:

- Click the Make Slop button in the corner of the Pigpen menu to create slop from bushels in your inventory (see Chapter 7 for more on bushels).

- Receive slop as a gift from a friend.

- Find slop when you harvest your Pigpen.

Figure 9-8: The Pigpen menu.

After you have slop, you can click any pig in your Pigpen to send it on a hunt for truffles on your neighbors' farms. Each pig has a chance of finding four different types of truffles, as detailed in Table 9-1. When you find a truffle on a neighbor's farm, you must first post that truffle to your neighbor's wall and then get that neighbor to click a link in the wall post to send the truffle back to you before using it to unlock the reward.

After hunting for a truffle, a pig has to rest for two days before it can hunt again.

Table 9-1	Possible Rewards for Truffle Discoveries	
Truffle Type	**Possible Rewards**	**Pig Most Likely to Discover It**
Brown	1/5 Fuel, Strawberry Pig, Black Pig, Ossabaw Pig	Pig (regular), Black Pig, Ossabaw Pig, Party Pig
Black	1 Fuel, Strawberry Pig, White Pig, 300 Coins	Saddleback Pig, Piglet, Strawberry Pig
White	5 Fuel Refills, White Pig, Pink Pot Belly Pig, 1,000 coins	Hot Pink Pig, Hula Pig, Island Pig, White Pig
Gold	10 Fuel Refills, Pink Pot Belly Pig, 5,000 Coins	Javelina, Miniature Pig, Pot Belly Pig, Pink Pot Belly Pig

10

Looking for Special Items and Events

In This Chapter

▶ Participating in limited-edition events

▶ Receiving mystery items

▶ Helping people in the real world through virtual farming

*P*erhaps you've heard some of these homespun bits of wisdom: Variety is the spice of life. Without mysteries, life would be very dull, indeed. A good deed is its own reward. These sayings are just as true in the virtual world of FarmVille as in the real world.

This chapter shows you how to add some variety to the standard set of items on your farm by purchasing limited-edition items. We also cover how to give and receive randomized mystery items and what specific items they may contain when opened. Finally, we tell you about how your virtual farming can help raise money for real people in need through FarmVille's philanthropic events.

Catching Limited-Edition Items and Events

Although most items in FarmVille are permanently available through the Market menu (see Chapter 6 for a thorough tour of this menu), a certain class of item is available for only a limited time. Such limited-edition items must be purchased before they disappear from the Market for good. In-game missions such as co-op jobs and collection sets are also sometimes available only for a limited time.

As discussed in Chapter 6 and shown in Figure 10-1, you can view all currently available limited-edition items by clicking the Specials button in the Market menu. These items are indicated by all the following:

- ✔ The Limited Edition theme on the item's picture
- ✔ An icon to the left of the picture that varies depending on the specific limited-edition event
- ✔ Red text detailing how much longer the item will be available in the Market

Limited-edition items remain on your farm even after they are gone from the Market. Some limited-edition items are occasionally re-released to the market at a later date, but no item is guaranteed for a future re-release. This fact makes these limited-edition items prized possessions for many farmers.

Figure 10-1: The limited-edition items section of the Market menu.

Discovering the benefits of limited-edition items

Different types of limited-edition items tend to have improved features over their permanently available counterparts, as described in the following sections.

Limited-edition seeds

Limited-edition seeds are usually relatively cheap in comparison to permanently available seeds. They also often feature shorter growth times, have higher coin yields when harvested, and earn more experience points (XP) when planted. Seize upon these advantages while you can.

In contrast to crops from other seeds, limited-edition crops do not provide bushels when harvested. Some limited-edition crops can be mastered — as indicated by the mastery stars under their pictures on the Market menu — but you have to harvest pretty quickly to earn that limited-edition crop mastery sign.

Limited-edition trees

In contrast to seeds, limited-edition trees tend to be more expensive to purchase than their permanently available brethren. However, limited-edition trees tend to provide more coins per harvest than other trees, making them some of the most lucrative purchases in the game on a long-term basis. Your initial purchase of a limited-edition tree also typically yields more XP than does the purchase of a regular tree.

Limited-edition animals

Although limited-edition animals, such as the Pinto Pony or Dwarf Goat, may look different from standard animals, they function similarly in terms of collecting coins and placement in animal shelters. As is true of most other animals, usually you can purchase limited-edition animals only with Farm Cash. These animals often provide inflated amounts of XP when purchased. They also take up much less space on a crowded farm than comparably priced limited-edition decorations and buildings. As a result, limited-edition animals are a great way to gain levels efficiently for those farmers willing to shell out the Farm Cash.

Limited-edition decorations and buildings

Most regular decorations and buildings don't serve any productive purpose on your farm, and the same holds true of limited-edition decorations and buildings. However, these rarely seen items are a great way to set your farm apart from the countless others that feature identical, permanently available decorations. Limited-edition decorations also often feature fanciful animations to add pizzazz to your farm.

Checking in for limited-edition events

If you log in to play FarmVille regularly, it's pretty hard to miss the limited-edition items being offered. Information about a limited-edition sale often appears on the FarmVille loading screen, as shown in Figure 10-2. New limited-edition events are also often noted by a pop-up notification when you log in to FarmVille.

If you somehow miss these clues, you can always see the currently available limited-edition items by clicking the Specials button in the Market menu (refer to Figure 10-1).

Figure 10-2: A limited-edition item notice, as seen on the FarmVille loading screen.

If you don't want to miss a limited-edition sales event, you should log in to FarmVille at least twice a week. Typically, new content, including limited-edition items, is added to the game on Tuesdays and Thursdays, but new stuff can in fact be released at any time. Limited-edition items can stay in the FarmVille Market for anywhere from two days to two weeks, so visiting your farm daily is the best way to absolutely ensure that you don't miss anything.

FarmVille loves celebrating holidays with limited-edition item sets, so be sure to check in more often around major holidays to be among the first to get your hands on the associated limited-edition items.

Solving the Mystery of Mystery Items

FarmVille offers quite a few items that you have to open, like presents, to reveal what's inside. After you find or receive a mystery item, it resides in your Gift Box until you click the Use button underneath its icon. When you click the Use button, the mystery item is replaced by the specific, no-longer-mysterious item inside, which remains in your Gift Box until you use or sell it as normal.

Mystery items come in a few different varieties. Read on to find out all about them!

Mystery Boxes and Games

Both the Mystery Box and Mystery Game are purchasable items that contain exclusive items that you can't purchase elsewhere in the Market. Either the Mystery Box or the Mystery Game, but not both, will always be featured as a limited-edition item in the Market menu. The precise price for these items varies, but it usually ranges between 16 and 22 Farm Cash.

Buying a Mystery Box or taking a chance at the Mystery Game always yields a limited-edition item, but you have no guarantee that the item will be one you want. You might even get a duplicate of a prize you've already received from a previous mystery purchase. You can usually find hints as to what prizes can be won from your purchase, but prizes are not revealed until you purchase.

Although Mystery Boxes are opened the same way other mystery items are — by clicking the Use button in your Gift Box — playing the Mystery Game is a bit more complicated. To play and earn mystery items from a Mystery Game, follow these steps:

1. **Click the Play button under the Mystery Game item in the Market menu.**

   A simple, interactive balloon-popping game appears, as shown in Figure 10-3. The cost is deducted from your Farm Cash balance at this point.

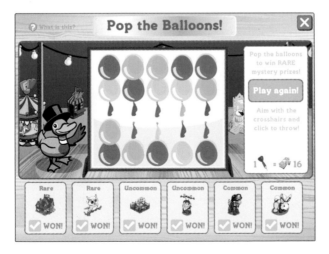

Figure 10-3: The balloon-popping Mystery Game.

2. **Click the Play button on the right side of the screen.**

    Your mouse pointer is replaced with a dart, which you can point at the balloons in the center of the screen.

3. **Click any balloon with your mouse.**

    A random limited-edition item is added to your Gift Box.

You can click the Buy or Buy More buttons at the bottom of the Mystery Game menu to purchase these items directly, or you can click Play Again to purchase another dart for the displayed cost in Farm Cash.

The first time you click Play to load the Mystery Game, you receive a free dart to throw without spending any Farm Cash. The resulting limited-edition item you earn is completely risk free, so trying the game at least once, just for fun, can't hurt.

Mystery Gifts

Mystery Gifts can contain all types of FarmVille items, including coin rewards, XP rewards, animals, trees, decorations, vehicles, Farm Cash, and fuel. Some items featured among the Mystery Gifts, such as the Chinchilla, are Mystery Gift exclusive items that you cannot find or purchase anywhere else in FarmVille.

You can send free Mystery Gifts to your neighbors via the Gifting page. The gift recipient then has to accept your gift through the FarmVille Requests page. We describe both sending and receiving gifts in more detail in Chapter 4.

Mystery Eggs

You find Mystery Eggs primarily by harvesting Chicken Coops on your farm (as discussed in Chapter 9) and by feeding chickens in your neighbors' Chicken Coops (as described in Chapter 4). Whenever you perform either of these actions, you have the chance to earn a Mystery Egg for your trouble. Your chance increases if you harvest from an expanded Coop or a Coop with lots of fed chickens.

A pop-up notification reveals whether you've received a Mystery Egg or just the normal coin or XP bonuses for your actions, as shown in Figure 10-4. If you find a Mystery Egg when feeding a neighbor's Coop, you can also share an extra egg with your neighbors through a news feed post.

Not all Mystery Eggs are created equal. Colored chickens produce eggs that match their color, and rarer chickens produce eggs with rarer and more valuable items inside. To keep things, well, mysterious, Zynga changes the specific items found in each type of Mystery Egg frequently. However,

Table 10-1 shows the chickens and other items that you can currently find randomly inside various types of Mystery Eggs, as of this writing. Note that some chickens and items found in Mystery Eggs also yield an XP bonus when hatched, as indicated in the table.

You found a Mystery Egg!

Do you want to share your Mystery Egg with your friends?

Share

Figure 10-4: A notification that you have found a Mystery Egg.

Opening Mystery Eggs is one of the best ways to get more chickens, which in turn fills up your Chicken Coop and increases your chances of finding more Mystery Eggs. Be sure to feed your neighbors' chicken coops frequently and expand your coop as necessary to increase your chances of finding more eggs.

Table 10-1	Possible Mystery Egg Prizes	
Egg Color	*Chickens*	*Possible Other Items*
White (regular)	Chicken (regular), Brown	1/5 fuel refill, 20 XP, common collectible, Chicken Gnome
Uncommon Brown	Brown, Black	1 fuel refill, 20 XP, common or uncommon collectible
Rare Black	Black, Golden	10 fuel refills, uncommon collectible
Treasured Golden	Golden (50 XP), Cornish (50 XP), Rhode Island Red (50 XP), Scots Grey (50 XP)	Gold Gnome (200 XP), School House, Wax Apple Tree, 1 Farm Cash, uncommon or rare collectible, farmhand, arborist
Treasured Cornish	Cornish (50 XP), Scots Grey (200 XP)	Chicken Gnome, Windmill, 20 fuel refills (500 XP), One Farm Cash, uncommon or rare collectible, farmhand, arborist, Orange Butterfly

(continued)

Table 10-1 *(continued)*		
Egg Color	*Chickens*	*Possible Other Items*
Treasured Scots Grey	Scots Grey (50 XP), Rhode Island Red (50 XP)	Chicken Gnome, Red Barn, 20 Fuel Refills (500 XP), 1 Farm Cash, uncommon or rare collectible, farmhand, arborist, Orange Butterfly
Rhode Island Red	Golden (50 XP), Cornish, Rhode Island Red	Chicken Gnome, Post Office, Wax Apple Tree, 20 fuel refills (500 XP), One Farm Cash, rare collectible, farmhand, arborist
Rainbow	Rainbow (400 XP), Cornish (50 XP), Scots Grey (200 XP), Rhode Island Red (50 XP)	Gold Gnome, Rainbow Cottage, 20 fuel refills (500 XP), uncommon collectible, Chicken Gnome

Giving Back: FarmVille Philanthropy in the Real World

Periodically, Zynga offers special limited-edition seed items called Sweet Seeds that support good real-world causes while also supporting your farm. These Sweet Seeds events let you purchase one-week licenses to plant limited-edition seeds — such as sweet yams and white corn — for a donation of a minimum of 25 Farm Cash. (You can donate more virtual currency if you want.)

The crops you can plant with these licenses tend to have very quick harvest times and a high profit ratio, as well as the unique ability to never wither! As a way of saying thank you for the donation, farmers who take part in the event also receive a Sweet Seeds flag that they can display on their farm.

Depending on the event, FarmVille publisher Zynga takes anywhere from 50 to 100 percent of the Farm Cash donations spent on these permits, converts them to real money, and sends that money to relief organizations such as FATEM (which serves people of Haiti) and the U.N. World Food Programme.

As of this writing, the three Sweet Seeds for Haiti limited-edition events have raised more than $3 million for food and school construction in some of the poorest areas of the earthquake-ravaged country. Zynga has committed to running more Sweet Seeds limited-edition events in the future, so keep your eyes peeled and help out your fellows while you help your virtual farm.

Part IV
Embracing FarmVille Fame and Community

The 5th Wave   By Rich Tennant

"Mr. President, North Korean President Kim Jong-il wants to co-op farm in FarmVille."

Whereas the previous parts cover the basics of farming and how to make money, this part covers the details of earning achievements. You can earn many types of achievements in FarmVille, including ribbons from bronze through gold, various types of collections, and crop mastery. We explain these achievements and how you obtain them so that you, too, can seek your FarmVille fame! This part ends with a chapter on co-operative farming missions, which give you a chance to embrace your FarmVille community and work toward a common goal for common benefits.

11

Earning Achievements

In This Chapter

▶ Earning ribbons

▶ Collecting collectibles

▶ Mastering crops

Although many people play FarmVille just for the Zen-like joy of tending to their crops and organizing their farms, most players like to receive some sort of recognition for the effort they put in. Of course, FarmVille provides in-game currency and experience points (XP) and levels to signify your progress, but those rewards can seem either too short-lived or too generic, in their turn. Where are the permanent rewards that recognize specific situations in which you've gone above and beyond your fellow farmers?

Well, they're in this chapter. Ribbons, collections, and crop mastery levels all provide micro-goals to focus on as you continue to pursue ever-higher levels of in-game currency and XP. They also provide a great way to set yourself apart from your neighbors as well as compare your farming skills with other players. In this chapter, we tell you all about these achievements and how to obtain them with the minimum of effort.

High Roller

All ribbons earned!

2,890,437

A Pretty Pen

All ribbons earned!

2,823,456

Cream of the

Harvest 25,000 crop

Ribbon. 11,000 to g

Earning Ribbons

Ribbons are simply FarmVille's way of recognizing when you've performed a specific action or collected a specific item a certain number of times. Ribbons come in four different colors (in order of attainment: yellow, white, red, and blue), and each color requires more actions or items than the previous one's did.

You can see the ribbons you've already earned, as well as the requirements for the next ribbon in each sequence, by following these steps:

1. **In the Tools menu, located at the bottom right of your FarmVille play area, click the Ribbon icon.**

   The Ribbons menu, shown in Figure 11-1, appears. Each row of this menu displays, among other information, the following:

   - The required action or item collection required for that ribbon (befriending neighbors for the Local Celebrity ribbon, for instance)
   - The specific number of the action or item you need to attain the next colored ribbon in that sequence
   - Your current progress toward the next ribbon in that sequence

2. **Click the right arrow to see information about more ribbons and your progress toward obtaining them.**

3. **Click the Stats icon in the upper-right corner of the play area to view the total number of each colored ribbon you've earned.**

   Checking this stat from time to time helps give a sense of accomplishment while also revving up your motivation!

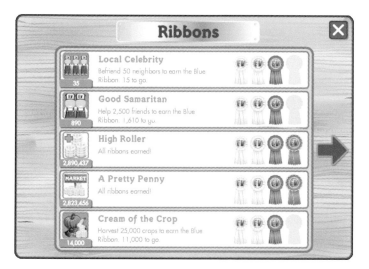

Figure 11-1: The Ribbons menu.

Collecting ribbon bonuses

Ribbons aren't just good for showing off. Each ribbon you earn comes with a bonus of coins and XP. Occasionally you'll also receive a bonus item in your Gift Box that's related to that ribbon's goal (a bonus tree for a tree collection ribbon, for instance).

Although there are some exceptions (see the upcoming section), the number of coins and XP you earn for most colored ribbons is shown in Table 11-1.

Table 11-1	Ribbon Coin & XP Rewards	
Ribbon Color	*Coin Reward*	*XP Reward*
Yellow	500 to 1,000 coins	10 to 50 XP
White	1,000 to 2,500 coins	20 to 100 XP
Red	5,000 coins	50 to 250 XP
Blue	10,000 coins	100 to 1,000 XP

Exceptions

The Pretty Penny, Pack Rat, and Pretty Garden ribbons do not come with any coin rewards. The Architect ribbon, on the other hand, comes with inflated XP rewards of 100 XP for the yellow ribbon, 250 XP for the white ribbon, 500 XP for the red ribbon, and the normal 1,000 XP for the blue ribbon. The Shutterbug and Crop Whisperer ribbons provide fewer coins than the normal amount that comes with the red and blue ribbons.

Sharing ribbon bonuses with neighbors

Collecting ribbons doesn't just earn you a bonus — you can also let your neighbors in on the celebration and share the wealth by posting a notice of your accomplishment to your Facebook news feed.

When you earn a ribbon, a pop-up notice like the one in Figure 11-2 appears to inform you of your achievement. Click the Share button on this notification to post a notice about your achievement to your news feed. Up to ten neighbors can click the link in that news feed post to receive a coin bonus, as follows:

- **Yellow ribbon:** 50 coins
- **White ribbon:** 100 coins
- **Red ribbon:** 250 coins
- **Blue ribbon:** 500

Figure 11-2: The Ribbon Bonus notification window.

Earning the next ribbon

Although the Ribbons menu outlines how many repetitions of a certain action you need to perform to earn the next ribbon in a sequence, some farmers want to plan ahead and figure out how many actions the following ribbon will require, without having to wait to find out. For those farmers, Table 11-2 lists the requirements for each colored ribbon. Simply replace the X in the Action column with the numbers in the various ribbon columns to figure out the requirements.

Table 11-2	Calculating Ribbon Requirements				
Ribbon	*Action*	*Yellow Ribbon*	*White Ribbon*	*Red Ribbon*	*Blue Ribbon*
Local Celebrity	Befriend X neighbors	4	8	25	50
Good Samaritan	Help X friends	20	150	500	2,500
High Roller	Earn X coins	25,000	50,000	500,000	1,000,000
A Pretty Penny	Spend X coins at the market	50,000	100,000	500,000	1,500,000
Cream of the Crop	Harvest X crops	10	1,000	5,000	25,000
Knock on Wood	Harvest X trees	20	250	1,500	5,000

Ribbon	Action	Yellow Ribbon	White Ribbon	Red Ribbon	Blue Ribbon
Zoologist	Harvest X animals	15	500	1,000	5,000
Architect	Own X buildings	2	6	15	30
Pack Rat	Own X decorations	25	50	100	250
Animal Shelter	Adopt X animals	2	3	4	15
Green Thumb	Harvest X unique crops	5	10	14	17
Tree Hugger	Harvest X unique trees	3	8	12	15
Noah's Ark	Collect from X unique animals	2	4	6	8
Not Spoiled, Gifted!	Have X unique gifts in your gift box	3	9	15	21
Crop Whisperer	Fertilize X crops on neighbors' farms	100	250	500	2,500
Flower Power	Harvest X flowers	15	500	2,500	10,000
Pretty Garden	Place X perfect bunches	5	10	25	50
King of Compost	Harvest X fertilized crops	75	150	300	600
They of Mystery	Open X mystery boxes	2	6	15	30
Fenced In	Place X fences	5	50	100	250
Baled Out	Place X hay bales	5	50	100	250
Lord of the Plow	Use the tractor to plow X plots	200	1,000	2,500	10,000
Need for Seed	Use the seeder to seed X plots	200	1,000	2,500	10,000

(continued)

Table 11-2 *(continued)*

Ribbon	Action	Yellow Ribbon	White Ribbon	Red Ribbon	Blue Ribbon
Cracked	Open *X* Mystery Eggs	5	50	75	150
Cat Lady	Brush *X* cats	5	50	100	250
Vegetable Virtuoso	Harvest *X* vegetables	15	500	2,500	10,000
Foremost Fruit Farmer	Harvest *X* fruits	15	500	2,500	10,000
Egg-cellent Discovery	Discover *X* Mystery Eggs in your Chicken Coop	5	25	50	100
Cunning Collector	Complete *X* collections	2	25	50	100
Horse Power	Collect *X* items from your Horse Stable	5	25	50	100
Employee of the Month	Complete *X* co-op jobs at gold as a helper	5	25	50	100
Fabulous Foreman	Complete *X* co-op jobs at gold as a starter	1	5	10	20
Best of the Rest	Be the MVP on *X* successful co-op jobs	1	10	20	40
Crafty	Craft *X* goods	5	25	100	250
Super Salesman	Sell *X* crafted goods to friends	5	25	100	250
Best Buyer	Buy *X* crafted goods from friends	5	25	100	250

Ribbon	Action	Yellow Ribbon	White Ribbon	Red Ribbon	Blue Ribbon
Gearhead	Upgrade X vehicles	2	6	15	30
Style Maven	Purchase X clothing items for your farmer	5	10	20	40

Collecting Collectibles into Collections

Farmers can amass their own collections of all sorts of decorations, vehicles, animals, and other items. Additionally, FarmVille has a special class of items meant specifically for collecting. After you reach level 10, you start finding these collectible items as you perform actions around your farm and your neighbors'.

You can't place these collectible items on your farm — rather, they go straight to your Collectibles menu, shown in Figure 11-3. You can access this menu at any time by clicking the Collectibles icon that appears when you hover over the Ribbon icon in the Tools menu. You can also reach the Collectibles menu by clicking the small pop-up notification that appears when you find a collectible, as shown in Figure 11-4.

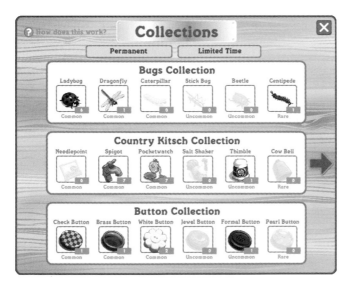

Figure 11-3: The Collections menu.

Figure 11-4: A notification that you've found a collectible.

Differentiating between permanent and limited-time collections

Each collectible you find is part of either a permanent collection or a limited-time collection. As their names imply, permanent collections are always available in the game, whereas items in limited-time collections can be found only briefly, usually for a period of six or seven weeks.

You can see the current limited-time collections, as well as items from retired limited-time collections, by clicking the Limited Time tab in the Collections menu shown in Figure 11-3. Doing so displays the Limited Time section of the Collections menu, as shown in Figure 11-5.

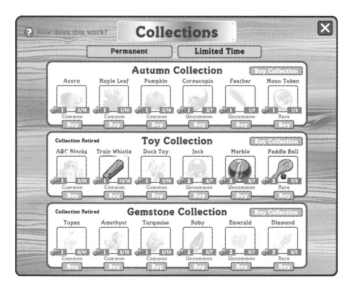

Figure 11-5: The Limited Time menu on the Collections menu.

Besides the difference in availability, limited-time collections also differ from permanent collections by requiring you to find multiple copies of each collectible in order to complete the collection. The number to the right of the slash under each limited-time collectible indicates how many of that collectible you need to acquire before storing the collection, whereas the number to the left indicates how many you have found thus far.

If you're having trouble finding that final collectible or two necessary to finish a limited-time collection, you can just buy it. To do so, click the Buy button under that collectible and then click the Buy button in the resulting pop-up notification to confirm your purchase. You can also click the Buy Collection button to purchase all the remaining collectibles you need for your limited-time collection.

For active collection, common collectibles cost 1 Farm Cash each, whereas uncommon collectibles cost 2 Farm Cash, and rare collectibles cost 3 Farm Cash. Retired limited-time collectibles can be purchased for 1 Farm Cash each. Note that you can't purchase permanent-collection collectibles this way — you have to earn them the hard way.

A countdown timer appears on your farm when a limited-time collection gets within a few days of retiring. After a limited-time collection is retired, you can collect those items only with a Farm Cash purchase rather than by finding items while farming, so complete those collections before your limited time runs out!

You can keep up to ten of each permanent-collection collectible at any time. As for limited-time collection collectibles, the sky's the limit on what you can own.

Acquiring collectibles

You can acquire collectibles in a number of ways, including:

- **Find a collectible while farming or helping a neighbor's farm.** See the upcoming Table 11-3 for advice on which farming actions turn up specific permanent-collection items.

- **Receive a collectible as a free gift from a neighbor.** Common collectibles are featured in the rotation of items on the FarmVille Gifting page, as discussed in Chapter 3. Usually, two different collectibles are featured on the page for several days before being rotated out to make room for a new collectible. Note that the giftable collectibles are randomized, meaning that neighbors don't necessarily see the same ones that other neighbors see on the Gifting page.

Also note that some permanent-collection collectibles are available only as gifts and can't be collected any other way. See Table 11-3 for more on these collectibles.

✔ **Find collectibles in Mystery Eggs.** Each Mystery Egg you open has a chance of containing a collectible. Mystery Eggs are eggs that yield special prizes when hatched from your FarmVille chickens that you can find when harvesting your Chicken Coop.

✔ **Click the collectible sharing links on a neighbor's news feed.** These news posts will be in the format [*Friend name*] Found Some Uncommon Collectibles and Wants to Share Them with You in FarmVille! or [*Friend name*] Has Completed a Collection in FarmVille." You can post similar links to your news feed when you find a collectible or complete a collection. See Chapter 4 for more on sharing items and bonuses using the Facebook news feed.

Finding permanent collectibles

Certainly, you can obtain all your collectibles as gifts or by clicking news feeds. Engaging in the activities involved in farming, however, is by far the most efficient way to complete your various collections.

Not every collectible is created equal, though. Some collectibles pop up much more frequently than others, as noted by the word Common, Uncommon, or Rare that appears under a given collectible in the Collections menu (refer to Figure 11-3 to see examples).

What's more, each different farming task gives you a chance of finding different collectibles in the permanent collections. The game cryptically alludes to these methods when you hover over a collectible on the Collections menu, but for those of you who find hints like "Look up!" too hard to decipher, we've outlined how to find each permanent collectible in in Table 11-3.

Table 11-3	How to Find Permanent-Collection Items	
Collectible	**Rarity**	**How to Get**
Gardening Tools Collection		
Gloves	Common	Can receive only as a gift
Trowel	Common	Find by plowing or hatching white Mystery Eggs
Cultivator	Common	Find by fertilizing neighbors' crops
Twine	Uncommon	Find by harvesting sheep
Pruning Saw	Uncommon	Find by harvesting trees or hatching gold Mystery Eggs
Shears	Rare	Find by fertilizing neighbors' crops

Collectible	Rarity	How to Get
Country Kitsch Collection		
Needlepoint	Common	Can receive only as a gift
Spigot	Common	Find by plowing or hatching Mystery Eggs
Pocketwatch	Common	Find by plowing
Thimble	Uncommon	Find by plowing
Salt Shaker	Uncommon	Find by plowing
Thimble	Uncommon	Find by plowing
Cow Bell	Rare	Find by collecting from cows or Dairy Farms
Bugs Collection		
Ladybug	Common	Find by fertilizing a neighbors' crops or hatching Mystery Eggs
Dragonfly	Common	Can receive only as a gift
Caterpillar	Common	Find by harvesting trees or hatching Mystery Eggs
Stick Bug	Uncommon	Find by harvesting trees
Beetle	Uncommon	Find by fertilizing a neighbor's crops or hatching Mystery Eggs
Centipede	RareFind by plowing	
Butterfly Collection		
Emperor Butterfly	Common	Can receive only as a gift
Painted Lady Butterfly	Common	Find by fertilizing a neighbor's crops or hatching Mystery Eggs
Blue Butterfly	Common	Find by harvesting trees or hatching Mystery Eggs
Swallowtail Butterfly	Uncommon	Find by fertilizing neighbors' crops
Zebra	Uncommon	Find by harvesting trees
Copper	Rare)	Find by harvesting trees or hatching Mystery Eggs
Feather Collection		
Green Plume	Common	Can receive only as a gift
Hen Feather	Common	Find by harvesting any colored chicken or Chicken Coop
Dapple Plume	Common	Find by collecting from Ducks
Red Feather	Uncommon	Find by fertilizing a neighbors' crops

(continued)

Table 11-3 *(continued)*

Collectible	Rarity	How to Get
Banded Quill	Uncommon	Find by harvesting Turkeys, Brown Geese, and Swans
Blue Feather	Rare	Find by harvesting trees
Button Collection		
Check Button	Common	Can receive only as a gift
Brass Button	Common	Find by fertilizing neighbors' crops
White Button	Common	Find by plowing
Jewel Button	Uncommon	Find by collecting from any colored chicken and in Chicken Coops
Formal Button	Uncommon	Find by plowing
Pearl Button	Rare	Find by plowing

Finding limited-time collectibles

As of this writing, all limited-time collectibles can be found on your farm while seeding crops. The only other way to acquire these collectibles is by purchasing them, as discussed in the "Differentiating between permanent and limited-time collections" section, earlier in this chapter.

Storing completed collections

After you've acquired all the collectibles you need for a complete collection, click the Store Collection button to turn that collection in for a bonus. You can exchange completed collections for the following:

- **Permanent collections:** Exchange for 5 tanks of fuel, 5,000 coins, and 250 XP

- **Limited-time collections:** Exchange for 200 XP and an exclusive prize that you can't purchase from the FarmVille Market (a prize that varies with the specific collection). Note that although you can redeem a limited-time collection multiple times (if you acquire the collectibles again), subsequent storage will not include any fuel bonus.

Mastering Crops

When you first start your farming career and are on the lower levels of the game, planting crops is all about earning XP and Farm Coins, as we describe in Chapter 3. When you reach level 10, however, you gain the ability to master crops that you plant frequently. Each crop you harvest after reaching level 10 is worth one mastery point for that crop. Collect enough mastery points for a crop and you'll earn mastery stars and other bonuses Keep reading to see how.

Crops planted before you reach level 10 do not count toward your crop mastery.

Earning mastery points

All permanent seeds (seeds that are always offered in the FarmVille Market) and some limited-edition seeds in the Market can be mastered. (See Chapter 6 for more on using the FarmVille Market menu to obtain seeds.) After you reach level 10, crops that can be mastered are indicated by a set of three brown stars under their name in the Seeds tab of the Market menu, as shown in Figure 11-6.

Figure 11-6: Crop mastery progress, as shown on the Market menu.

When you harvest a crop after level 10, a small pop-up message saying "+1 Mastery" appears, showing that you've earned 1 point toward mastering that crop. Note that you receive mastery points by only harvesting crops — planting and deleting a crop before it is ripe doesn't earn you any mastery points.

As you earn more mastery points, the blue progress bar below the stars on the Market menu fills up. When it's completely full, you earn a star representing the next mastery level for that crop, as well as a bonus. After a crop has reached mastery level 3, it is fully mastered, and you earn a mastery sign for that crop (as discussed in the "Earning mastery bonuses" section, later in this chapter).

You can also hover your mouse over the progress bar to see how many mastery points you've already earned and how many you need to achieve the next mastery level, as shown for the tomato crop in Figure 11-6.

You can use bushels to receive two mastery points per harvested plot rather than one! See Chapter 7 for more on finding and using bushels.

Each crop requires a different number of mastery points to reach each crop mastery level, as detailed in Table 11-4. Note that the mastery points counter resets every time you earn a mastery level, so after earning 500 mastery points to reach the first mastery level for strawberries, for instance, you have to earn 1,000 more mastery points before reaching mastery level 2. For simplicity, the Total Mastery Points column in the table shows how many points it takes to earn full mastery of the given crop.

Some crops also require you to master a previous crop before they'll be unlocked in the Market menu. These crops are indicated in the Mastery Prerequisites column. See Chapter 8 for more on what levels are required to unlock each crop.

Table 11-4   Crop Mastery Requirements

Seed	Mastery Level 1	Mastery Level 2	Mastery Level 3	Total Mastery Points (for Full Mastery)	Mastery Prerequisites
Strawberries	500	1,000	3,750	5,250	
Eggplant	200	400	600	1,200	
Wheat	500	1,000	1,500	3,000	
Soybeans	300	600	900	1,800	
Peanuts	275	550	825	1,650	
Squash	200	400	600	1,200	
Lilac	450	900	1,350	2,700	
Pumpkin	500	1,000	1,500	3,000	
Spinach	300	600	900	1,800	
Artichokes	125	250	375	750	
Rice	400	400	2,000	2,800	
Raspberries	1,500	3,000	4,500	9,000	
Daffodils	200	400	600	1,200	
Cotton	150	300	450	900	
Cranberries	450	650	2,900	4,000	
Chickpea	400	800	1,200	2,400	Soybean Mastery
Bell Peppers	350	270	455	1,075	
Rhubarb	480	960	1,440	2,880	
Peppers	425	850	1,275	2,550	

(continued)

Table 11-4 (continued)

Seed	Mastery Level 1	Mastery Level 2	Mastery Level 3	Total Mastery Points (for Full Mastery)	Mastery Prerequisites
Morning Glory	500	1,000	1,500	3,000	
Aloe Vera	800	1,600	2,400	4,800	
Pineapples	425	325	550	1,300	
Red Tulips	500	1,000	1,500	3,000	
Pattypan Squash	350	700	1,050	2,100	
Blueberries	1,000	2,000	3,000	6,000	
Watermelon	150	300	450	900	
Grapes	425	850	1,275	2,550	
Tomatoes	750	1,500	2,250	4,500	
Pink Roses	450	338	590	1,378	
Potatoes	150	300	450	900	
Rye	900	1,800	2,700	5,400	
Carrots	500	1,000	1,500	3,000	
Coffee	350	700	1,050	2,100	
Corn	200	400	600	1,200	
Sunflowers	575	1,150	1,725	3,450	
Ghost Chili	1,200	2,400	9,000	12,600	
Cabbage	500	375	665	1,540	

Table 11-4 (continued)

Seed	Mastery Level 1	Mastery Level 2	Mastery Level 3	Total Mastery Points (for Full Mastery)	Mastery Prerequisites
Zucchini	550	1,100	1,650	3,300	Pattypan Squash Mastery
Gladiolus	1,600	3,200	4,800	9,600	Daffodils Mastery
Green Tea	750	1,500	2,250	4,500	
White Grapes	1,200	2,400	3,600	7,200	
Black Berries	1,200	2,400	3,600	7,200	
Red Wheat	250	500	750	1,500	
Lavender	450	338	590	1,378	
Sugar Cane	1,300	1,300	8,400	11,000	
Peas	600	1,200	1,800	3,600	
Yellow Melon	150	300	450	900	
Onion	825	825	4,125	5,775	
Broccoli	550	1,100	1,650	3,300	
Lilies	500	1,000	1,500	3,000	
Acorn Squash	1,000	2,000	3,000	6,000	
Asparagus	825	825	4,125	5,775	
Purple Poppies	750	1,500	2,250	4,500	
Elderberry	825	825	4,125	5,775	
Purple Pod Peas	525	1,050	1,575	3,150	Peas Mastery

(continued)

Table 11-4 (continued)

Seed	Mastery Level 1	Mastery Level 2	Mastery Level 3	Total Mastery Points (for Full Mastery)	Mastery Prerequisites
Ginger	650	1,300	1,950	3,900	
Cucumber	820	1,640	2,460	4,920	
Columbine	2,200	4,400	6,600	13,200	
Iris	600	1,200	1,800	3,600	
Basil	1,200	2,400	3,600	7,200	
Lemon Balm	2,200	4,400	6,600	13,200	
Square Melon	700	1,400	2,100	4,200	Watermelon and Yellow Melon Mastery
Oats	1,850	3,700	5,550	11,100	
Posole Corn	1,500	3,000	4,500	9,000	Corn Mastery
Heirloom Carrot	1,400	2,800	4,200	8,400	Carrots Mastery
Orange Daisies	720	1,440	2,160	4,320	Gladiolus Mastery
Bamboo	1,200	2,400	3,600	7,200	
Carnival Squash	2,000	4,000	6,000	12,000	Pattypan Squash Mastery
Saffron	1,500	3,000	4,500	9,000	
Clover	2,500	5,000	7,500	15,000	
Amaranth	1,200	2,400	3,600	7,200	
White Roses	900	1,800	2,700	5,400	Pink Roses Mastery
Forget-Me-Not	1,100	2,200	3,300	6,600	

Earning mastery bonuses

When you earn a crop mastery level, you also earn a bonus of coins and XP, indicated by a pop-up notification, as shown in Figure 11-7. You can also click the Share button on this notification to post a coin bonus link for your neighbors on your Facebook news feed. The specific bonuses for each mastery level are detailed in Table 11-5.

Figure 11-7: A bonus notification for a level 2 crop mastery bonus.

Table 11-5		Crop Mastery Bonuses	
Mastery Level	*XP*	*Coins*	*Coins for Neighbors (via News Feed Link)*
1	25	500	50
2	75	1,500	100
3	250	5,000	150

Other perks you can earn by mastering crops include:

✔ **Crop mastery signs:** When you reach mastery level 3 for a crop, a mastery sign for that crop appears in your Gift Box. You can place these mastery sign decorations on your farm, as shown in Figure 11-8, or in storage (Chapter 9 tells you about storage). You can't purchase these signs from the FarmVille Market — you can only earn them — so they're a good way to show off your elite farming skills.

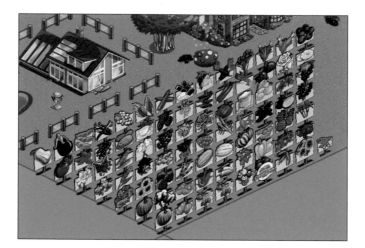

Figure 11-8: Mastery signs displayed on a farm.

- **More XP from harvests:** When you reach mastery level 3 for a crop, each seed you plant of that crop type has a chance of being a premium crop. These premium seeds look slightly bigger than regular crops and yield bonuses of anywhere from one to eight XP when you harvest them, depending on the crop. The only way to receive this randomized premium crop bonus is by planting fully mastered crops, so get cracking on earning those mastery points!

- **Bushel and market stall bonuses:** When you find a bushel while harvesting a crop, you receive a bonus bushel for each level of mastery you've attained for that crop. (See Chapter 7 for more on finding and using bushels.) For instance, if you've reached mastery level 2 on Strawberries, you receive three total bushels every time you turn up a bushel when harvesting those berries. These bushels are also available in your Farmers Market stall for eight hours longer than they were for your previous mastery level.

Let's Cooperate: Co-op Farming

In This Chapter

▶ Grasping the basics of co-op farming

▶ Navigating the Co-op Farming menu

▶ Starting and completing co-op farming jobs

On April 2, 2010, FarmVille developer Zynga introduced cooperative farming jobs to FarmVille. These jobs give you an opportunity to work together with your FarmVille neighbors toward a common goal. Co-op farming is one of the most social aspects of this already very social game.

In this chapter, we explain what co-op farming is, how to navigate the Co-op Farming menu, and how to complete co-op jobs in FarmVille. We also explain why you'd want to bother with co-op farming in the first place by outlining the benefits of completing co-op farming jobs. Read on for everything you need to know!

WARNING!

You can't start or join in a co-op farming job until you've reached level 20. If you're not at level 20 yet, see Chapter 8 for more on gaining new levels, and come back here when you're able to join in.

How Do Co-op Jobs Work?

Cooperative farming jobs, also known simply as co-op jobs, involve farmers working together by combining their resources and efforts for mutual benefit. Just as real world co-op farming does, FarmVille's version involves having each participant share in both the work and rewards of a job.

For the most part, co-op farming is just like regular farming in FarmVille, except that it requires a little extra planning and cooperating (obviously)! Crops still grow and wither at the same rate when you're on a co-op job, but now you have the added the constraint of a specific time limit for reaching your harvest quota. Think of it as a crop-growing race: If you and your friends can reach the finish line before the timer runs down, you win a medal!

Each co-op job asks you and your neighbors to grow a set number of specific crops within a set, real-world time limit. Depending on the completion time, the job can earn your co-op group gold, silver, or bronze medals, each of which comes with various coin and experience point (XP) rewards for each member. Gold-medal performances on co-op jobs come with unique reward items, as well, and crafting jobs also come with extra bushels for a gold-medal performance. (If you need to know more about getting and using bushels, see Chapter 7.)

Although you don't technically *need* to work with any neighbors to complete co-op jobs, they are designed to be hard — if not impossible — for any single farmer to complete alone. For example, even a farming veteran with a massive plantation would have trouble harvesting 1,275 grape plots in two days to get the gold medal on the Fashion Bug co-op job. With the help of even a few friends with smaller farms, however, the entire group should have no trouble making the deadline with some diligent harvesting and replanting.

Starting or Joining a Co-op Job

Before you start a co-op job, you have to let the game know that you and your friends plan to attempt it. You notify FarmVille of this through the Co-op Farming menu, shown in Figure 12-1.

Crops planted on your farm before you start or join a co-op job don't count toward the job's goal, so make sure your plots are plowed and empty before starting a new co-op job.

To start a co-op job, follow these steps:

1. **Click the Co-Op Farming icon in the upper-right corner of the Tools menu.**

   This icon appears only if you've unlocked co-op farming by reaching level 20. Clicking it brings up the Co-op Farming menu (refer to Figure 12-1). This menu shows all the available co-op jobs you can participate in, including jobs already under way by your neighbors.

Figure 12-1: The Co-op Farming menu.

2. **Browse the Co-op Farming menu to choose the job you want.**

   For each job, you can see the maximum potential reward in coins and XP, as well as the amount of time you and your co-op team will have to complete that job. For jobs already in progress, you'll also see pictures of the neighbors who are participating in the job and what percentage of the job they've already completed.

   Be sure to click the Next button in the corner to scroll through all the pages of available jobs. Also note that you can use the tabs at the top of the Jobs menu to filter the menu by the type of co-op job you're looking for. Crafting jobs offer a special bushel reward for gold-medal completion. (For more about bushels, see Chapter 7.)

3. **Click the green Start or Join button next to the job you're interested in.**

   Don't worry if you're not 100 percent sure that you want to take the job at this point — clicking this button just displays the Jobs menu, shown in Figure 12-2. This menu shows exactly how many of each crop you and your team will need to grow to complete the job, as well as the various time limits you all have to beat to receive each colored medal. For jobs that have already been started by neighbors, this menu also shows how many of the appropriate seeds have been seeded and harvested.

   To find out what the Gold Reward prize is for each specific co-op job, simply scroll or mouseover the Gold Trophy icon, as shown in Figure 12-3. If the specifics of the job you're looking at don't interest you for any reason, simply click the Cancel button to go back to the Co-op Farming menu referred to in Step 1.

Figure 12-2: The Co-op Jobs menu.

Figure 12-3: Hovering over the trophy to see the Gold Reward.

 4. **Click the Green Start or Join button on the Jobs menu.**

    Congratulations, you're now part of a co-op job. A pop-up notification asks whether you want to share news of your new job with your Facebook friends.

5. **(Optional) Click Share to post a notification to your Facebook wall or Cancel to skip it.**

   Clicking Share notifies your neighbors via a Facebook news feed post that you have started a job. (If you click Cancel, no news feed is posted. See Chapter 4 for more details on posting notifications to your Facebook news feed.)

   The Active Job menu, shown in Figure 12-4, appears. This menu shows the following:

   - How many crops in the job have been seeded and harvested.

   - How many of each type of crop still needs to be seeded.

   - How much time is left to get each colored medal for the job.

   - Pictures of each person involved in the current co-op job. Hover the mouse pointer over any picture to see that neighbor's name. (Note that co-op participants who aren't on your Neighbors list appear as anonymous outlines with a question mark over the shadow-face.)

   To return to the Co-op Farming menu at any time during your current job, just click the Co-op Jobs icon on the Tools menu.

Figure 12-4: The Active Job menu.

6. **Click the Return to Game button at the bottom right to return to your farm.**

   Time is constantly counting down on your co-op job, so better get planting!

Recruiting Friends to Help

Now that you're part of a co-op job, you want to get as many friends as possible helping you out. To do so, follow these steps:

1. **Click the Recruit Friends button in the Co-op Jobs menu.**

   A pop-up notification appears.

2. **Click the Share button in the notification box.**

   The Facebook message posting dialog box, shown in Figure 12-5, appears.

3. **Enter a message and then click Publish to post the notice on your Facebook wall.**

   Your neighbors can click a link that automatically appears in the news feed post to join your co-op job.

Figure 12-5: Posting a note about your co-op job to the Facebook news feed.

Neighbors can also join your co-op jobs by visiting the Co-op Jobs menu. Jobs currently under way by neighbors are shown first in the Co-op Jobs menu, so any of your neighbors can easily join your job just by clicking the Join button in their game.

Because you need to rely on your neighbors' participation to complete a co-op job, it's vital that you not only have neighbors join the job but also communicate with them. Before you start planting, you should coordinate with your fellow co-op participants and decide who should grow what crops and in what quantities.

Working on a Co-op Job

After you have your friends involved and coordinated, there's not much to co-op farming. Simply plow, seed, and harvest your crops as normal to work toward your goals. Remember, time is of the essence in co-op jobs, so be sure to harvest and replant your plots as quickly as possible.

You can check on your team's progress toward the co-op job goal at any time by clicking the Active Job tab in the Co-op Farming menu (refer to Figure 12-4). Then click the Friends tab to see how many crops have been seeded and harvested by each friend, as shown in Figure 12-6. You can click the Send Message button next to your friend's name on this menu to post a message on his or her Facebook wall and better coordinate your efforts.

Figure 12-6: The Active Job menu's Friends tab.

Quitting a co-op job

Note that you can't start a second co-op job until your current job is finished. If you're really eager to move on with your co-op farming career, you can quit your current job early by clicking the Quit Job button in the lower-left of the Active Job Progress tab of the Co-op farming menu (refer to Figure 12-4) and then clicking Quit Job again on the pop-up notification to confirm your choice. Note that if you started a co-op job, you have to see it through to the bitter end when either the time limit for the bronze (lowest) medal expires or your team completes the job.

Consequences of quitting a job before it's done

After you quit a co-op job, you forfeit your right to any rewards that come from the completion of that job. Also note that any progress you've contributed to the current job will be lost when you quit, meaning that you'll be leaving the neighbors who were depending on you that much further from their goal. That said, if it looks as though you and your team will have no chance to complete your job before time runs out, cutting your losses early might not be a bad idea. Also note that you can't quit a job that you yourself started if other neighbors have already joined your job.

Farm Cash buys more time for the job

If you're worried that you won't make the deadline for your current co-op job, you can spend Farm Cash to buy an extension. Just click the Purchase button in the bottom-left corner of the Co-op Farming menu and then click the Purchase button on the resulting pop-up notification to confirm your purchase (or click Cancel if you think better of it). Time extensions cost 15 Farm Cash and extend the amount of time remaining for each medal level, though the specific amount of time varies depending on the specific co-op job. It's a high price, but if your co-op team's pride is on the line, it might be worth it.

Completing a Co-op Job

A co-op job ends when the bronze medal time limit has expired or your co-op team has harvested the required number of crops. The appropriate amount of bonus coins and XP are automatically deposited in your account as soon as the co-op job is completed — no need for any additional action on your part. If you earned a gold medal, an exclusive prize is also automatically deposited in your Gift Box. Yeehaw!

Note that completing a co-op job is an all-or-nothing proposition. Even if you've singlehandedly completed 90 percent of a co-op job and your good-for-nothing neighbors have barely lifted a finger to help, you'll receive no bonus if the bronze medal time limit runs out before you reach 100 percent. If it looks as though your team won't be able to complete your job, it might pay off to quit and cut your losses (see the previous section).

When your current job is complete, a white arrow appears, pointing to the Co-op icon on the toolbar. You can view the results by clicking the Co-op icon to open the Co-op Jobs menu. These results will live on in the Job History tab of the Co-Op Jobs menu, as shown in Figure 12-7. The Job History menu keeps track of the total number of co-op jobs you've successfully completed, as well as the total number of medals of each color you've received. The Job History menu also shows details about your current job completion streak and average and largest co-op team sizes.

Click the Details tab to see more complete information about your successfully completed co-op jobs, as shown in Figure 12-8. That information includes the following:

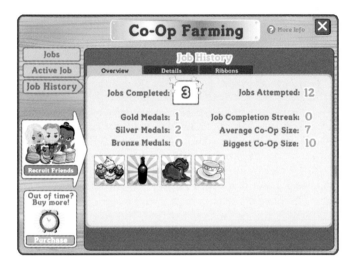

Figure 12-7: The Job History menu of the Co-op Farming menu.

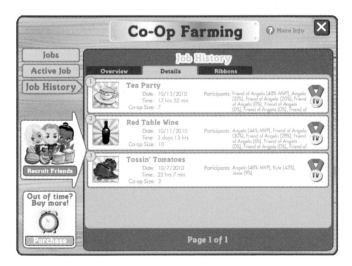

Figure 12-8: The Details tab of the Co-op Farming Job History menu.

　　　↵ Date

　　　↵ Time to completion

　　　↵ Size of your team

　　　↵ How much each member of the team contributed to the job

Click the Ribbons tab in the Job History menu to see your progress toward collecting co-op–related ribbons. (Go to Chapter 11 to find details about earning ribbons.)

Rewards You Earn from Co-Op Farming

The specific XP and coin rewards you receive for a co-op job depend on the particulars of that job. Generally, jobs that require you to grow more crops yield more rewards. Each completed co-op job earns you coins, XP, and an exclusive prize.

Every member who signs up to participate in a successful co-op job receives the full reward for that job. This benefit applies even to participants who contributed literally no planting or harvesting to the effort, meaning that a lot of jobs will attract a lot of do-nothing hangers-on when the job nears the finish line. Many farmers get angry when slacker neighbors leech off their hard work without contributing, but just remember that their success doesn't diminish your hard-won achievement.

Finishing co-op jobs helps you toward earning three ribbons — Fabulous Foreman, Best of the Rest, and Employee of the Month. Also remember that you can earn bragging rights as the MVP — the farmer who contributes the most harvested crops to a successful co-op Job.

You can also earn special, additional prizes for completing a co-op job within the strict, gold-medal time limit. These gold-medal exclusive prize vary depending on the co-op job. Basic jobs reward you with special items, most of which can't be purchased in the FarmVille Market. For example, you can get a Grape Sheep by completing the Fashion Bug co-op job, or a Mini Pagoda for completing the Stirring Things Up co-op job. Crafting jobs reward you with three bushel sets for the appropriate recipe when you earn a gold medal.

To find out what the gold reward prize is for each specific co-op job, simply scroll or mouse over the Gold Trophy icon (refer to Figure 12-3).

Part V
Staying Safe and Up-to-Date on FarmVille

The 5th Wave   By Rich Tennant

"He saw your laptop and wants to know if he can check on his tomato crop in FarmVille."

*F*armVille is a browser-based game, meaning that it's available to anyone with Internet access and a Web browser. This part of the book focuses on keeping you knowledgeable and safe as you play the game online. We provide you with some tips for avoiding common FarmVille scams, information on contacting FarmVille's developer Zynga, links to Web resources for extracurricular farming activities, and advice on other technical matters. Read this part and you are sure to be a technologically savvy farmer.

zynga

CONNECTING THE WORLD THROUGH GAMES

Let us help you get back in the game!

Sub-Forums : FarmVille

Forum
Rules
All you need to know about FarmVille's rules and guidelines.
Updates and Announcements
Get the latest information about new releases and stay up to date with FarmVille news.
User Support
Game related questions? Come here for player-provided support.

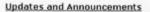

13

Staying Secure
and Finding Support

In This Chapter

▶ Avoiding FarmVille scams

▶ Spotting fake news feed posts

▶ Contacting Zynga support

▶ Finding more FarmVille information on the Web

With tens of millions of players, FarmVille has attracted a lot of attention from unscrupulous characters looking to exploit some player's lack of technical knowledge through FarmVille-related scams. This chapter shows you how to spot some of the most common of these scams so that you can avoid being drawn in.

Despite our best efforts, this book may not be able to answer all your support questions about FarmVille. Some issues you encounter may require the help of Zynga support to fix, and we tell you in this chapter how to contact that support. Other issues may have to do with new features introduced after this book goes to press. As a result, in this chapter we recommend some good Web resources for keeping up with these frequent changes, as well.

Avoiding FarmVille Scams

Unfortunately, numerous scams targeted at unsuspecting FarmVille players are floating around out there. Most of these scams are designed to make you believe they originate from FarmVille itself, or from its publisher, Zynga, while asking you to reveal private information about you or your account.

Each FarmVille player needs to take responsibility to protect his or her personal security while playing the game. Keep an eye out for these common types of scams.

"Free" Farm Cash offers

As discussed in Chapter 5, Zynga provides links to numerous offers and promotions that purport to provide free in-game Farm Cash upon completion. Just because these third-party offers are linked to the FarmVille page, though, doesn't mean they're trustworthy.

Some offers claim to require only a free trial subscription on the link but then demand an up-front payment after you click through. Others simply refuse to work unless you choose one of the paid options they offer, despite having been advertised as free offers. Still others simply never deliver the Farm Cash they promise after you complete the offer.

In general, if an offer comes from a major, well-known national brand, it's most likely safe. Be wary of offers from unknown companies that ask you to provide your cell phone number or mailing address. Giving out cell phone numbers in these offers can be especially dangerous because unscrupulous companies can use them to place unwanted charges on your cell phone bill. Always read the fine print on any offer page to make sure you know what you're agreeing to.

If you do run into an offer that you feel is fraudulent in some way, contact Zynga using the methods discussed later in this chapter. After an outcry from many players, the company is now pretty good about responding to complaints and cleaning up problems on its Offer page.

Also, it should go without saying that you shouldn't trust any other Web site besides FarmVille's that provide links to supposedly free Farm Cash offers. As a general rule, if you didn't find it on the FarmVille game page, don't trust it — and even if you did find it on FarmVille, be cautious.

FarmVille guides

A quick Internet search for FarmVille turns up countless guides that promise to make you a better FarmVille player by giving you secrets, tips, and strategies that aren't available to the general public. Of course, you have this book, which does all those things already, so you don't need to go searching out those guides, anyway.

If you do go searching around, however, be cautious of guides that ask for any sort of up-front payment before providing a download. The PDF products they offer are usually no better than the information freely available online (or in a book like the one you're holding!). In extreme cases, the guide itself may not exist, a fact you'll discover only after your credit card has been charged.

Fake FarmVille Facebook groups

Searching for FarmVille-related groups on Facebook easily turns up hundreds if not thousands of groups that claim to offer free Farm Cash or other items if you become a fan, as shown in Figure 13-1. Without exception, these groups are all scams that use unfulfillable promises of free stuff to attract members. The only legitimate ways to receive free Farm Cash are listed in Chapter 5 of the book. Disregard any Facebook groups that say otherwise.

Figure 13-1: Examples of false FarmVille promises made by Facebook scam group invites.

Fake news feed links

Although clicking legitimate news feed links is a good way to get in-game bonuses (as discussed in Chapter 4), many scammers post illegitimate links that actually take you to phishing sites or other dangerous corners of the Internet. The differences between these fake news feed posts and real FarmVille news feed posts can be quite subtle. As shown in Figures 13-2 and 13-3, the only noticeable difference might be a small misspelling of the game name.

Figure 13-2: A legitimate FarmVille news feed post. Note that the game name is spelled correctly as "FarmVille."

Figure 13-3: A fake FarmVille news feed post. The game's name is misspelled as "farmville."

To check the veracity of a news feed post without having to rely on a sharp eye for misspellings, simply hover the mouse over the suspect link *without clicking* and look in the lower-left corner of your Web browser window. There, a Web address should show where the news feed link leads. If that Web address starts with `http://apps.facebook.com/onthefarm/`, it is a legitimate link. If it starts with anything else, it is a fake link, and you should ignore or delete it.

Protecting Yourself on Facebook

Protecting yourself while playing FarmVille doesn't just mean avoiding scams — it also means protecting your Facebook account. If your Facebook account is accessed illegitimately by a hacker, Zynga will not be held responsible for any items, Farm Cash, or Farm Coins that might be lost. The same applies even if you purposely share your Facebook account with a supposed friend who proceeds to ruin your farm.

Allowing other people to access your Facebook account obviously carries other serious personal privacy risks, as well. Follow these tips to help protect your Facebook account from illegitimate access:

- **Never share your Facebook account information with other Facebook users, third-party Web sites, or anyone else.** If a person or site says it needs your Facebook information to give you access to a free item or to unlock privileged game features, ignore that request. Your login information should always remain private and known only to you. Type your Facebook password only into the Facebook login page at Facebook.com, as discussed in Chapter 2.

- **Use a strong password.** A strong password includes lowercase and capital letters and numbers and symbols, and it doesn't include words commonly found in a dictionary. Try adapting your password from the first letters of an easy-to-remember phrase or song lyric, or use an easy-to-remember pattern of key positions on your keyboard. Insert memorable dates and numbers into the password for added security. Remember, longer passwords are harder for hackers to figure out.

✔ **Use unique login information.** Don't use the same e-mail address and password information for more than one Web site. For simplicity and memorability, try adding some variation of the current site's name to the end of your standard password.

✔ **Avoid clicking Facebook news feed links from unknown parties.** As we explain earlier, in the "Fake news feed links" section of this chapter, fake links often try to fool you into entering your Facebook login information so that a third party can record it.

Be especially careful if Facebook unexpectedly asks you to enter your login information after clicking a link; you may not actually be on Facebook, even if the page looks legitimate. Check the URL in the address bar carefully.

✔ **Download a virus scanner and run regular virus scans.** Anti-Virus Gold offers a relatively robust, free virus scanner at `http://free.avg.com`.

✔ **Log out after using Facebook on a public computer.** If you don't log out, the next person to use that computer will have full access to your Facebook account. Log out by clicking the Account button in the upper-right corner of any Facebook page and then clicking the Logout button in the drop-down menu that appears.

Contacting Zynga

If you run into a technical, billing, or gameplay issue with FarmVille that you can't fix using the information in this book, you can contact the game's publisher, Zynga, for help. The following sections describe ways to seek help from Zynga.

General user support

You can find Zynga's support page for FarmVille by visiting `http://zynga.custhelp.com/app/home/gameid/63/`, shown in Figure 13-4. From here, you can click links to more information about some of the most common issues currently affecting FarmVille players.

More likely, though, you'll want to skip these links and search for the specific information you're looking for. In the Search box midway down the page on the right side, type a few keywords describing your problem and then click the Search button to display a list of possible answers to your issue. Click the links on the Results page to read more information about that issue from Zynga's support database.

Figure 13-4: Zynga's FarmVille support page.

If you don't find an answer to your issue there, click the See More link on the main support page. Then click the Email Us link on the right sidebar to bring up the Zynga e-mail support form, as shown in Figure 13-5. Use the drop-down menus and text areas to detail the problem you're having; then click the Submit button to send your question to Zynga. The company usually responds to e-mail queries in anywhere from 24 to 48 hours.

Zynga's support page also contains a nifty section of the most current hot topics called "the hottest issues and answers for Farmville." Click any of the links in this section to find answers to some of the most common issues affecting FarmVille players at that moment.

Replacing lost items

Lost items are one of the most common FarmVille problems requiring support from Zynga. The company has specific criteria for when and how lost items can be replaced.

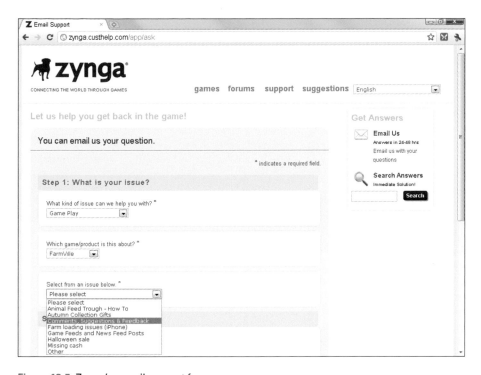

Figure 13-5: Zynga's e-mail support form.

In general, if you lost an item because of an in-game error or glitch, Zynga gladly replaces the purchase or refunds the purchase price in Farm Cash or Farm Coins. However, items lost because of user error — such as accidentally deleting or selling an item — will not be replaced. Likewise, your money will not be refunded for an accidental purchase of an item from the Market menu.

Please note that as of this writing, Zynga doesn't restore free gifts that are lost because of in-game bugs. Zynga also doesn't refund purchases of gifts sent to the wrong person, including both free gifts and those purchased with Farm Cash. The company doesn't replace free gifts that are lost in transit, nor any free gift that has been accidentally sold or deleted.

If your Facebook account is compromised by another user, with or without your consent, Zynga doesn't replace any item that might have been lost or deleted as a result. Please take necessary precautions to secure your account, as discussed earlier in this chapter.

You can read more details about FarmVille's full Item Restoration Policy by visiting http://zynga.custhelp.com/app/answers/detail/a_id/796.

Web Resources

Even though this book is a handy reference for nearly everything you need to know about FarmVille, the game changes much faster than this book can keep up with. For the most up-to-date information on the latest happenings in and around FarmVille, try the Web sites described in the following sections.

The Official FarmVille Forum

`http://forums.zynga.com/forumdisplay.php?f=91`

Zynga hosts an official forum, shown in Figure 13-6, in which farmers can discuss the game and any other topics of interest. Besides being a great place to swap tips and observations with other players, the forum serves as Zynga's repository for official posts containing information about new game features.

Figure 13-6: The Official FarmVille Forum.

The official forum is also an excellent place to post general feedback about the game for community discussion. Zynga pays attention to what players are talking about in this forum, and what you discuss there may affect the direction the game takes in the future.

If you don't feel like registering for a specific account on the official FarmVille Forum, you can click the Connect With Facebook button under the login menu to use your Facebook credentials to represent yourself in the forum.

The Official FarmVille Podcast

`http://www.youtube.com/user/farmville`

Zynga schedules a biweekly podcast to discuss the current happenings in FarmVille. The podcast addresses gameplay tips and happenings throughout the FarmVille community in a short, pithy format. The most exciting part of the podcast might be the Coming Soon segment, which gives information about upcoming FarmVille game features, limited-edition items, and special events.

Though podcast episodes are officially hosted as YouTube videos at the address noted previously (and shown in Figure 13-7), the regular Zynga information dumps have no visual conponent, meaning that if you prefer reading to listening, you can find transcripts of each podcast on Zynga's Official FarmVille Forums at `http://forums.zynga.com/forumdisplay.php?f=245`.

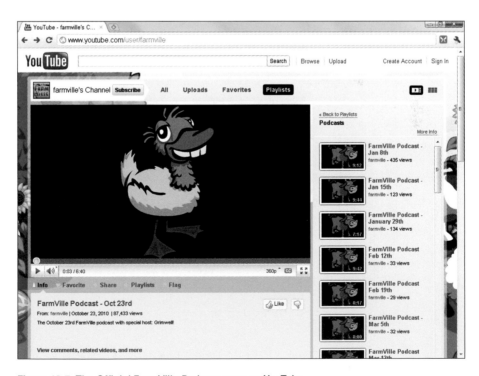

Figure 13-7: The Official FarmVille Podcast page on YouTube.

FarmVille Freak

http://www.farmvillefreak.com

If you can't get your farming fix from the official Zynga sources listed in previous sections, just search for FarmVille in your favorite search engine to turn up countless fan sites devoted to the game. One of the oldest and most well-regarded of these sites is FarmVille Freak, which is maintained by *FarmVille For Dummies* coauthor Angela Morales.

FarmVille Freak, shown in Figure 13-8, is updated several times per day with FarmVille's lastest happenings, including new item releases and features, guides, tips, reviews, and general news.

Figure 13-8: The FarmVille Freak home page.

Technical Matters: Troubleshooting and Game Enhancements

In This Chapter

▸ Taking a screenshot of your farm

▸ Dealing with game updates

▸ Dealing with common FarmVille bugs and glitches

*E*ven though FarmVille is well over a year old as of this writing, the developers at Zynga are constantly developing new features and updating content. Although this constant development means that you get to try out new features as they're added to the game, it also means that the game may not be as stable as your average retail release.

In this chapter we tell you how to deal with some of the more common technical problems you may encounter while playing the game, and show you how to take advantage of some of the more technically advanced features in the game.

Taking a Picture of Your Farm

Although your neighbors can see your farm at any time with a quick in-game visit, showing your farm off to people who don't play the game can be a little tougher. Facebook provides an in-game camera that lets you save a picture of your farm in a Facebook photo album, but this camera has some limitations, including a tiny frame that makes taking aerial shots or full-view images of your farm difficult. To get around these limitations, you can use your computer to capture a screenshot and save it as a digital image by following the steps in the next sections.

Getting ready to take a screenshot

Whether you're on a PC or a Mac, take these steps to prepare to capture an image of your screen:

1. **Turn on high-quality graphics by clicking the Eye icon in the upper-left corner of the play area until the icon turns white.**

   Doing so ensures that your screenshot will be of the best quality available.

2. **Click the Full Screen button in the Tools menu.**

   The play area expands to take up your entire monitor, increasing the size of in-game details and how much you can see of your farm.

3. **Arrange the scene to your liking by positioning and zooming the camera to focus on the parts of your farm you want to show.**

   See Chapter 3 for more on controlling the in-game camera.

Taking a screenshot on a Windows PC

Here are the steps to capturing a shot of your farm if you're on Windows:

1. **Press the Print Screen key on your keyboard.**

   You usually find this key near the Insert, Home, Delete, and End keys on the right side of the keyboard. Press Print Screen (it might be labeled Prt Sc or PrtScn or some other variation) to save a copy of your current screen to the Clipboard (a temporary storage area).

2. **To get the image off the Clipboard, open Microsoft Paint by clicking Start⇨Programs⇨Accessories and then locating the Paint program.**

   The application may simply be called Paint on some Windows systems, and may be found under All Programs. If you are comfortable using a different image editing program, you can open it instead.

3. **Choose Edit⇨Paste.**

   This places a copy of the screen you captured in Step 1 on the Paint (or other image-editing application's) canvas. You may need to click and drag the blue square in the lower-right corner to resize your picture and capture the entire captured screen.

4. **Edit your picture as desired.**

You may want to add text or cut off certain unsightly elements.

5. **Choose File⇨Save As.**

The Save Picture dialog box appears.

6. **Enter a filename and select a location and file type for your image; then click Save.**

The picture of your farm is now saved on your computer.

Taking a screenshot on a Mac

Apple's Mac OS offers a few convenient keyboard shortcuts for taking shots of your farm or any other elements on your screen. You can access the most useful of these by pressing the Command+Shift+3 keyboard combination. Doing so saves the current screen to your desktop in a PNG file containing the words "Screen shot" and the date and time in the filename.

Alternatively, press Command+Shift+4 to transform your cursor into a crosshair. Click and drag this crosshair to describe a box around the area of the screen you want to capture; next, release the mouse to save a PNG file of the captured section to your desktop.

Troubleshooting Common Bugs and Glitches

Although FarmVille is generally pretty stable, bugs and glitches can occasionally interrupt your game play, which can be very frustrating when all you really want to do is harvest your strawberries! These glitches can be anything from having trouble loading the game to losing crops and game items. This section outlines some of the most common problems you might encounter while playing Farmville as well as some simple ways to deal with them.

You can resolve many issues by reloading the FarmVille Web page, restarting the Web browser, or restarting the computer. If other suggested fixes don't work, try those potential solutions in that order. Also note that many issues are simply caused by temporary problems on Zynga's servers and may be resolved by the next time you load the game.

Out of sync

The problem: The game reports that the current game state is out of sync with the server, as shown in Figure 14-1. All this technical mumbo-jumbo simply means that Zynga's game servers are having trouble tracking and saving the current status of your farm (which, as we describe in Chapter 1, is stored in the "cloud" of Zynga's servers). These errors can happen at any time, but performing a lot of farming tasks in a short period of time or placing large quantities of animals, decorations, and trees too rapidly seems to cause these errors to appear more often.

Your game state is out of sync with the server. Please refresh the page to continue.

Okay

Figure 14-1: An out-of-sync error message.

The solution: As the game suggests, clicking the Refresh button on your Web browser should re-sync the game with Zynga's servers. Any farming actions you performed in the last few minutes may not appear after your farm has reloaded, but don't worry — you can still perform those actions again.

Note that if you continue farming without refreshing the browser after receiving an out-of-sync warning, all your hard work may be lost. Be sure to refresh your farm as soon as possible after the warning appears to avoid losing more work.

Facebook news feed posting

The problem: The game freezes when you attempt to share an item with friends through your Facebook news feeds, or the Facebook news feed dialog box fails to appear.

The solution: Actually, this occasional problem has no known fix. Reloading your browser page allows you to continue playing, but you may no longer be able to share the item you were trying to post. Rest easy knowing that it's your neighbors, not you, who will suffer most from this error.

Performance

The problem: Game animation appears choppy or laggy, or the game takes longer than normal to respond to mouse clicks.

The solution: Try clicking the Eye icon in the upper-left corner to reduce the graphic quality of the game. If that doesn't help, try closing other programs or browser tabs that are open on your computer, or try loading FarmVille in a different browser.

Loading

The problem: The game fails to load, either freezing on the loading screen or displaying a blank white screen where your farm should be. Alternatively, Adobe Flash Player may report that the plugin has crashed, as shown in Figure 14-2.

The solution: Try closing your browser completely and reloading the page Often the game will go ahead and work on the second loading. If the problem persists, try clearing the cache in your Web browser and reloading your farm. (See your Wcb browscr's hclp filc for information on clearing the cache.) If that doesn't work, try installing the latest version of Adobe's Flash player, as detailed in Chapter 2. You may need to uninstall your current Flash player before taking this step.

Figure 14-2: An Adobe Flash Player plugin crash.

Gifts

The problem: Gifts don't appear in your Gift Box after you've clicked a link from your Facebook Requests page, or gifts that were previously in your Gift Box are no longer there.

The solution: Although no technical fix for this error exists, Zynga may be able to replace the gifts you've lost. Read more about contacting Zynga customer support about gift refunds in Chapter 13.

Requests

The problem: When trying to send gifts or invite new neighbors, the box from which you usually select friends to share with is blank and the list of your FarmVille neighbors is missing.

The solution: First, try refreshing the page. If this doesn't work, click the Invite Friends tab and see whether it is also blank. If it is, refresh the page and do the same with the Free Gifts tab. If the problem persists, contact Zynga support, as detailed in Chapter 13.

Saving

The problem: Farming actions performed during the last play session are not reflected when you load the game the next time. Problems with saving most commonly occur right after users expand their land and rearrange their farms to accommodate their new space. In addition to sometimes nullifying hours of work, in extreme cases these saving issues can cause you to lose in-game currency with nothing to show for it, or to lose accumulated XP.

The solution: Zynga recommends staying on your farm for at least 15 minutes before closing your Web browser or leaving the FarmVille page to avoid problems with saving your actions. If you do need to leave the FarmVille page for any reason, Zynga recommends clicking the Facebook logo to return to your Facebook home page before moving on to other Web pages.

If a saving issue causes you to lose any in-game currency or experience, try contacting Zynga support using the methods detailed in Chapter 13.

Also, this should go without saying, but if a pop-up message tells you that your farm is saving and "Please do not close your browser," as shown in Figure 14-3, take it seriously. Please do not close your browser!

Figure 14-3: Do not close your browser when you see this message.

Neighbors' profile pictures

The problem: Your neighbors' profile pictures don't appear as they should in the Neighbors bar at the bottom of the play area.

The solution: Restarting your browser and clearing your cache can sometimes fix these problems. If the issue persists, Zynga's servers might be acting up — try coming back later to see whether the issue is resolved.

Strangely clad neighbors

The problem: One or more of your neighbors are shown wearing what appears to be underwear rather than their usual clothing when you hover over their names in the Neighbors bar.

The solution: If this issue is occurring for only a few of your neighbors, it's probably because those neighbors have uninstalled the FarmVille application from their Facebook accounts and are no longer playing the game. See Chapter 3 for more on removing these defunct neighbors from your Neighbor list.

If this issue affects all your neighbors, it is probably a temporary glitch that will be solved the next time you load the game.

Full Screen mode not working

The problem: Clicking the Full Screen button does not cause the game to enter Full Screen mode as it should.

The solution: Sorry, but there isn't one at this time. Try refreshing the page or use other general fixes listed at the beginning of this section.

Avatar not displaying

The problem: Your farmer avatar appears as a white silhouette when your farm loads.

The solution: No one has a solution as of this writing. Try the general fixes listed at the beginning of this section.

Missing items on farm

The problem: Previously purchased items no longer appear on your farm.

The solution: Contact Zynga support (see Chapter 13 for how to do so). Zynga will either place the item in your Gift Box or refund the price of the missing item.

Random text in pop-up messages

The problem: Pop-up notifications appear with random text rather than the correct message, as shown in Figure 14-4. Common replacement text includes error code names, repeated requests to "give me a hand" or the word "null" in place of a player's name.

The solution: This problem should fix itself when you refresh your Web browser.

Figure 14-4: A pop-up notification with incorrect text.

Handling the "FarmVille Has Been Enhanced" Notification

One of the most exciting pop-up notifications in all of FarmVille is the message that "FarmVille Has Been Enhanced," as shown in Figure 14-5. This means that Zynga has just released a new version of FarmVille with new features or gameplay fixes. When you see this notification, click the Okay button to reload your farm.

Often, when your farm reloads, additional pop-up notifications let you know that new items, events, or promotions are now available on your farm. This new content often includes limited-edition items that are available for only a short time. (See Chapter 10 for more about limited-edition items.) These updates can also include new game features that are explained via the pop-up notification.

Figure 14-5: The Farmville Has Been Enhanced notification.

If no new pop-up notifications show up when your farm reloads, the new updates probably applied primarily to behind-the-scenes fixes, including improvements to the game's stability and security. Even so, you should check the Market menu to see whether any new items are available, just in case.

Zynga usually deploys these types of updates to FarmVille at least twice a week, so you shouldn't have to wait long for something new to show up.

Part VI
The Part of Tens

The 5th Wave   By Rich Tennant

"These are the parts of our life that aren't on Facebook."

The final part of this book consists of a series of lists containing ten juicy topics that make playing FarmVille fun. Read about ten different types of farming personalities and see where you fit in on the list. We've also provided a list of the ten most wanted items that FarmVille players continue to crave. Finally, the last chapter in this book lists the ten go-to crops that you can never "grow" wrong with.

Ten Farming Personalities

In This Chapter

▶ Play your own way

▶ Hoarders, breeders, collectors . . . oh, my!

▶ What type of farmer are you?

*O*ne of the best things about FarmVille is how much it lets you customize the playing experience. No two farmers have to play the game the same way, although, in practice, players tend to fall into one of a few broad categories. Most players find that they have a mixture of these farming personalities, and that's okay, too.

This chapter outlines ten different types of FarmVille players. Which one describes you best?

The Functional Farmer

Functional farmers don't have room on their farm for the frills of FarmVille. Their basic attitude is that every plot counts and anything else takes up precious space. Their farms are easy to spot by their ample fields of prosperous crops with a lack of decorations. Farm expansion is a key concern for these farmers, who maximize their profit by growing as many crops as quickly as possible.

Functional farmers make great co-op partners because of their ability to grow a large amount of crops in a short time limit. Visiting a functional farmer is a treat, too, because his or her extremely basic farm loads quickly and usually has plenty of plots that need fertilizing.

The Exterior Decorator

The exterior decorators' main focus is the physical appearance of their farms. These farmers are interested in having the most visually appealing farm possible, even if it takes them a little longer to earn Farm Coins and experience points (XP).

Exterior decorators usually change their decorations constantly, trying to match their farm's appearance with their mood or with the season. Although exterior decorators need to keep some crop space available to fund their decorating habits, this functional space is usually not more than a small corner of the farm.

Visiting these neighbors is always an interesting experience because you can sample the latest seasonal décor without having to spend any coins or Farm Cash.

The Leveler

As their name implies, levelers are concerned primarily with earning XP and raising their level as high as possible. Although each leveler might have his or her own technique for leveling up, the goal of each one is the same — getting that number next to his or her name to tick up as quickly as possible.

Levelers tend to be some of the most competitive farmers out there, and many see farming as a blood sport. You can find these farmers' names at the extreme right edge of your Neighbors toolbar, with XP numbers so high they get cut off because they spill outside the available space.

Visiting a leveler's farm usually isn't very interesting. Orderly rows filled with crops that yield a lot of experience often sit next to disorganized piles of hay bales, perhaps with a few high-cost, high-experience buildings dotting the field.

The Happy Hoarder

"It's not hoarding; it's collecting!" is the defensive cry of this farmer. Happy hoarders are interested in accumulating as many decorations, animals, buildings, and other tangible property as they can, often amassing truly ridiculous amounts of their favorite item in carefully organized rows.

Limited-edition items are of particular interest to happy hoarders. Land expansions are also a priority because they let the hoarder pile more junk on his or her fields.

Because every square inch of a happy hoarder's farm is typically covered with different items, you have to be very patient when visiting to allow all that content to load. After it does, though, be ready for your senses to be assaulted by a veritable cornucopia of color and variety.

The Breeder

Breeders are interested in animals — specifically in using animal shelters to produce rare offspring, as discussed in Chapter 9. Regular baby foals and calves grow like weeds on their farms, but the limited-edition animals are the breeder's real pride and joy.

Breeders usually have deep virtual pockets full of Farm Cash, which they keep funded because of their need to purchase as many limited-edition animals as possible from the FarmVille Market.

It's a joy to be neighbors with breeders because they usually share their rare offspring with you via posts to their Facebook news feed. As a result, you get to adopt plenty of cute baby animals for your own farm without doing any of the hard work. Don't feel bad for mooching — the breeder is happy to spread the pleasure of baby animals around.

The Farm Master

A farm master wants to become an expert in everything FarmVille-related. Crops, crafts, trees — if you can earn mastery stars and signs for it, the farm master is interested in it.

Even though mastering these various items takes more time than it does any particular skill, these farmers take pride in the sense of accomplishment they get from excelling at everything the game throws at them You can spot a farm master from afar by the dense forest of mastery signs that clog a corner of his or her farm.

The Artist

FarmVille artists use their farm as a canvas. This creative farmer strives to do something entirely unique with his or her farm, thinking outside the box to find some exciting new uses for common FarmVille items. For example, artists might craft hay bales into beautiful, three-dimensional works of art.

Although artists still grow crops as every other farmer does, these crops are just a means to an end — the menial work that lets them pursue their true artistic passion.

Artists often get a lot of visits from their neighbors because everyone is eager to check out the ever-evolving projects on their farms.

The Collector

FarmVille collectors do just that — collect one specific item type as many times as possible. In contrast to happy hoarders, FarmVille collectors aren't interested in accruing just any old FarmVille decoration or item. Instead, collectors concentrate on completing a collection that suits their fancy. You encounter gnome collectors, building collectors, sheep collectors, tree collectors . . . collectors for pretty much any type of FarmVille item you can name.

Collectors are obsessed with limited-edition items that fit with their collection, checking the FarmVille Market obsessively and breaking out their wallets to spend as much Farm Cash as necessary to secure their latest bauble.

Visiting a collector's farm is always a fun experience because their prized collection is usually displayed with pride.

The Zoologist

FarmVille zoologists are known for their penchant for collecting as many animals as possible. Some strive to have at least one of every type of animal released. Others focus on specific animal breeds. In contrast to breeders, zoologists are not concerned with an animal's breeding capabilities. All zoologists let their general love for animals override all other possible focuses on their farm.

Zoologists need a lot of Farm Cash to pick up all the rare, new, limited-edition animals that pop up frequently in the FarmVille Market. Animal storage is another major concern for zoologists, who need a lot of animal shelters to save space as well as to make harvesting all those animals a little easier.

Visiting zoologists is, unsurprisingly, like taking a visit to a virtual zoo. Such visits can be a little annoying, though, if the zoologist doesn't have any open plots of land that you can plow or fertilize for XP.

The Overachiever

The main focus of overachievers is to earn ribbons and achieve other distinctions in the game. They gear every farming action toward some ribbon and aren't satisfied until they've collected every blue ribbon available.

For an overachiever, getting a ribbon is more important than making a profit, collecting a specific item, or helping out neighbors — unless those activities are needed to earn that next ribbon, that is! After they've acquired all the ribbons, overachievers often become listless and complacent before devoting their farming energies to some other effort, which frequently leads them to morph into one of the other types of farmers listed here.

Overachievers can be founts of useful information for methods to quickly gain new ribbons.

The Ten Most Wanted FarmVille Items

In This Chapter

▶ Owning the rarest FarmVille items

▶ More land and more storage!

*N*ot all FarmVille items are created equal. This much should be obvious to anyone who's scanned the prices in the FarmVille market. But some items are more unequal than others. These items are the rarest of the rare — the most coveted and most useful items in the entire game.

Some of them are available only during brief, limited-edition events. Others cost a dear sum in Farm Cash, or have been permanently discontinued from the game.

In any case, if you manage to get your hands on any of these ten items, consider yourself among the lucky few. And try not to rub it in your neighbors' faces too much, eh? No one likes a show-off.

Unwither Ring

The Unwither Ring, shown in Figure 16-1, is one of the most expensive and coveted possessions that a FarmVille farmer can call his or her own. If you have an Unwither Ring, you'll never need to worry about your crops withering again, meaning that you can come visit and harvest your crops entirely on your own schedule.

Figure 16-1: The Unwither Ring as it appears in the Market menu.

As of this writing, the Unwither Ring has been available only three times, always for a beefy cost of 250 Farm Cash (which represents at least $40 in real world currency). When the ring was first made available for purchase as part of a Valentine's Day limited-edition theme — February 9 through February 14, 2010 — it could be purchased only as a gift for a FarmVille neighbor, making it even harder to obtain than most limited-edition items. To the relief of many farmers, when the ring was re-released for limited availability, farmers could purchase the Unwither Ring for themselves.

You can modify an Unwither Ring using a customized band and your choice of stone, making each ring as unique as its owner.

Lawn Jockey

The Lawn Jockey was a decoration that was available only during the earliest days of FarmVille. Because of a controversy over the somewhat racist historical associations of many real-world Lawn Jockey decorations, the FarmVille version was removed from the game on August 28, 2009. However, players who had already purchased jockeys got to keep them, lording their acquisition over their neighbors and proving they've been playing FarmVille since nearly the beginning. You can check out a lucky farmer's Lawn Jockey in Figure 16-2.

Even though Lawn Jockeys weren't a limited-edition item, the only way to purchase them was with 8 Farm Cash, making them slightly rarer than other items of that time. However, whereas limited-edition items are sometimes re-released, it's probably safe to say that the Lawn Jockey will never be coming back to the FarmVille Market.

Figure 16-2: The Lawn Jockey
as it appears on a farm.

Although no farmer who owns a Lawn Jockey is likely to sell it, a farmer can get 50 Farm Coins if he or she decides to part with one of the rarest and most coveted items in all of FarmVille.

White Stallion

Stallions are needed to breed horses, which makes owning one a must for farmers who want a lot of foals around. Most farmers have to rely on randomly finding a wandering Stallion, which stays in a Horse Stable only temporarily. If you're lucky enough to own a White Stallion, shown in Figure 16-3, however, your days of hoping for wandering Stallions to appear will be behind you forever.

Figure 16-3: A White
Stallion.

As of this writing, White Stallions have been available only three times. The White Stallion's first appearance was from February 9 through 14, 2010, when it could be found in a Valentine's Day–themed Mystery Box. The second appearance was on May 11, 2010, when farmers found it in a Mystery Chest. Its final appearance thus far was on August 15, 2010, as part of the day's Mystery Game.

If the White Stallion comes back into the FarmVille Market — and it's a good bet that it will one of these days — you'll get 400 experience points if and when you put it on your farm. The White Stallion can be resold for 2,000 Farm Coins and can be harvested for 84 Farm Coins every day if it is in a Horse Stable, or every three days if it's outside a Stable.

Black Stallion

The elusive Black Stallion, shown in Figure 16-4, is coveted for the same reasons as any other Stallion — its ability to breed foals. This Stallion was one of the rare prizes that appeared as part of the first Mystery Game, released July 14, 2010. Its only other appearance in FarmVille was during an extremely short, unannounced few minutes when it was available for purchase in the FarmVille Market. Some lucky farmers who just happened to be browsing the FarmVille Market at the time were able to snag one, but everyone else is still waiting for the day when these majestic horses are made available once again.

Figure 16-4: A Black Stallion.

Villa

At one point, the purely decorative Villa was the most expensive item you could purchase without Farm Cash, weighing in at a cool million Farm Coins to purchase. The Villa, shown in Figure 16-5, was — and still is — coveted because of its high cost and because of the requirement that a farmer reach level 34 before purchasing one. The 10,000 XP you receive for purchasing a Villa is enough to gain an entire level in one fell swoop, making it a useful purchase as a well as a beautiful one.

Figure 16-5: The Villa.

Although the Villa has since been surpassed as the most expensive item by the 5,000,000 Farm Coin Mansion, the prestige associated with this rare and beautiful decoration has not fully diminished.

Platinum Gnome

Gnomes are purely decorative items; they serve no productive purpose on the farm. The Platinum Gnome, however, which is shown in Figure 16-6, distinguishes itself as a limited-edition item that was available only as a silver Mystery Box prize from December 1 through December 7, 2009. Lucky farmers who found a Platinum Gnome in their box were also rewarded with 300 XP.

You can sell a Platinum Gnome for 1,500 Farm Coins, but the prestige of having one on your farm is worth much more than that to many farmers.

Figure 16-6: A
Platinum Gnome.

Farmhands and Arborists

As the first truly productive items on our list, Farmhands and Arborists are coveted for the immense time-saving services they provide. When faced with a farm full of hundreds of ripe trees or animals, a handy Farmhand (for animals) or Arborist (for trees) can save a farmer literally hundreds of clicks and provide thousands of Farm Coins at the same time.

Although you can purchase both Farmhands and Arborists directly from the FarmVille Market for five Farm Cash each, gaining them is more enjoyable when you find them while farming or receive them as a free gift.

Lake Nessy

Lake Nessy is a limited-edition decoration based on Scotland's fabled Loch Ness monster. This limited-edition item was available as part of FarmVille's April Fool's Day celebration — March 31 to April 6, 2010. The prominent size of Lake Nessy, as shown in Figure 16-7, easily distinguishes it from other FarmVille decorations.

Figure 16-7: Lake Nessy, shown with a farmer avatar for scale.

Nessy instantly became a treasured item thanks to its high 56 Farm Cash price tag and limited availability. It continues to be a favorite among farmers who appreciate its unique design and large physical size, which towers over farmers and most other decorations.

Farm Expansion

Even though it's not a limited-edition item, or even an item you need to spend precious Farm Cash on, farm expansion is still one of the most sought-after items in FarmVille. Farm expansions can be purchased with Farm Cash or Farm Coins in the FarmVille Market. Many farmers purchase an expansion for their farm as soon as they can, and soon thereafter find themselves wanting more virtual land to quench their appetite for more FarmVille items and farming space.

Unlimited Storage

Besides farm expansion, more storage is one of the most common requests from veteran farmers. With their virtual pitchforks in hand, disgruntled famers are constantly demanding more storage from FarmVille developer Zynga. This is especially true of farmers interested in collecting limited-edition items — as their prized collections of decorations, animals, and buildings grow, they continue to run out of space on their farms.

Farmers can use storage buildings and a Storage Cellar to hold up to 500 extra items that won't fit on their farm, as discussed in Chapter 9. This number was smaller in the past and may well increase in the future as more and more farmers see their farms filling up with items. Unless Zynga implements some sort of unlimited storage option, though, the storage limits will likely always seem stifling to the most devoted FarmVille players.

Ten Go-to Crops

In This Chapter

▶ Knowing what crops to plant, and when

▶ Maximizing Farm Coin and experience point yields

▶ Choosing the best crops for each level of the game

A quick glance at the FarmVille Market is enough to show you that you have a lot of seeds to choose from. Even if you aren't at a high enough level to purchase all those seeds, choosing which crop to plant for each situation can seem overwhelming.

So how do you know what to grow on your farm? You can start by selecting seeds that you know will be available to harvest when they ripen. You might also want to consider the profit in Farm Coins and the number of experience points (XP) gained from each plot of the crop you plant. You really can't go wrong with any of the seeds listed in this chapter. Note that even though we don't include any limited-edition crops in this list, such crops usually yield high profits and have quick ripening times, making them quite lucrative and smart choices for planting.

Costs and benefits listed for the crops in this chapter don't include the 15 Farm Coin cost and 1 XP from plowing a plot of land.

Peas

- ✔ **Unlocked at:** Level 32
- ✔ **Harvest time:** 1 day
- ✔ **Cost per plot:** 190 Farm Coins
- ✔ **Harvest value:** 381 Farm Coins
- ✔ **XP per harvested plot:** 3

Peas are a favorite of long-time farmers and are considered one of the best crops in the game because of the three XP they generate in a single, one-day planting. The 176 Farm Coin per-day profit for each plot, which includes the cost of plowing, doesn't hurt, either. You should definitely start growing fields full of peas as soon as you can.

Raspberries

- ✔ **Unlocked at:** Level 8
- ✔ **Harvest time:** 2 hours
- ✔ **Cost per plot:** 20 Farm Coins
- ✔ **Harvest value:** 46 Farm Coins
- ✔ **XP per harvested plot:** 0

Although raspberries do not yield XP when harvested, their short growing time more than makes up for that disadvantage. Because raspberries are one of the quickest-growing crops in the game, a really dedicated farmer can plant and harvest 11 fields of raspberries in a single, sleep-free day. Besides the quite decent per-hour Farm Coin bounty from such manic harvesting, remember that all that plowing is worth XP as well, making the quick turnover quite effective for your leveling up.

Asparagus

- ✔ **Unlocked at:** Level 37
- ✔ **Harvest time:** 16 hours
- ✔ **Cost per plot:** 220 Farm Coins

✔ **Harvest value:** 357 Farm Coins

✔ **XP per harvested plot:** 2

Asparagus is a great mid-level crop to grow, bringing healthy rewards of XP and coins in every 16-hour growing cycle.

Black Berries

✔ **Unlocked at:** Level 29

✔ **Harvest time:** 4 hours

✔ **Cost per plot:** 75 Farm Coins

✔ **Harvest value:** 117 Farm Coins

✔ **XP per harvested plot:** 1

On a per-hour basis, black berries (yes, the game spells it as two separate words; don't ask us, we just work here) are one of the best crops for gaining a lot of XP quickly, provided that you can commit to keeping up with multiple four-hour growing cycles per day. The Farm Coin rewards aren't nearly as lucrative as some other crops but still provide a nice bonus for your efforts.

After you reach level 70, try growing clover for a similar schedule of quick experience points.

Pumpkin

✔ **Unlocked at:** Level 5

✔ **Harvest time:** 8 hours

✔ **Cost per plot:** 30 Farm Coins

✔ **Harvest value:** 68 Farm Coins

✔ **XP per harvested plot:** 1

Pumpkins are a great crop for beginner farmers who haven't unlocked some of the more lucrative crops yet. As the game's quickest-growing vegetable, they provide relatively quick experience and XP rewards, and help you rapidly earn vegetable-related ribbons.

Onion

- **Unlocked at:** Level 34
- **Harvest time:** 12 hours
- **Cost per plot:** 170 Farm Coins
- **Harvest value:** 275 Farm Coins
- **XP per harvested plot:** 1

Onions provide some of the heaviest per-harvest coin profits among crops unlocked at the middle levels of the game. Their 12-hour growing also means that you can easily squeeze in a couple of harvests per day, or let them ripen overnight for an early-morning harvest.

Rice

- **Unlocked at:** Level 7
- **Harvest time:** 12 hours
- **Cost per plot:** 45 Farm Coins
- **Harvest value:** 96 Farm Coins
- **XP per harvested plot:** 1

Among crops with low-level requirements, rice is one of the best at providing a high profit in Farm Coins in a short growing time, making it an early favorite for building up your fortune. The not-too-long, not-too-short 12-hour growing time allows fields of rice to turn around quickly — but not so quickly that you have to be stuck to your computer.

Tomatoes

- **Unlocked at:** Level 20
- **Harvest time:** 8 hours
- **Cost per plot:** 100 Farm Coins
- **Harvest value:** 173 Farm Coins
- **XP per harvested plot:** 1

The 53-coin profit that a tomato plot provides every 8 hours can be a quick path to a FarmVille fortune for diligent farmers.

Grapes

- ✔ **Unlocked at:** Level 19
- ✔ **Harvest time:** 1 day
- ✔ **Cost per plot:** 85 Farm Coins
- ✔ **Harvest value:** 270 Farm Coins
- ✔ **XP per harvested plot:** 2

Grapes take a full day to grow, but the wait is worth it for many farmers who love the well-rounded coin and XP yields that the fruit provides. Planting grapes is a great way for busy farmers who don't have time to check in to their farms more than once a day to still make a good profit on their farms.

Sunflowers

- ✔ **Unlocked at:** Level 25
- ✔ **Harvest time:** 1 day
- ✔ **Cost per plot:** 135 Farm Coins
- ✔ **Harvest value:** 315 Farm Coins
- ✔ **XP per harvested plot:** 2

Like grapes, sunflowers provide a good mix of Farm Coins and XP for each daily harvest. Sunflowers also have the added advantage of generating occasional "perfect bunches," which can be stored in a flower stall and then placed around your farm. And who could say no to free decorations?

Index

• A •

Abram, Carolyn
  Facebook For Dummies, 22, 54
abstract design, 10
abusive comment, 37
Acai tree, 49
accepting
  gift, 66–69
  help from neighbor, 63
  neighbor request, 34–35, 55
account
  Facebook, 19–22
  how this book is organized, 2
  Zynga company, 90–91
achievement. *See also* mastery point;
    ribbon; XP
  how this book is organized, 3
  how to earn, 181
  overview, 14
Active Job menu, 205, 207
addiction, 13
Adobe Flash Player platform, 17
adoption, animal, 46
age requirement, Facebook account, 20
animal
  adoption, 46
  baby, 167–168
  decorative, 46
  diversifying your farm, 45–46
  earning Farm Coin, 77
  frugal farming, 112
  game concept, 11–12
  harvesting, 63
  helping neighbor with, 63
  humane harvest, 46–47
  knowing your, 77
  limited-edition item, 173
  lost, 46
  pet, 46–49
  pink indicator icon above, 45
  purchasing, 46
  receiving as gift, 46
  selling, 46
  viewing information about, 97–98
animal shelter. *See also* storage facility
  Beehive, 168
  Chicken Coop, 164–166
  Dairy Farm, 166
  Horse Stable, 166–167
  moving item to, 157
  Nursery Barn, 167–168
  Pigpen, 169–170
  removing animal from, 158
  types, 164
Animals tab (Market menu), 97–98
Anti-Virus Gold scan, 217
Apple Safari browser, 16–18
Arborist
  how to use, 110
  as most wanted item, 246
Architect ribbon, 183
artist personality, 237–238
Asian Pair tree, 49
asparagus, 250–251
Available Goods menu, 128–129
avatar
  clothing, 102
  farmer customization, 42–43
  profile picture, 21
  troubleshooting, 229
  walking the farm, 39

• B •

baby animal, 167–168
Baig, Edward C.
  iPhone For Dummies, 4th Edition, 27
Bailed Out ribbon, 147
bakery. *See* crafted good
balloon-popping Mystery Game, 175–176
Barn
  description, 159
  storage space, 161

barn raising, 155–156
Beehive
  description, 164
  Honeybee, 168
  Queen Bee, 168
Best of the Rest ribbon, 210
big-ticket item, 150–152
biplane vehicle, 107–109
Birch tree, 48
black berry, 251
Black Stallion, 244
blocking
  center of farm, 70
  farmer, 50–51
bonus. *See also* reward; XP
  bushel harvest, 120–121, 200
  harvest, 200
  market stall, 200
  mastery point, 199–200
  ribbon, 183
  sharing, 77
bookmarking, 24
breeder personality, 237
Bugs collectible, 191
building material
  Farm Cash purchased, 79
  as gift, 64
buildings
  crafted good, 122–123, 131–132
  limited-edition item, 173
  market stall, 114–118
  storage facility, 154–155
  viewing information about, 98
Buildings tab (Market menu), 98–99
bushel
  benefit of helping neighbor, 64
  bonus, 120–121, 200
  collecting, 114–117
  to craft goods, 122
  description, 113
  for pig slop, 122
  for planting and harvest bonus, 120–121
  sharing, 118–120
Butterfly collectible, 191
Button collectible, 192
Buy button (Market menu), 95
Buy Farm Coins & Cash menu, 81–82
buying. *See* purchasing

● *C* ●

cache, 19
camaraderie, 11
cash. *See* Farm Cash
chicken
  feeding, 63, 165
  helping neighbor with, 63
  limit, 164
Chicken Coop
  description, 164
  expansion, 165
  free, 166
  harvesting chicken from, 164
  Mystery Egg, 165–166
  storing chicken in, 164
Chinchilla gift, 176
Chrome browser (Google), 16, 18
cleared farm space, 145–147
clothing, 43
Clothing tab (Market menu), 102
coin. *See* Farm Coin
Coin Display icon, 36
collectible
  acquiring, 189–192
  as gift, 189–190
  level required for, 187
  in Mystery Egg, 190
  notification, 187–188
  permanent and limited-time, 188–189
  rarity, 190–192
  storage, 192
  trading for fuel, 192
  types, 190–192
collecting bushel
  from co-op job, 117
  from Farm Cash purchase, 117
  from harvesting crop, 114–115
  limit, 116
  from neighbors' market stall, 115–117
  from news feed, 117
collector personality, 238
Collier, Marsha
  PayPal For Dummies, 82, 91
color
  Mystery Egg, 177–178
  pet, 47
  ribbon, 181

Combine vehicle, 107–108
comment
  abusive, 37
  adding, 36
  copying to neighbor wall, 37
  leaving as message sign, 37
Comments icon, 38
Comments menu, 36–38
competitive gameplay, 9
completing co-op job, 208–210
computer
  crash, 19
  Internet connection, 16
  lag, 17–18
  Web browser, 16–17
concept, game
  animal, crop, and tree, 11–12
  decoration, 12
  expansion, 12
  helping neighbor, 12
  in-game tool, 11–12
  leveling up, 14
  overall, 7–8
  owning a farm, 11
connection, Internet, 16
construction, storage facility, 154–155
consumable item (Market menu), 95
Co-Op Farming icon (Tools menu), 41
co-op job
  active job, 205
  benefit of helping neighbor, 64
  completing, 208–210
  crafted good, 203
  description, 201–202
  extension, 208
  Fashion Bug, 210
  Gold Reward prize, 203–204, 210
  jobs in progress, 203
  joining, 203–205
  neighbor etiquette, 70
  news feed, 205–206
  quitting, 207–208
  recruiting help with, 206
  reward, 210
  starting, 202–203
  Stirring Things Up, 210
  viewing available job, 203
  working on, 207–208
copying comment, 37

Country Kitsch collectible, 191
crafted good
  benefit of helping neighbor, 64
  building, 122–123, 131–132
  bushel to craft, 122
  co-op job, 203
  leveling up, 126–128
  making, 123–126
  mastery point, 126–128
  profit, 122
  purchasing, 128–129
  recipe, 124–126
  selling, 130–131
  selling and earning Farm Coin through, 77
  trading, 129–130
crash, computer, 19
Create New List menu, 59
creativity, 10
credit card, 81–82
crop
  earning Farm Coin, 77
  fast-growing, 52
  game concept, 11–12
  helping neighbor with, 62
  high profit, 233, 249–252
  knowing your, 77
  mastery point, 193–200
  maximizing profit, 111
  maximizing space, 52
  neighbor etiquette, 69
  ripened, 45
currency. *See* Farm Cash; Farm Coin
Customize My Farmer menu, 42–43

Dairy Farm
  description, 164
  expansion, 166
  harvesting, 166
decoration
  diversifying your farm, 49
  game concept, 12
  limited-edition item, 173
  purchasing, 49
  uses for, 49
  viewing information about, 99
  waiting to decorate, 50

Decorations tab (Market menu), 99
decorator personality, 236
design, abstract, 10
dog, 48
Dogwood tree, 48

• *E* •

earning
    experience point (XP), 136–138
    Farm Cash, 78–79
    Farm Coin, 76–78
    mastery point, 193–194
    ribbon, 181–184
ease of play, 8–9
e-mail
    allowing acceptance from FarmVille, 23
    Facebook account setup, 19
    inviting friend through, 56
    Morales, Angela, 4
    Orland, Kyle, 4
Employee of the Month ribbon, 210
enabling JavaScript, 17–18
entertainment, 11
etiquette, neighbor, 69–70
Expand Storage menu, 156–157
Expand tab (Market menu), 101
expansion. *See also* farm expansion
    Chicken Coop, 165
    Dairy Farm, 166
    game concept, 12
    Horse Stable, 167
    land, 101
    Nursery Barn, 167
    storage facility, 155–156
experience point. *See* XP
extension, co-op job, 208
eye icon, 36

• *F* •

Fabulous Foreman ribbon, 210
Facebook. *See also* news feed
    account, 19–22
    age requirement, 20
    bookmarking FarmVille on, 24
    danger of placing personal information on, 19

description, 15
friend, inviting unconverted, 55–56
friend, turning into FarmVille neighbor, 27–28
history of, 21
illegitimate access, 216–217
logging out, 217
password, 20, 216–217
photo, 21
privacy settings, 22, 59–60
profile information, 21
scam group, 215
security, 216–217
Security Check page, 20
setting up, 19–21
sign-up/login page, 19–20
valuation, 21
Facebook For Dummies (Abram and Pearlman), 22, 54
facial feature, 42
Falling Blossom tree, 48
farm. *See also* farm expansion
    blocking off center of, 70
    cleared space, 145–147
    diversifying, 45–49
    helping neighbor with, 61–64
    moving item in, 40–41
    screenshot, 223–225
    upgrade, 99–100
    viewing, 38–39
    walking the, 39
Farm Aides tab (Market menu), 99–100
Farm Cash
    earning, 78–79
    farm expansion cost, 101
    free, 87–91
    game concept, 11
    hidden, 78
    overview, 75
    purchasing, 81–82
    scam, 214
    third-party offer, 87–88
    uses for, 78
    when to use, 79–80
Farm Cash Display icon, 36
Farm Coin
    earning, 76–78
    farm expansion cost, 101

frivolous spending, 76
game concept, 11
overview, 75
purchasing, 81–82
farm expansion
cost and requirements, 101
earning farm coin, 78
Farm Cash purchased, 79
maximizing profit, 112
as most wanted item, 247
neighborly assistance, 64
farm master personality, 237
Farm Name icon, 37
farmer
blocked-in, 50–51
clothing, 43
facial feature, 42
gender, 42
Farmers Market. *See also* Market menu
bushel collection, 114–117
bushel sharing, 118–120
bushel uses, 120–122
crafted good mastery star, 126–127
crafted good purchasing, 128–129
crafted good recipe, 124–126
crafted good selling, 130–131
crafted good trading, 129–130
crafting building, 122–123
description of, 113
exiting, 117
how this book is organized, 2
market stall, 114
Farmhand
how to use, 110
as most wanted item, 246
FarmVille app installation, 22–23
FarmVille Freak Web site, 220–222
FarmVille Requests tab, 34–35
FarmVille Web site, 24–26
Fashion Bug co-op job, 210
fast-growing crop, 52
FATEM relief organization, 178
Feather collectible, 191–192
feeding
chicken, 63, 165
neighbor etiquette, 69
pet, 48

fertilizer, 166
finding
additional neighbors, 57–60
fuel, 109–110
Firefox browser (Mozilla), 16, 18
Flash Player platform (Adobe), 17
forum, 57, 220–221
free Farm Cash, 87–91
Free Gifts tab, 30–32
friend
inviting unconverted, 55–56
turning into FarmVille neighbor, 27–28
Friend Selection page, 31–32
frozen game problem, 226
frugal farming, 112
fuel
finding, 109–110
gauge, 109
purchasing with Farm Cash, 79
trading collectible for, 192
trading crafted good for, 129–130
Fuel Display icon, 38
Full Screen mode
toggling between, 39
troubleshooting, 229
functional farmer personality, 235

• **G** •

Game Bar installation, 23, 88–90
Game Card
FarmVille, 83–84
as online gift, 85–86
purchasing, 83–84
reason for, 84
redeeming, 84–85
Zynga, 85–86
Game Card tab, 34, 84
game concept
animal, crop, and tree, 11–12
decoration, 12
expansion, 12
helping neighbor, 12
in-game tool, 11–12
leveling up, 14
overall, 7–8
owning a farm, 11

gameplay
  competitive, 9
  ease of play, 8–9
  time-sensitive, 7–8
Garage
  description, 159
  storing item in, 162
  vehicle, 162
Garden Shed
  description, 159
  storing item in, 162–164
Gardening Tools collectible, 190
gender
  Facebook account setup, 20
  farmer, 42
  pet, 47
general user support, 217–218
Get Farm Cash tab, 34
gift
  accepting, 66–69
  animal as, 46
  as benefit of helping neighbor, 64
  blue present icon representation, 41
  building material as, 64
  collectible as, 189–190
  Game Card as, 85–86
  limit, 66
  locked, 31
  Mystery Gift, 176
  neighbor etiquette, 70
  pending request, 67
  re-gifting, 69–70
  rejecting, 67
  returning, 70
  selling, 69
  sending, 30–32, 65–66
  tangible and intangible objects, 68
  thanks for, 68
  tree as, 49
  troubleshooting, 227
  vehicle part as, 64
Gift Acceptance confirmation page, 67–68
Gifts icon (Tools menu), 41
Ginko tree, 49
Give a Game Card menu, 85–86

Gnome
  as most wanted item, 245
  as Mystery Egg prize, 177–178
Gold Reward prize, 203–204, 210
gold star level indicator, 138
Google Chrome browser, 16, 18
grape, 253
graphic, 19, 36
Green Pastures landscape, 102
guide scam, 214

• H •

Haiti limited-edition event, 178
happy hoarder personality, 236–237
harvest
  animal, 63
  bonus, 200
  bushel collection, 114–115
  Dairy Farm, 166
  earning experience point through, 136
  earning Farm Coin through, 76
  full harvest day, 111
  game concept, 11–12
  humane, 46–47
  maximizing profit, 111
  ripened crop, 45
  tree, 63
hay bale
  abstract design, 10
  leveling up method, 145–147
helping neighbor
  with animal, 63
  benefits of, 64
  with chickens, 63
  with crop, 62
  earning experience point through, 137
  earning Farm Coin through, 77
  game concept, 12
  with plowing, 62–63
  with tree, 63
  visiting neighbor farm, 61
hidden Farm Cash, 78
high profit crop, 233, 249–252
highest level, 139
hoarder, 236–237

Hobby Farming For Dummies (Husarik), 1
Homes tab (Market menu), 98
Honeybee, 168
Horse Stable
 description, 164
 expansion, 167
 purchasing horse for, 166
Hot Rod vehicle, 79, 107–108
humane harvest, 46–47
Husarik, Theresa A.
 Hobby Farming For Dummies, 1

• *I* •

icon
 how this book is organized, 3–4
 informational, 36–39
 Options menu, 35–36
 Tools menu, 39–41
iDevice, 26–27
inactive neighbor, 33, 61
inactive tab, 34
informational icon, 36–39
installation
 FarmVille app, 22–23
 Game Bar, 23, 88–90
interface, 29–30
Internet
 connection, 16
 Web browser, 16–17
Internet Explorer browser (Microsoft), 16, 18
The Internet For Dummies, 12th Edition
 (Levine and Young), 16
Invite Friends tab, 33–34
iOS device, 26–27
iPhone For Dummies, 4th Edition (Baig and
 Levitus), 27

• *J* •

Jacaranda tree, 48
Jackfruit tree, 49
JavaScript, 17–18
job. *See* co-op job
Job History menu, 208–210

• *K* •

Kerin, Dimitar (politician), 13

• *L* •

lag, computer, 17–18
Lake Nessy, 246
land expansion, 101
Landscape tab (Market menu), 102
Lawn Jockey, 242–243
level. *See also* leveling up
 defined, 138
 game concept, 12
 gold star indicator, 138
 highest, 139
 as in-game progress, 135
 limit, 138–139
 starting the farm level, 42–45
 unlocked features, 139–144
leveler personality, 236
leveling up. *See also* level
 big-ticket item, 150–152
 crafted good, 126–128
 earning Farm Cash through, 78
 game concept, 14
 hay bale method, 145–147
 news feed method, 149–150
 soy bean method, 147–149
 unlocking new item and feature by, 139
Levine, John R.
 The Internet For Dummies, 12th Edition, 16
LeVitus, Bob
 iPhone For Dummies, 4th Edition, 27
limit
 bushel collection, 116
 chicken, 164
 gift, 66
 level, 138–139
 limiting gameplay time, 13
 neighbor, 60–61
limited-edition item
 animal, 173
 availability time, 103
 benefit of helping neighbor, 64

limited-edition item *(continued)*
  benefits of, 172–173
  building, 173
  collectible, 188–189, 192
  decoration, 173
  description of, 171
  event, 173–174
  Farm Cash exclusive, 79
  for Haiti event, 178
  red text indicator, 172
  seed, 172–173, 178
  theme, 102
  tree, 173
  viewing, 102
loading problem, 227
locked gift, 31
locked item (Market menu), 94–95
lost animal, 46
lost item
  support, 218–219
  troubleshooting, 229
Lychee tree, 49

● *M* ●

Mac, 225
Magnolia tree, 48
Market icon (Tools menu), 41
Market menu. *See also* Farmers Market
  Animals tab, 97–98
  Buildings tab, 98–99
  Buy button, 95
  Clothing tab, 102
  consumable item, 95
  Decorations tab, 99
  Expand tab, 101
  Farm Aides tab, 99–100
  Homes tab, 98
  Landscape tab, 102
  locked item in, 94–95
  More Info button, 94
  navigation, 94
  opening, 93–94
  Others tab, 98
  overview, 93–94

  Pets tab, 97
  Preview button, 94
  Seeds tab, 96
  Specials button, 102–103
  tangible item, 95
  Trees tab, 96
  Vehicles tab, 102
  viewing products in, 94
market stall
  bonus, 200
  collecting bushel from, 115–117
  crop-sharing reward notification, 118–119
  looking inside, 121
  multiple, 114
  setting up, 114
  sharing bushel through, 118
mastery point
  bonus, 199–200
  counter, 194
  crafted good, 126–128
  crop, 193–200
  earning, 193–194
  requirements, 195–198
maximizing profit, 111–112
message posting, 70–71
Microsoft Internet Explorer browser, 16, 18
mobile device, 26–27
money. *See also* Farm Cash; Farm Coin
  Farm Coin and Cash purchase, 81–82
  nontraditional payment method, 82–83
  Platinum Purchase Program, 80
Morales, Angela
  e-mail address, 4
More Info button (Market menu), 94
most wanted item
  Arborist, 246
  Black Stallion, 244
  farm expansion, 247
  Farmhand, 246
  Lake Nessy, 246
  Lawn Jockey, 242–243
  unlimited storage, 247
  Unwither Ring, 241–242
  Villa, 244–245
  White Stallion, 243–244

Move tool (Tools menu), 40
moving
  animal to shelter, 157
  farm item, 40–41
  item to storage facility, 157
  plot, 40–41
Mozilla Firefox browser, 16, 18
Multi tool icon (Tools menu), 39–40
music note icon, 36
My Neighbors tab, 27–28, 32–33
My Sales menu, 131
Mystery Box, 175–176
Mystery Egg
  collectible in, 190
  description, 63
  egg color, 177–178
  notification, 176–177
  opening, 177
  prize, 177–178
  sharing, 176
  XP bonus, 138
Mystery Game, 175–176
Mystery Gifts, 176

• N •

name
  Facebook account setup, 19
  pet, 47
neighbor. *See also* helping neighbor
  benefits of having, 53
  co-op job help, 206
  etiquette, 69–70
  finding more, 57–60
  game concept, 12
  inactive, 33, 61
  limit, 60–61
  non-neighbor, 32
  pending request, 32, 55
  purchasing crafted good from, 128–129
  recruiting more, 33–34
  removing, 60–61
  request, accepting, 55
  request, sending, 54–57
  sending gift to, 30–32

  sharing ribbon bonus with, 183
  strange neighbor problem, 229
  stranger as, 58–60
  turning Facebook friend into, 27–28
Neighbor bar, 38
new feature notification, 230–231
news feed (Facebook)
  collecting bushel from, 117
  co-op job, 205–206
  leveling up method, 149–150
  posting to, 70–71
  publishing box, 70–71
  scam, 215–216
  security, 217
  sharing bushel through, 119–120
  troubleshooting, 226
  watching the, 51
non-neighbor, 32
notification
  collectible, 187–188
  crop-sharing, 118–119
  Mystery Egg, 176–177
  new feature, 230–231
  preventing pop up of, 40
  ribbon, 183–184
Nursery Barn
  baby animal, 168
  description, 164
  expansion, 167

• O •

offer, free Farm Cash, 87–88
official forum Web site, 220–221
onion, 252
online payment, 81–83
optimization, performance, 18–19
Options menu, 35–36
organization, 2–3
Orland, Kyle
  e-mail address, 4
Others tab (Market menu), 98
out-of-sync error, 18, 225–226
overachiever personality, 239

● *P* ●

Pack Rat ribbon, 147, 183
password, Facebook account, 20, 216–217
patience, 112
PayPal account, 81–82, 91
PayPal For Dummies (Rosenborg and Collier), 82, 91
PC, 224–225
Pearlman, Leah
  Facebook For Dummies, 22, 54
peas, 250
pending gift request, 67
pending neighbor request, 32, 55
performance
  optimization, 18–19
  troubleshooting, 226–227
permanent collectible, 188–192
permission, 22–23
personality
  artist, 237–238
  breeder, 237
  collector, 238
  decorator, 236
  farm master, 237
  functional farmer, 235
  happy hoarder, 236–237
  leveler, 236
  overachiever, 239
  zoologist, 238
pet
  color, 47
  diversifying your farm, 46–48
  feeding, 48
  gender, 47
  name, 47
  purchasing, 46–48
Pet Customization menu, 47–48
Pets tab (Market menu), 97
photo
  Facebook account, 21
  troubleshooting, 228–229
pig slop, 122, 169–170
Pigpen
  description, 164
  placing pig in, 169–170
  truffle, 170
pink indicator icon, 45

planting
  earning experience point through, 136
  schedule, 111
Platinum Gnome, 245
Platinum Purchase Program, 80
play area
  game concept, 11
  refreshing, 32
Play tab, 32
playing
  from FarmVille Web site, 24–26
  from mobile device, 26–27
  Mystery Games, 175–176
plot
  arranging for vehicle, 105
  moving, 40–41
  plowing, 44
  seeded, 44
Plow icon (Tools menu), 41
plowing
  earning experience point through, 136
  helping neighbor with, 62
  process, 44
podcast, 221
popularity of game, 8
posting to news feed, 70–71
premium item, 78–80
Pretty Garden ribbon, 183
Pretty Penny ribbon, 183
Preview button (Market menu), 94
privacy settings
  Facebook account, 22
  strange neighbor, 58–60
Privacy Settings page (Facebook), 59–60
profile information, Facebook account, 21
profile picture
  troubleshooting, 228–229
  uploading or taking, 21
profit
  crafted good to increase, 122
  high profit crop, 233, 249–252
  maximization, 111–112
pumpkin, 251
puppy, 48
purchasing
  animal, 46
  clothing, 102
  crafted good, 128–129

decoration, 49
Farm Cash, 81–82
Farm Coin, 81–82
fuel, 79
Game Card, 83–84
market stall, 114
pet, 46–48
seed, 44
tree, 48–49

• Q •

Queen Bee, 168
quitting co-op job, 207–208

• R •

rarity, collectible, 190–192
raspberry, 250
reason to play
  challenge of self-improvement and
    competition, 9
  creativity, 10
  ease of play, 8–9
  entertainment and escape, 11
recipe, 124–126
Recycle tool (Tools menu), 40
red text limited-edition item indicator, 172
Redeem Your Game Card menu, 84–85
refreshing
  out-of-sync error, 226
  play area, 32
re-gifting, 69–70
rejecting gift, 67
removing
  animal from shelter, 158
  item from storage facility, 157–158
  neighbor, 60–61
Report Abuse button, 37
request
  accepting, 34–35, 55
  pending, 55
  sending, 54–57
  troubleshooting, 227–228
  viewing all, 67
Request for Permission page, 22–23
Restoration Policy, 219

Return Home button (Tools menu), 61–62
reward. *See also* bonus; XP
  co-op job, 210
  experience point as, 137–138
  Gold Reward prize, 203–204
  for helping neighbor, 62–63
  how this book is organized, 3
  truffle discovery, 170
ribbon
  as benefit of helping neighbor, 64
  Best of the Rest, 210
  bonus, 183
  color, 181
  earning, 181–184
  earning Farm Coin, 77
  Employee of the Month, 210
  Fabulous Foreman, 210
  hay bale purchase, 147
  notification, 183–184
  order of attainment, 181
  overachiever personality, 239
  requirement, 184–187
  types, 184–187
Ribbons icon (Tools menu), 41
rice, 252
ripened crop, 45
ripening time, 48
Rosenborg, Victoria
  PayPal For Dummies, 82, 91

• S •

Safari browser (Apple), 16–18
safety, 3
saving problem, 228
scam
  description, 213
  Facebook group, 215
  Farm Cash, 214
  guide, 214
  news feed, 215–216
schedule
  gameplay, 13
  planting, 111
screenshot, 223–225
scroll wheel, 38
security, 216–217

Security Check page (Facebook), 20
seed
  crop mastery requirements, 195–198
  frugal farming, 112
  limited-edition item, 172–173, 178
  purchasing, 44
  Sweet Seed, 178
  types, 195–198
  viewing information about, 96
Seeder, 106–108
Seeds tab (Market menu), 96
self-improvement, 9
selling
  animal, 46
  crafted good, 130–131
  gift, 69
sending
  gift, 30–32, 65–66
  neighbor request, 54–57
sharing
  as benefit of helping neighbor, 64
  bonus, 77
  bushel, 118–120
  Mystery Egg, 176
  neighbor etiquette, 70
  ribbon bonus, 183
shelter. *See* animal shelter
shovel, 160–161
Sign Post icon, 36
Sign Up button (Facebook), 20
site. *See* Web site
Skip This Tutorial button, 42
social gaming, 9
sound, 36
soy bean, 147–149
spa. *See* crafted good
speaker icon, 36
special. *See* limited-edition item
Specials button (Market menu), 102–103
sponsored link, 88
stall. *See* market stall
starting
  co-op job, 202–203
  the farm (Level 1), 42–45
Stats icon, 37–38

Stirring Things Up co-op job, 210
storage
  collectible, 192
  unlimited, 247
Storage Cellar
  depth, 160–161
  description, 159
  placing on farm, 160
  shovel, 160–161
storage facility. *See also* animal shelter
  Barn, 161
  building material and construction,
    154–155
  description, 153–154
  expansion, 155–156
  Garage, 162
  Garden Shed, 162–164
  moving item to, 157
  removing item from, 157–158
  Storage Cellar, 159–161
  Tool Shed, 161
  types, 159
Storage Inventory menu, 157–158
sunflower, 253
support
  general user, 217–218
  lost item, 218–219
  Web resource, 220–222
Sweet Seed, 178

• T •

tab
  Animals, 97–98
  Buildings, 98–99
  Clothing, 102
  Decorations, 99
  Expand, 101
  Farm Aides, 99–100
  FarmVille Requests, 34–35
  Free Gifts, 30–32
  Get Farm Cash, 34
  Game Card, 34, 84
  Homes, 98
  inactive, 34

Invite Friends, 33–34
Landscape, 102
My Neighbors, 27–28, 32–33
Others, 98
Seeds, 96
Trees, 96
Vehicles, 102
Take a picture icon, 39
tangible item (Market menu), 95
text problem, 230
tickling puppy, 48
time-sensitive gameplay, 7–8
Toggle Full Screen icon, 38
tomato, 252
Tool Shed
  description, 159
  storage space, 161
Tools menu
  features and icons, 39–41
  Return Home button, 61–62
top menu, 29–30
Tractor, 106–108
trading
  collectible, 192
  crafted good, 129–130
tree
  diversifying your farm, 48–49
  earning Farm Coin, 78
  frugal farming, 112
  game concept, 11–12
  harvesting, 63
  helping neighbor with, 63
  highly-sought after, 49
  limited-edition item, 173
  lucrative, 49
  purchasing, 48–49
  receiving as gift, 49
  ripening time, 48
  types, 48–49
  viewing information about, 96
Trees tab (Market menu), 96
trick, dog, 48
troubleshooting
  avatar, 229
  frozen game, 226
  Full Screen mode, 229

gift problem, 227
loading problem, 227
lost item, 229
news feed posting, 226
out-of-sync error, 225–226
performance problem, 226–227
profile picture, 228–229
request problem, 227–228
saving issue, 228
strange neighbor problem, 229
text problem, 230
truffle, 170

● *U* ●

U.N. World Food Programme, 178
unlimited storage, 247
Unwither Ring, 241–242
upgrade. *See also* expansion
  crafting building, 131–132
  farm, 99–100
  vehicle, 107
Use Goods menu, 130
user interface, 30
user support, 217–218

● *V* ●

vehicle
  basic, 106, 108
  biplane, 107–109
  Combine, 107–108
  cost and benefit of farming with, 105
  fuel, 109–110
  garage for, 162
  Harvester, 107–108
  Hot Rod, 79, 107–108
  parts, as gift, 64
  plot arrangement, 105
  Seeder, 106–108
  selection, 104
  Tractor, 106–108
  types, 106–107
  upgrade, 107
Vehicles tab (Market menu), 102

Villa
  as most wanted item, 244–245
  sign of high status, 143
V.I.P. (Very Important Player), 80
virtual farming, 1
virtual money. *See* Farm Cash; Farm Coin
virus scan, 217

• *W* •

walking the farm, 39
Web browser, 16–17
Web site
  FarmVille, 24–26
  FarmVille Freak, 222
  official forum, 220–221
  YouTube podcast, 221
White Stallion, 243–244
winery. *See* crafted good

• *X* •

XP (experience point). *See also* bonus;
    reward
  comparing to neighbor, 136
  earning, 136–138

game concept, 12
level requirements, 139–144
ribbon bonus, 183
white bar indicator, 136
XP & Level Meter icon, 36

• *Y* •

Young, Margaret Levine
  The Internet For Dummies, 12th Edition, 16
YouTube podcast, 221

• *Z* •

zoologist personality, 238
Zoom In icon, 38
Zoom Out icon, 38
Zuckerberg, Mark (Facebook co-creator), 21
Zynga company
  account, 90–91
  browser suggestions, 16
  co-op job introduction, 201
  forum, 57
  Game Card, 85–86
  support, 217–219

& Macs

or Dummies
-470-58027-1

e For Dummies,
dition
-470-87870-5

ook For Dummies, 3rd
n
-470-76918-8

OS X Snow Leopard For
nies
-470-43543-4

ess

keeping For Dummies
-7645-9848-7

terviews
ummies,
dition
-470-17748-8

nes For Dummies,
dition
-470-08037-5

ng an
e Business
ummies,
dition
-470-60210-2

Investing
ummies,
dition
-470-40114-9

ssful
Management
ummies
-470-29034-7

Computer Hardware

BlackBerry
For Dummies,
4th Edition
978-0-470-60700-8

Computers For Seniors
For Dummies,
2nd Edition
978-0-470-53483-0

PCs For Dummies, Windows
7 Edition
978-0-470-46542-4

Laptops For Dummies,
4th Edition
978-0-470-57829-2

Cooking & Entertaining

Cooking Basics
For Dummies,
3rd Edition
978-0-7645-7206-7

Wine For Dummies,
4th Edition
978-0-470-04579-4

Diet & Nutrition

Dieting For Dummies,
2nd Edition
978-0-7645-4149-0

Nutrition For Dummies,
4th Edition
978-0-471-79868-2

Weight Training
For Dummies,
3rd Edition
978-0-471-76845-6

Digital Photography

Digital SLR Cameras &
Photography For Dummies,
3rd Edition
978-0-470-46606-3

Photoshop Elements 8
For Dummies
978-0-470-52967-6

Gardening

Gardening Basics
For Dummies
978-0-470-03749-2

Organic Gardening
For Dummies,
2nd Edition
978-0-470-43067-5

Green/Sustainable

Raising Chickens
For Dummies
978-0-470-46544-8

Green Cleaning
For Dummies
978-0-470-39106-8

Health

Diabetes For Dummies,
3rd Edition
978-0-470-27086-8

Food Allergies
For Dummies
978-0-470-09584-3

Living Gluten-Free
For Dummies,
2nd Edition
978-0-470-58589-4

Hobbies/General

Chess For Dummies,
2nd Edition
978-0-7645-8404-6

Drawing
Cartoons & Comics
For Dummies
978-0-470-42683-8

Knitting For Dummies,
2nd Edition
978-0-470-28747-7

Organizing
For Dummies
978-0-7645-5300-4

Su Doku For Dummies
978-0-470-01892-7

Home Improvement

Home Maintenance
For Dummies,
2nd Edition
978-0-470-43063-7

Home Theater
For Dummies,
3rd Edition
978-0-470-41189-6

Living the
Country Lifestyle
All-in-One
For Dummies
978-0-470-43061-3

Solar Power Your Home
For Dummies,
2nd Edition
978-0-470-59678-4

ble wherever books are sold. For more information or to order direct: U.S. customers visit www.dummies.com or call 1-877-762-2974.
ustomers visit www.wileyeurope.com or call (0) 1243 843291. Canadian customers visit www.wiley.ca or call 1-800-567-4797.

Internet

Blogging For Dummies,
3rd Edition
978-0-470-61996-4

eBay For Dummies,
6th Edition
978-0-470-49741-8

Facebook For Dummies, 3rd
Edition
978-0-470-87804-0

Web Marketing
For Dummies,
2nd Edition
978-0-470-37181-7

WordPress
For Dummies,
3rd Edition
978-0-470-59274-8

Language & Foreign Language

French For Dummies
978-0-7645-5193-2

Italian Phrases
For Dummies
978-0-7645-7203-6

Spanish For Dummies,
2nd Edition
978-0-470-87855-2

Spanish For Dummies,
Audio Set
978-0-470-09585-0

Math & Science

Algebra I For Dummies,
2nd Edition
978-0-470-55964-2

Biology For Dummies,
2nd Edition
978-0-470-59875-7

Calculus For Dummies
978 0 7645 2498 1

Chemistry For Dummies
978-0-7645-5430-8

Microsoft Office

Excel 2010 For Dummies
978-0-470-48953-6

Office 2010 All-in-One
For Dummies
978-0-470-49748-7

Office 2010 For Dummies,
Book + DVD Bundle
978-0-470-62698-6

Word 2010 For Dummies
978-0-470-48772-3

Music

Guitar For Dummies,
2nd Edition
978-0-7645-9904-0

iPod & iTunes
For Dummies,
8th Edition
978-0-470-87871-2

Piano Exercises
For Dummies
978-0-470-38765-8

Parenting & Education

Parenting For Dummies,
2nd Edition
978-0-7645-5418-6

Type 1 Diabetes
For Dummies
978-0-470-17811-9

Pets

Cats For Dummies,
2nd Edition
978-0-7645-5275-5

Dog Training For Dummies,
3rd Edition
978-0-470-60029-0

Puppies For Dummies,
2nd Edition
978-0-470-03717-1

Religion & Inspiration

The Bible For Dummies
978-0-7645-5296-0

Catholicism For Dummies
978-0-7645-5391-2

Women in the Bible
For Dummies
978-0-7645-8475-6

Self-Help & Relationship

Anger Management
For Dummies
978-0-470-03715-7

Overcoming Anxiety
For Dummies,
2nd Edition
978-0-470-57441-6

Sports

Baseball
For Dummies,
3rd Edition
978-0-7645-7537-2

Basketball
For Dummies,
2nd Edition
978-0-7645-5248-9

Golf For Dummies,
3rd Edition
978-0-471-76871-5

Web Development

Web Design
All-in-One
For Dummies
978-0-470-41796-6

Web Sites
Do-It-Yourself
For Dummies,
2nd Edition
978-0-470-56520-9

Windows 7

Windows 7
For Dummies
978-0-470-49743-2

Windows 7
For Dummies,
Book + DVD Bundle
978-0-470-52398-8

Windows 7 All-in-One
For Dummies
978-0-470-48763-1

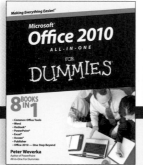

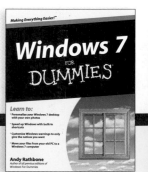

Available wherever books are sold. For more information or to order direct: U.S. customers visit www.dummies.com or call 1-877-762
U.K. customers visit www.wileyeurope.com or call (0) 1243 843291. Canadian customers visit www.wiley.ca or call 1-800-567-4797.